D0280937

interrogating TEXTS

General Editors
PATRICIA WAUGH AND LYNNE PEARCE

To Denise and Alec

Practising
POSTMODERNISM
Reading
MODERNISM

PATRICIA WAUGH
Lecturer in English, University of Durham

Edward Arnold
A member of the Hodder Headline Group
LONDON   NEW YORK   SYDNEY   AUCKLAND

Edward Arnold is a division of Hodder Headline PLC
338 Euston Road, London NW1 3BH

First published in the United Kingdom 1992

3 5 7 6 4
95 97 99 98 96

Distributed exclusively in the USA by St Martin's Press Inc.
175 Fifth Avenue, New York, NY 10010, USA

British Library Cataloguing in Publication Data
Waugh, Patricia
Practising Postmodernism / Reading Modernism. -
(Working with Theory Series)
I. Title   II Series
809

ISBN 0 340 55050 3

Typeset in Palatino by Wearset, Boldon, Tyne and Wear
Printed and bound in the United Kingdom by
J W Arrowsmith Ltd, Bristol

CONTENTS

ACKNOWLEDGEMENTS

I first became interested in Postmodernism in its early (peaceful?) days in the seventies. I have remained grateful to David Lodge who inspired my initial interest in it and taught me how to begin to read it. Since then, many friends and colleagues have contributed to this and to my general interest in modern literature and theory. I would like to thank Jo Caitlin, John Coggrave, Andrew Crisell, Peter Dempsey, David Fuller, Jonathan Harris, Barry Lewis, Lynne Pearce, Richard Terry, Colin Trodd, Irving Velody and the Forster Triumvirate for conversations and suggestions. My fondest thanks to Denise Brown whose friendship and affection constantly bears out my feminist critique of Postmodernism and my postmodern critique of the institution – her support has been sustaining and invaluable. I would like to acknowledge the help and encouragement as ever of Alec, Rob, Jane, Eileen and Eric. I am grateful to Durham University for a term's research leave and to Irving Velody and Jim Goode for organising a thoroughly stimulating Centre for the History of the Human Sciences lecture programme on modernity and postmodernity. Finally, I would very much like to thank the staff at Edward Arnold for their support and helpful suggestions for this project. This book is dedicated to a thoroughly postmodern couple – Denise and Alec.

A Note on Organization

The first half of this book examines Postmodernism: as a 'period' term for a cultural epoch; as an aesthetic strategy and as a philosophical critique. Although I have tried to examine the main positions in the debate, this book does develop its own view of Postmodernism. This is basically that Postmodernism as a theoretical 'mood' is an extension of aestheticist assumptions (which reach back to Romantic poetics) into areas other than the strictly aesthetic. I suggest that Postmodernism should be understood within this context of thought and that its elucidation should, therefore, involve close attention to works of art. The second half of the book examines the implications of this argument for the construction of Modernism and challenges the elucidation of modernist writing in terms of theories of autonomy. If I have my own theoretical position it is a 'New Humanism': an existential aesthetics which can learn from, whilst remaining critical of, aspects of the postmodern. The book offers close readings of three 'postmodern' and four 'modernist' texts though, as the inverted commas suggest, the readings aim to deconstruct the categories. Most readers approaching this book will be familiar with the term 'postmodernism'; some will be familiar with its theorisation. To avoid tedium for those with some acquaintance, I have used footnotes in the early part of the book to offer summaries of the basic postmodern positions. I suggest, therefore, that inexperienced readers may wish to consult the footnotes, whereas more experienced grapplers with the postmodern may simply get on with the argument.

Part One

READING POSTMODERNISM

Modernity and its Discontents

1

INTRODUCING POSTMODERNISM

*The Romance
of the Aesthetic
and Post-Romantic Aesthetics*

I

Introduction

What we call the beginning is often the end
And to make an end is to make a beginning.
The end is where we start from.
(T. S. Eliot, *Four Quartets*)

Postmodernism is normally conceived of as a condition beset by a sense of ending. But as the quotation from Eliot suggests, endings must always involve retrospective construction of beginnings or origins. Where is the beginning of Postmodernism? Instead of accepting Postmodernism on its own terms as a radical break with previous Western modes of knowledge and representation, it may be more fruitful to view it as a late phase in a tradition of specifically *aestheticist* modern thought inaugurated by philosophers such as Kant and embodied in Romantic *and* modernist art. In these terms, Postmodernism as an aesthetic and body of thought can be seen as a late-flowering Romanticism. What distinguishes its mood from earlier Romanticisms, however, is that its aesthetic impulses have spilled out of the self-consciously defined sphere of art and into the spheres of what Kant referred to as the cognitive or scientific on the one hand and the practical or moral on the other. This mood reveals itself on both sides of the Atlantic. In its European forms, it tends to draw on a theoretical or philosophical tradition through writers such as Nietzsche, Bataille, Artaud and post-phenomenological critiques arising out of thinkers such as Heidegger, Derrida and post-structuralists such as Lacan. In America, although given definition by writers such as Ihab Hassan who draw on an eclectic mix of European philosophy, Postmodernism has largely found expression in the form of cultural artefacts conceived in relation both to an indigenously defined and a European Modernism.

However, a further meditation in Eliot's poem expresses the view that 'there is only a limited value/In the knowledge derived from experience./ The knowledge imposes a pattern, and falsifies,/For the pattern is new in every moment/And every moment is a new and shocking/Valuation of all we have been' (1969, p. 179). Thus, if *Romanticism* (and Romantic thought) is constructed as a 'beginning' for Postmodernism, it may be possible to loosen Modernism itself from its traditional critical moorings by viewing its texts through an engagement with postmodern aesthetic discourses. This book will inevitably, therefore, be as much engaged with an attempt to problematise the construction of Modernism as with the elucidation of Postmodernism: in my view, neither activity can be pursued without involving the other. Of course, *any* engagement with ideas or literary texts through period concepts will be fraught with the pitfalls of generalisation, but it is hoped that a dialectical conversation across such concepts may produce genuine insights as well as inevitable blindnesses. My aim in arguing against a radical break theory of the relation of Postmodernism to earlier aesthetic practice and theory is not to fall into the opposite error of a naive evolutionism, but to consider continuities *and* discontinuities and the possibility of perceiving new relationships.

In beginning here as the end of my argument effectively returns Postmodernism to a context of specifically aesthetic debate which is where its critical formulation most emphatically arose in the nineteen fifties. Few of the numerous contemporary discussions of the concept refer to this history or consider its implications. Yet the term Postmodernism first appeared in the context of literary criticism as a way of describing aesthetic practices which seemed to be related to those of Modernism but also to have moved beyond them. It entered American criticism in the fifties to describe Charles Olson's attempt to define the existence of a new non-anthropocentric poetry whose Heideggerian anti-humanism was directed at seeing 'man' as a being in the world, as radically situated as any other object. The same tendency appears at this time in the French New Novel and its theorisation in the writing of Alain Robbe-Grillet and in Susan Sontag's rejection of an 'intellectualised' depth/surface model of interpretation for an acceptance of the experience of art as sensuous *surface*, an 'erotics' of literature. John Barth talked of abandoning the literature of exhaustion for the essentially parodic mode of replenishment, Leslie Fiedler of a new art which would bridge the gap between high and mass culture and undo the elitist 'autonomy', the aesthetic withdrawal from mass culture, which he associated with modernist writing. For both Sontag and Ihab Hassan, in particular, Postmodernism, an art of the surface, was the contemporary period's answer to Adorno's 'negative aesthetics' of Modernism: an art which in making itself opaque and resistant to interpretation would, in its effective silence, refuse consumption even as it partook of a culture of consumption.[1]

[1]   See Charles Olson *Causal Mythology*, San Francisco, 1969. Alain Robbe-Grillet, 'Nature, Humanism and Tragedy' (1958) and 'New Novel, New Man' (1961), in *Snapshots and Towards a New Novel*, trans. Barbara Wright: London, 1965. Susan Sontag *Against Interpretation*, New

By the early eighties, however, the term shifts from the description of a range of aesthetic practices involving playful irony, parody, parataxis, self-consciousness, fragmentation, to a use which encompasses a more general shift in thought and seems to register a pervasive cynicism about the progressivist ideals of modernity. 'Postmodernism' now expresses the sense of a new cultural epoch in which distinctions between critical and functional knowledge break down as capitalism, in its latest consumerist phase, invades everything including the aesthetic, the post-colonial world and the unconscious (what Lionel Trilling had seen as that bit of biology radically opposed to culture), leaving no remaining oppositional space. At this point, the term becomes inflected with a kaleidoscope of meanings drawn from those human sciences variously engaged in the production of a theoretical palimpsest where the specific *aesthetic* origins of the term are almost entirely obscured. However, as we shall see, there are good reasons for returning to an aesthetic point of origin in order to think about 'working with' postmodern theory in the context of literary studies.

Firstly, a common element in the bewilderingly diverse range of theoretical Postmodernisms is a recognition and account of the way in which the 'grand narratives' of Western history have broken down. Without such metanarratives (God, history as purposefully unfolding immanent dialectic, Reason), history itself becomes a plurality of 'islands of discourse', a series of metaphors which cannot be detached from the various institutionally produced languages which we bring to bear upon it (Foucault), or a network of agonistic 'language games' where the criteria are those of performance not truth (Lyotard).[2] The implication of this is that 'truth'

York, 1966. John Barth 'The Literature of Replenishment', *The Atlantic*, 1980, pp65–71. Leslie Fiedler 'Cross the Border – Close that Gap: Postmodernism', *Sphere History of Literature*, 9, ed. Marcus Cunliffe, London, 1975. Ihab Hassan *The Dismemberment of Orpheus: Towards a Postmodern Literature*, New York, 1971 and *The Right Promethean Fire*, Illinois, 1980. By the eighties, writing by Derrida, Foucault, Kristeva, Lyotard and Barthes had begun a thoroughgoing critique of Structuralism, involving an attempt to give priority to the signifier over the signified, to demonstrate the radical indeterminacy of textual meaning. This post-Structuralist theory produced a number of radical critiques of traditional philosophy, and in particular the notion of 'foundationalism': the idea that knowledge is the reflection of 'truth' and that there is a stable foundation for it. Literary critics like Hassan joined the 'new' philosophers and political theorists who were turning to an alternative 'dark' tradition of Western thought: Bataille, de Sade, Nietzsche, Artaud, Heidegger as part of an ongoing critique of the rationalist Cartesian tradition. Postmodernism in its current form was born out of this congeries of thinkers and theorists. Gradually the challenge to art and philosophy came to be seen as a manifestation of a new cultural epoch: economists, political theorists and sociologists now entered the debate. Postmodernism exists as an area of overlap of these three groups of preoccupations: a critique of foundationalist thought, an aesthetic practice, a description of a cultural epoch. The first part of this book attempts to unravel their associations.

2   Foucault's work has been a major influence on postmodern theory. His writing has evolved in a complex process from an initial focus on the way in which subjectivities are constructed to a final emphasis on the capacity of the subject aesthetically (drawing on the Greek notion of *techne*) to fashion and produce itself. Throughout, however, he has been consistently critical of the Enlightenment equation of reason with progress and emancipation, turning to writers such as Bataille and Nietzsche in order to examine ways in which a pervasive will to power is enacted through formations of knowledge. He has resisted the allure of 'total theories': theories which claim to account for all aspects of human existence

cannot be distinguished from 'fiction' and that the aesthetic, rather than disappearing, has actually incorporated everything else into itself. For the philosopher Richard Rorty, therefore, we should embrace the potential this offers to us to reshape our world by abandoning altogether an outworn rhetoric of metaphysical truth. Instead of seeing knowledge through the image of mind as mirror of eternal truths, a 'Glassy Essence', we should see it 'as a matter of conversation and of social practice' and thus 'we will not be likely to envisage a metapractice which will be the critique of all possible forms of social practice' (1980, p17). In a more recent book, Rorty extends this insight to the view that literature, rather than philosophy, can more usefully provide the model for a new form of social knowledge, for 'a poeticised culture would be one which would not insist we find the real wall behind the painted ones, the real touchstones of truth as opposed to touchstones which are merely cultural artefacts' (1989, p52). Instead of trying to rebuild the collapsing foundations of Western knowledge we should rather concentrate our energies on refurbishing the interior. And poets and novelists, who have always dealt with the contingencies of 'style' and human particularity rather than the universal absolutes of systematic 'truth', may be the philosophers of the future. Their modes of irony and contingency may come to provide the possibility of imaginative expansion of human sympathy and empathy as a basis for that social and political solidarity no longer available in the philosophical, historical or religious grand narratives of the past. Though 'postmodern' in its emphasis on irony and contingency and in its critique of analytic philosophy, Rorty's vision of the aesthetic as the basis for a new social consensus is, however, hardly a radical departure from a firmly established tradition of Western *aesthetics* running from the work of Schelling through Arnold to cultural pessimists from Theodor Adorno to T. S. Eliot.

Postmodern theory can be seen and understood as the latest version of a long-standing attempt to address social and political issues through an aestheticised view of the world, though it may be more *thoroughly* aestheticising than any previous body of thought. The aesthetic has now entered the 'hard' core of the human sciences: philosophy, political theory, social science. One of the problems confronting readers, however, is that

---

and focused his critical attention on the 'other' excluded by and constructed through such theories. His interest in transgression, the 'other' of reason (desire, body, madness, multiplicity, micropolitics), and his critique of theories which claim transcendence, 'a view from nowhere', has had a powerful influence on postmodern thought. For Foucault, power is omniscient but not omnipotent: there are no pure spaces of liberty, but equally there is no oppression without the possibility of resistance.

Lyotard is the thinker most centrally associated with Postmodernism, particularly since the publication of his book *The Postmodern Condition* in 1979 (translated into English in 1984). Like Foucault, his writing has consistently provided a critique of totalising forms of thought and he too shifts from an initial interest in the politics of desire (influenced by Bataille etc.) to a concern with ethics and with possibilities of non-oppressive order. His critique of metanarratives, the idea of grand orders of knowledge which can legitimate foundationalist claims, and his preference for context-specific agreements, heterogeneity and pragmatism, are central points of reference for all postmodern theory.

increasingly, although its models are aesthetic, its theorists rarely discuss actual works of *art*. Surely in seeking to understand Postmodernism, in particular, art must illuminate theory as well as theory offer conceptual frameworks and methodological approaches to art. We must regard Postmodernism firstly as a mood or style of thought which privileges aesthetic modes over those of logic or method; secondly as an aesthetic practice with an accompanying body of commentary upon it; and thirdly as a concept designating a cultural epoch which has facilitated the rise to prominence of such theoretical and aesthetic styles and which may or may not constitute a break with previous structures of modernity. The first half of this book will examine Postmodernism understood in the light of each of these formulations of it. The second half will offer a reading of key modernist texts in relation to those issues foregrounded in the theoretical debate. If theory is in some sense always conceptualisation after the event (as much as a mode of prediction), it may be interesting to return to the literary text precisely as an 'event' and to see how the 'postmodern' has always, perhaps, inhabited the 'modern'.

II

Apocalypse Now

Postmodernism and Cultural Pessimism

George Eliot's Mr. Brooke could not have known as he reflected upon the perils of reading Adam Smith that his reservations about the benefits of a little theory would become central to current late twentieth-century aesthetic debate: 'The fact is, human reason may carry you a little too far-over the hedge in fact. It carried me a good way at one time; But I saw it would not do. I pulled up; I pulled up in time. But not too hard.' Gentle deceleration is preferred, as he goes on to explain, because we 'must have Thought else we shall be landed back in the dark ages' (1972, p39). Reading much postmodern theory, however, it is difficult to avoid the feeling that not only may we be heading for a new Dark Age, a new barbarism, but that the rationalisms of Enlightenment thought were the instruments which accelerated this process. Though there are many forms of Postmodernism, they all express the sense that our inherited forms of knowledge and representation are undergoing some fundamental shift: modernity is coming to an end, strangled by its own contradictory logic, born astride of the grave which is now its abyss. Just as Greek civilisation ended or the Feudal system waned or as Nietzsche had announced the death of God (though not of grammar) a century earlier, so postmodernists like Foucault have forecast the end of modern Western Man, a face in the sand eroded by an ever encroaching sea.

So the historian Arnold Toynbee was the first to use the term outside the specific literary critical sense when he announced in the fifties that we were entering the postmodern age: the fourth and final phase of Western history and one dominated by irrationalism and helplessness.[3] In this world, not only self but also consciousness is discovered to be adrift, increasingly unable to anchor itself to any universal ground of justice, truth or reason, and is thus itself 'decentred' (to use a term much favoured by post-structuralists): no longer agent, origin, author, but a function through which impersonal forces pass and intersect – Dover beach, perhaps, displaced by an international airport lounge. There are a number of ways to respond to this scenario within the context of aesthetic debate. First, the negative view. One form of this is articulated by a character in Kurt Vonnegut's novel *Breakfast of Champions* who says, 'I have no culture', but realises that 'I can't live without a culture any more' (1973, p15). It is a common enough view of the postmodern as a fall from the oppositional autonomy of Romanticism and Modernism into the commodified complicity with mass culture which is the most obvious sign that capitalism has at last invaded all, leaving no space outside its logic of appropriation. In this view, formal innovation once experienced as a mode of political dissent (as in the works of Joyce or Brecht, for example), is now given over to the radical chic of the marketplace and its versions of Pop: opposition and confirmation have collapsed so indiscriminately into each other that we can no longer talk of Art at all. 'Style' is commodity, art loses its identity along with its autonomy and like everything, including knowledge, is recycled as a consumer product. This is the most familiar negative version of the postmodern and it is a powerful one. While recognising its force, however, it may be more challenging to see if an attempt to connect Postmodernism with a post-Romantic aesthetic tradition produces a more positive sense of the aesthetic (even a postmodern one) as offering some possibility of personal, social or political redemption. Nietzsche proclaimed in *The Birth of Tragedy* (1966) that art should be the highest task of life: it should provide us with all the metaphysics we need. In his vision of the capacity of art to reconstitute into a whole the fragments of a dismembered God, he connects a Romantic concern with the possibility of reconciliation through art with a postmodern sense of the role of the aesthetic in shaping an existence whose foundations seem on the verge of imminent collapse.

One way of viewing modernity, however, is to see it not so much as a collapse, but as a *proliferation* of value which, far from destroying our powers of self-determination, offers them new forms and contexts: new possibilities for creatively shaping or inhabiting our human environment and of renegotiating the boundaries of identity in ways which, without necessitating total abandonment of Enlightenment thought, may release us from the hidden tyrannies of universalising modes and their invisible exclusionary tactics. One cannot ignore the dangers here (and a later chapter on feminism and Postmodernism will address them in some detail). It is easy to move from a critique of metanarratives to the claim that if truth is only an effect of rhetoric, it is, therefore, simply a product of

---

[3]   Toynbee's six volume *A Study of History* appeared in 1947. D. C. Somervell suggested the term 'postmodern' to describe Toynbee's focus, and Toynbee himself subsequently took up the term in later work. He uses it in much the same way that Spengler had talked of the modern age in his earlier *Decline of the West*.

power. Similarly, if all interpretative models are contingent and provisional, then far from being the unacknowledged legislators of mankind, poets
are simply doing what everyone is doing, creating fictional scripts: simply
existing – Baudrillard's postmodern life as consumer lifestyle.[4] Equally, if
all is fiction, how to say that one fiction is better than another, or one
course of action more ethical than an alternative one? It is not surprising
that Postmodernism has been seen by its critics as neo-conservative or that
Rorty describes himself as a 'postmodernist bourgeois liberal'. One can see
how the erosion of the notion of oppositional critique from a transcendent
viewpoint can be used to confirm the freemarket pluralistic 'anything goes'
of capitalism in its most rapacious modes, or suggest a return to consensus
or interpretative communities which is equally resistant to the idea of
political critique or disinterested humanitarian progress. Any attempt to
formulate a positive sense of the postmodern in relation to post-Romantic
aesthetics must proceed tentatively in an awareness that every position on
Postmodernism is hedged about with its own dangers.

That the process must be tentative is suggested by the very term
'Postmodernism'. 'Post' implies after but with no indication of whither
next. The sense of transition is powerful, but inevitably accompanied by
the spectre of decadence: the feeling that we are at the end of an era.
Postmodernism is Apocalyptic. Or, if not in the full Christian millenarian
sense of a Last Judgement ushering in a New Jerusalem, then Apocalyptic
at least in its sense of crisis. The old verities may be breaking down, but
there is no clear sense of what is to replace them. Although it will become
apparent that the postmodern sense of crisis is bound up with specific
changes in the contemporary world, crisis thinking is as old as the
Judeo-Christian tradition itself. In both modes, redemption can only come
after revolution (internal or external). The new world may be revealed if
there is a destruction of the old (the Greek *apokalypsis* meaning revelation).
Once both the redemptive framework of Christianity and the rationalist
Enlightenment belief in progress cease to provide foundational certainty,
however, the possibility of a New Jerusalem may begin to seem a
chimerical projection of desire: an image which provides aesthetic play or
functions as a form of psychological compensation and no more. Or if
nihilism has, indeed, come to stand at the door, the image of the future
may be the shape of that rough beast slouching its way towards a new and
monstrous birth. Postmodern apocalypticism tends, therefore, to be tera-

---

[4] Baudrillard is another theorist centrally associated with Postmodernism. His focus has
been largely technologically determinist, developing earlier theories of modernity as a 'society
of the spectacle' into the notion of a culture of the 'simulacrum'. By the 1970s his work moves
entirely away from analysis of political economy to a concern with the culture of 'hyperreal-
ity': models replace the real and determine the real, Disneyland becomes America, hyperreal-
ity is everyday reality. Media messages saturate the cultural and social field so entirely that
the 'masses' are reduced through this overload of information to an inert and silent majority.
All social meaning thus 'implodes' into a black hole which is the universe of simulacra. In
effect, he takes the post-Structuralist critique of reference to an extreme and nihilistic limit.
Like Lyotard's *The Postmodern Condition*, his books *Simulations* (1983), *In the Shadow of the Silent
Majorities* (1983) and more recently, *The Ecstasy of Communication* (1988), have given him a
central place in the postmodern debate.

togenic in its imaginings: plagued by catastrophe, disease, images of final burnout; post-Auschwitz versions of the falling stars and floating wombs, for example, in D. M. Thomas's critique of scientific rationalism and portrait of a postmodern poetic Freud in his novel *The White Hotel*; the stumbling and silent dumb beasts who people Baudrillard's vignettes of the contemporary 'moronic inferno'.

Again these are familiar biblical images. Yet the idea of a condition which is 'post' modernity suggests an epochal break. Nietzsche, writing on *modernity*, though, saw the idea of a break, even here, as illusory. He saw his age still propelled by a temporal consciousness which has arisen with Christianity and entailed a view of history as a progressive movement towards a redemptive moment out of time and one of epoch as constituted by a revolutionary moment in time (the incarnation). Arguably, such impulses still inhabit those notions of temporal crisis articulated within Postmodernism. Epiphany as a redemptive moment outside time, for example, is a commonly expressed Romantic and modernist transforma-tion of a Christian concept which reappears in various guises throughout postmodern writing though often attached to an immanentist aesthetics of the human body as the site of redemptive experience (the maternal body in Kristeva, for example, or the primordial drives of the biological 'libidinal band' in Lyotard). In the writings of both of these and of Foucault, Deleuze and Bataille, the idea is bound up with the vocabulary of transgression which is a reworking of Christian mysticism involving a reuniting of the erotic with the sacred.[5] The epiphanic moment is supposedly immanent rather than transcendent, but similarly involving a return to a state of primordial unity before the division into subject and object, mind and body. It appears in the writing of Georges Bataille in images of the dissolution of the monadic subject through rapturous bodily experience involving terror, excess and the sexual: images of Bacchanalian waste which can subvert the rational structures of capitalist utility and efficiency. Foucault's interpretation of this is that if we live in a world where, indeed, God is dead, then 'transgression supplies the sole manner of discovering the sacred in its unmediated substance' (1977, p32). The aesthetic remains the prime vehicle for this, exploding its logic of the other into the world of

[5]   The 'politics of desire' represents one of the positive, liberatory modes of the postmodern as opposed to its culturally pessimistic forms. It is most closely associated with Gilles Deleuze and Felix Guattari, the former a philosopher and the latter a psychoanalyst. Their most influential book is *Anti-Oedipus*, first published in 1972. Their work is, in effect, an extension of earlier theories concerned with the political possibilities of liberation of desire (Marcuse, for example) and challenges subject-centred philosophies of consciousness through a Nietz-schean attention to the body. They reject utterly the Kantian ideal of a unified and rational subject in order to focus on multiple desiring 'intensities' which have been restricted, controlled and repressed through the orders of modernity. They develop a form of critique referred to as 'schizoanalysis' which posits a monadic primacy of desire over material production as constructive of social reality. There are obvious problems, however, with this sort of analysis. It is unclear how the promulgation of desire in this form is finally inseparable from the dynamic of consumer culture. Equally, it is unclear how the substitution of desire for reason as the basis for human activity does not replace Enlightenment foundationalism with a new foundationalism of the body which is just as reductive of human potential.

the logic of the Same. So that, in a new version of Isaiah, the wolf and the lamb shall feed together but, perhaps, through a new foundationalism of body rather than Spirit.

If theorists of this form of Postmodernism are concerned to rediscover modes of immediate experience as an impulse towards plenitude, however, they are equally aware of the unavoidability of mediation. Again, one sees that essentially Romantic struggle with the finite limits of the material which produced Romantic Irony and prompted Shelley in *The Defence of Poetry* to liken the mind in creation to a fading coal which has lost the brightness of original non-embodied vision, or Eliot to draw attention in the *Four Quartets* to the 'intolerable wrestle with words', that recalcitrance of the material, or what Wallace Stevens called the 'inaccessibility of the abstract' (1966, p434). Such awareness presses towards some expression of aesthetic self-referentiality, for even a pure idea of the Symbol embodying a reality beyond itself is ever poised on the edge of recognition that its own linguistic materiality will, unavoidably and subversively, interpose itself. Even for a postmodernist like John Barth, it may be a question of 'Oh God comma, I abhor self-consciousness'. Yet, within the terms of such recognition, there is still an impulse towards transcendence. For if the subject matter of poetry cannot be that 'collection of solid static objects extended in space', and must be the reality of composition itself as an 'artifice that the mind has added to human nature', composition can still be recognised as 'a power embedded in human nature' (Stevens, 1951, pp25, 37), the possibility of an art of life as well as the life of art – a familiar postmodern paradox. Yet, even here, one can see how postmodern textualism expresses a late form of Romantic Irony where, if the metaphysical framework of Idealist thought has collapsed, what is still with us is the sense of art as both ontologically distinct from the world but also a fundamental aspect of existence in it. Now, however, that world is only one of many possibilities. Later in *The Necessary Angel*, Wallace Stevens argued that 'modern reality is a reality of decreation in which our revelations are not the revelations of belief, but the precious portents of our own powers' (Stevens, 1951, p175). We create our own realities through reformulation of what is to hand. We still play God imaginatively, but ironically and provisionally.

The postmodern self-conscious awareness of the finitude of the material and the plasticity of the imagination (now producer of fictions by which to live rather than mediator of absolute vision), is often expressed through parody: a mode which explicitly speaks through the reformulation of an existing discourse. The materiality of language becomes the concern of theorist and imaginative writer alike. Postmodernism is nearly always parodic, acknowledging its implication in a pre-existing textuality, creating through decreation, displacing that secure perspective of a stable vantage point from outside (Romantic Vision or Enlightenment transcendental ego as pure reason). Indeed, even its apocalypticism is subjected to its own irony and rendered suspect. Here is Derrida in an essay entitled 'Of an Apocalyptic Tone in Recent Philosophy', in parodically apocalyptic vein, implicitly raising the question of the sort of psychological compensations offered by Apocalypse (in its postmodern as its Judeo-Christian modes), and of the extent to which it is always, like desire itself, as much a condition of discourse as of unmediated historical fact:

> It is not only the end of this here but also and first of that there, the end of
> history, the end of the class struggle, the end of philosophy, the death of God,
> the end of religions, the end of Christianity and morals ... the end of the
> subject, the end of man, the end of the West, the end of Oedipus, the end of
> the Earth, Apocalypse now, I tell you, in the cataclysm, the fire, the blood, the
> fundamental earthquake ... the end of literature, the end of painting, art as a
> thing of the past, the end of the past ... the end of phallocentrism and
> phallogocentrism and I don't know what else (Derrida, 1984).

Derrida's style is itself 'postmodern', hesitating between Joycean 'jocose-
rious' overkill and concerned engagement, like a tub-thumping preacher
piling up figures of repetition: epimone (repeating the same word for
emphasis); antanaclasis (repeating a word but using different senses of it);
polysyndeton (repeating a conjunction) and mingling them with interjec-
tions of the personally emphatic 'I told you so' variety. As long as he talks,
however, the end is deferred in a self-generating hypertrophy of discourse
where rhetoric seems ultimately to assert only its own existence. Derrida's
rhetorical self-referentiality undermines the truth effect of his assertions to
imply that Apocalypse is in fact a theoretical construction, or, as Wallace
Stevens observed, that imagination is always at the end of an era (1951,
p27). But as Kermode saw in his book *The Sense of an Ending* (1966), people
with no clear sense of their ending will always fabricate one. Concordances
are reassuring: they produce the illusion of retrospective significance.
Postmodernism is itself, in this respect, another Grand Narrative, but one
about the End of Grand Narratives. It is impossibly tied up with performative contradictions. It may even be the case that in a world offering
increasingly less space for speculative idealism, the impetus for postmodern thought comes from the diminishing speculators themselves, intellectual theorists anxious to construct a version of world history which can
preserve some significant place for themselves as prophets of its doom.

We shall see that the first problem for Postmodernism is an extension of
a Romantic dilemma: how to separate the object to be observed or studied
from the critical discourse which in some sense constructs it? How to know
what we give and what we receive? Is Postmodernism a phenomenon in
the world or a theoretical construction projected on the world for whatever
pragmatic, psychological or institutional reasons? The modernist writer
Virginia Woolf famously saw her world changing utterly in December
1910. Did she literally believe this? One can detect in the statement a
certain tongue-in-cheek irony: the comically exact dating of the modernist
apocalyptic moment also has the effect of undermining the statement as an
assertion of truth. The date was, of course, a specifically *aesthetic* turning
point – the month of the Post-Impressionist exhibition organised by Roger
Fry – and, as in Derrida, aesthetic self-referentiality renders the statement
half-playful. It acts as a reminder that crisis thinking is hardly new, nor is
the confusion about where to locate the crisis. Postmodernism again
appears to be an intensification of aspects of modern Western thought
rather than a radical break with them.

Nietzsche saw this self-conscious mode as characteristic of end of era
thinking generally and described it in these terms:

What is the mark of every literary decadence? That life no longer resides in the whole. The word becomes sovereign and leaps out of the sentence, the sentence reaches out and obscures the meaning of the page, and the page-comes to life at the expense of the whole – the whole is no longer a whole. This, however, is the simile of every style of decadence: every time there is an anarchy of atoms.[6]

For Nietzsche, however, there are two sorts of decadence. One is unself-conscious. This is the mode of the liar who deceives by imitating truth. It is the mode of conventional morality, a sickness masquerading as health and producing that attitude of 'ressentiment' or revengefulness against life which is anchored in self-deception and characteristic of the herd mental-ity. Against this, he advocates the need for a *positive* decadence; a self-conscious awareness of our fictionalising powers which will prevent us accepting another's fictionalised will to power as the collectively validated truth of myth. We must heighten subjectivity to the point where it dissolves itself and with it the principle of individuation which produces that anarchy of atoms which is modern life. We must destroy the false myths which chain us to beliefs in subject-centred reason in order that the atoms may be seen for what they are and that we may begin self-consciously and aesthetically to reshape them and become who *we* are. If there is no whole, then better self-consciously to construct one's own provisional fiction and consciously reshape the anarchy of atoms than to believe the fragment can express any pre-existent whole. Thus liberated, we can recognise that those systems given the moral prestige of 'truth' are actually life-denying illusions which turn us into craven animals who cannot use our own imaginative powers. Nietzsche includes Romantic 'vision' as an idealism implicated in the decadence of the principle of individuation. However, he too is caught up in the belief that not to invent one's own system is to be enslaved to someone else's. The full *postmodern* version (in Lyotard's terms), would be the recognition that passively to accept as universal the boundaries of any one powerful language game, is to render oneself powerless to manipulate the rules which performatively (in the speech act sense) constitute it. To be thus deprived is to be unable to contest it with another which would allow one self-consciously to produce oneself at their point of intersection.

More recently, Fredric Jameson has characterised this verbal self-consciousness and nostalgia for the whole (implied by the fragment) as the characteristic modes of the apocalypticism of the postmodern. For Jame-son, it manifests itself in forms of pastiche and linguistic self-reflexivity which constitute a denial of historicity and are simply a commodified version of 'art for art's sake' (Jameson, 1984). Again though, I would wish to argue that this is an exacerbation of a tendency with a long history which is clearly articulated within Romantic thought. A consideration of this tradition supplies an alternative way of looking at the concept of nostalgia. Apocalyptic modes always tend to express a sense of a fall from an original state of harmony into a fragmentation which, in the Christian

---

[6] Quoted from *The Case of Wagner* by Walter Kaufmann in *Nietzsche, Philosopher, Psychologist, Antichrist*, Princeton, New Jersey, 1974, p72.

(and Romantic) version, may be redeemed through integration into a higher unity of Spirit outside ordinary temporality (though not necessarily outside history). Although postmodern apocalypticism is primarily thought of as expressing absolute fragmentariness, in my view it is, if covertly, as much concerned with reconciliation and reintegration as it is with their impossibility. The aesthetic is still the vehicle for this, but it has now invaded the spheres of science and philosophy.

Schiller was one of the first writers to express the centrality of the aesthetic as the redemptive hope for an age of increasingly instrumental rationality. He saw that the reproduction of a culture must involve the life of the senses as well as that of consciousness. In his letters *On the Aesthetic Education of Man*, first written in 1793 (during the Reign of Terror after the French Revolution), Schiller proposed an aesthetic solution to the intractable political problems thrown up by the failure of rationalising logic evident in all the political vocabularies of his time (still largely our own even if in the midst of a crisis of legitimation). As an alternative to force or law, both as an activity valuable in its own right and a model for a new political order, he recommended the idea of the aesthetic as a disinterested realm of play and semblance. He described it as an autonomously existing state which could release us from the constraints imposed by utilitarian pressures. It could thus allow a reintegration of all those human faculties which had become fragmented and subjected to hierarchisation through the capitalist division of labour driven by 'interest' (in its full variety of meanings). Again in another important essay on 'Naive and Sentimental Poetry' (1795), he expressed the idea of the fortunate fall by emphasising the redemptive possibilities of the aesthetic. Here, he argues that reintegration into a lost harmonious world cannot be fully effected through a passive regression to a child-like unself-conscious state of nature but only through a self-conscious and strenuous *aesthetic* attempt to reintegrate thought and feeling into a state of equilibrium at a higher level in aesthetic activity. There are echoes of this idea throughout Nietzsche (both a Late Romantic and early postmodernist) and in those currents of Postmodernism which view the aesthetic in terms of self-conscious activity rather than rapturous dissolution. Throughout Romantic thought, repossession of the world as a healing of division is to be achieved as much through self-conscious aesthetically crafted distance (emotion recollected in tranquillity) from the immediate time or space of experience as through images of immediate dissolution. Romantic transcendence always involves Romantic irony and vice versa. Self-conscious detachment, paradoxically, allows one to see with a different eye from the 'despotic' one which looks immediately and instrumentally at an inert object outside itself. It allows one therefore to suspend interest and to experience the object as if one were not looking at it through the frame of purposive logic but in its own terms. As in Postmodernism, art becomes a model of existence as a dialectic of immersion in and detachment from world which allows one to shape the self but always in relation to the other (natural, human, divine). In its postmodern forms, however, the aesthetic is no longer simply model or catalyst occupying an autonomous realm of its own. It has entered the lifeworld and invaded the spheres of knowledge and ethics in a new version of a longstanding attempt fully to integrate body with mind and self with world.

What connects Romanticism and Postmodernism most obviously is a shared crisis mentality connected to a sense of the fragmentariness of the commercialised world with which Enlightenment reason is seen to be complicit: in both the aesthetic becomes the only possible means of redemption. As a redeeming power, it is both stronger and weaker in Postmodernism. Stronger in that, in either post-Nietzschean or post-Heideggerian modes (what I shall call those of radical fictionality and those of situatedness), it is finally seen as so inseparable from world or knowledge that no distinction remains between truth and fiction; but weaker in that it is no longer grounded as the expression of a metaphysical foundation (a repetition of the Divine I AM). The artist can no longer, therefore, legislate for humankind in the manner of the Romantic poet-seer or poet-prophet. What is preserved in Postmodernism, however, is a fundamental sense of the aesthetic (derived from Kantian thought) as a form of knowing and presenting which is sensuously embodied, an alternative to conceptual knowledge because, ontogenetically, it realises worlds and experiences for which we had no concepts until they came into existence. Implicitly then, at least, the aesthetic is both an epistemology and an ontology.

Postmodernism makes explicit a number of paradoxes which are rather more implicit in Romantic thought. For both Schiller and Kant, art must be autonomous in that it cannot exist otherwise in full purposive purposelessness. The artist must in some way withdraw from this world to build an alternative one. However, for each of them, as for other Romantic poets, art must also effect a reconciliation with the world, bring us back to a perception of it without the veil of habit imposed by ratiocinative thought. In this view, art allows us to recognise our implication in the world as a condition of reciprocal being where each is shaped through the other and part of a mutual situatedness through which the same breeze blows. Art is thus in the world experientially and cannot be divorced from living. Postmodernism is often identified *exclusively* with such an aestheticist position (viewed either positively or negatively) in order to set it off from so-called Romantic withdrawal or modernist autonomy. Yet Postmodernism also teaches us that autonomy is a fiction of the critical imagination arising out of a particular interpretation of Kant (and most obviously disseminated by the New Criticism). One could alternatively view Postmodernism as a *culmination* of an aestheticism which has its roots in two basic modes of Romanticism. (And which appear as the Symbolist and Imagist tendencies in modernist writing.) Even within its particular Idealist frame, one can see in Romantic writing an orientation, on the one hand, to a radical fictionalising mode and, on the other, to situatedness in the world. Each of these represents a particular orientation in an ongoing critique of Enlightenment which attempts to oppose its Cartesian separation of subject and object as a rationalising consciousness shaping an inert material object. Both attempt to articulate a mode of being in which mind and body, subject and object, may be seen to be inextricably part of each other. The aesthetic offers a form of non-conceptualising embodied language as an alternative way of knowing and being. Postmodernism is not simply a mode of counter-Enlightenment, it is, fundamentally, a late modern Romanticism.

Philosophically, each orientation has been expressed in ways most relevant to the postmodern debate by Nietzsche (whose radical fictionality can be traced back to Coleridge and forward to Wallace Stevens or Thomas Pynchon or critics such as Ihab Hassan and Frank Kermode's *The Sense of an Ending*) on the one hand, and Heidegger (whose concept of situatedness or Being-in-the-world connects Wordsworth with writers such as Charles Olson or critics such as Susan Sontag) on the other.[7] I have said that the critique is ongoing, however, and we will have to take account of the effects on this process of the gradual diminishment of the efficacy of grand narratives which has been seen as the hallmark of the postmodern apocalypse. If Romanticism is 'spilt religion' then perhaps Postmodernism is 'spilt Romanticism'. Thus I will see Postmodernism as a distinctive shift, but not a radical break. It is a new vocabulary as much as a new condition, though one arising out of actual material changes in the historical world. I do not believe we inhabit a 'post'-modern world in the radical break sense, though I do believe we inhabit a much *later* modern one than the Romantic writers to whom I have referred. Indeed, the very extent to which our theoretical formulations of it continuously and reflexively feed back into our experience of the contemporary world, is one aspect of our different situation. Postmodern theory itself increases our self-conscious awareness of the proliferation of 'little narratives' as it implicitly substitutes itself in the place of those overarching grand narratives which provided the framework for Romantic thought. One can see it as a foundationalism of the aesthetic which was always, in fact, implicit in Romantic thought. The difficulty will be in deciding whether it carries a similarly oppositional potential or whether it can only function as the theoretical justification for a commercially aestheticised consumer culture.

---

[7]   Nietzsche has been read in a number of ways by postmodernists. He has been seen as a philosopher of 'intensities', a proponent of Dionysian 'excess', by theorists of desire; Foucauldian theory has taken up his notion of the pervasiveness of power in order to develop a critique of Enlightenment reason; others, including Foucault in his late work, have been interested in the idea of 'life as Literature', existence as aesthetic shaping and artistic control. Similarly, Heidegger's writing has entered Postmodernism through a variety of doorways. William Spanos and the journal *Boundary 2* developed an interest in his work in the seventies, drawing on it to argue the case for a new postmodern 'existential' aesthetics of temporality which was opposed to the formal autonomy and 'spatial' aesthetics of Modernism. I am more interested in the way in which Heidegger's critique of subject-centred reason and his notion of Being-in-the-world is compatible with a particular way of seeing Modernism as much as Postmodernism. Although the idea that there can be no position from outside culture from which to judge culture is most obviously associated, via hermeneutic theory, with Postmodernism, it is a powerful aspect of aesthetic thinking with its roots in the counter-Enlightenment tendencies in Romantic thought. That it should be viewed currently as a challenge to Western thought seems to me to be simply a consequence of its extension out of aesthetic theory into other demesnes of knowledge traditionally associated with 'truth'.

III
From Autonomy to Aestheticism
Tradition and Innovation

A recent account of Postmodernism offers this conventionally held view of its relation to Modernism:

> Aesthetic modernity is, by the conventions of most art historians and literary critics, dated from the last decades of the nineteenth century. It constitutes a break with representation, hence a certain self-referentiality and above all a set of formalisms. Commentators such as Foucault and Richard Rorty have noted similar phenomena taking place approximately concurrently in epistemology, moral philosophy and the social sciences. The postmodernity of the 1960s on the other hand, consider for example Peter Brook in theatre and Sylvia Plath's poetry, means a break with formalisms, a break with the signifier; it means a new primacy of the unconscious, of the bodily and the material, of desire, of libidinal impulses. The work of Foucault, Lyotard, and Deleuze not only clarifies this new aesthetic substrate and indicates its ethical and political implications; the work of these writers is part and parcel of theoretical postmodernism itself (Lash, 1985, p3).

In fact, what is referred to here is not aesthetic modernity *per se*, but a tenacious and dominant critical formulation of it. The second half of this book will draw on Postmodernism to challenge this critical construction and to attempt to account for its institutional power. Postmodernists themselves often endorse it in order to claim a radical break. Critics of Postmodernism draw upon it to see the postmodern as a fall from modernist grace. However, in my view, postmodern writing itself enables us to see ways in which 'autonomy' has functioned as a critical label used to obscure important concerns of Romantic and modernist writers (such as their politics). Postmodernism reveals continuities of aestheticist concern across all three of these modern movements. In fact, if one looks at the features singled out by Lash as definitive of the postmodern 'break': the unconscious, desire, the bodily and the material, they are precisely those elements Schiller and other Romantics foregrounded as features of human existence destroyed by industrial modernity and preserved through their own aesthetic activity and theory. Schiller does argue for the necessary autonomy of the aesthetic, but he uses the term autonomy in its Kantian sense. Although the formalist version of this (used to designate the self-contained, self-referential and linguistically self-legitimating nature of the literary work) is derived from the Kantian, there are important differences.

In Kant, as in Schiller, the notion of autonomy as the separation of art *from* life paradoxically also implies a form of aestheticism, the existence of art *in* life. Neither espouses a full aestheticist position which projects artistic models onto the entire lifeworld as a means of understanding and shaping it (which is a Nietzschean extension of a way of seeing art less recommended than made possible by Kant). Equally, however, for neither did autonomy mean a withdrawal into a realm utterly distinct from the historical world and having no bearing upon it whatsoever. As we shall see later, the full return of aestheticism in postmodern theory suggests perhaps that it was denied in the earlier New Critical construction of Modernism. The Enlightenment concept of agency as autonomous self-determination through reason was challenged by the Romantic notion of the imagination conceived of as a non-conceptualisable and effectively divine power within human beings. Freedom is now to be discovered through the foundational form of Imagination not Reason. Once the metaphysical frame of Idealism began to weaken, however, the concept of autonomy began to be transferred from self entirely to the work of art itself conceived of as an internally coherent, self-contained system (culminating in the New Critical construction of Modernism). By this stage, autonomy as the basis for legitimation and freedom within modernity, is emphasised at the expense of the articulation of the aesthetic *as an aspect of the existential.* Art is radically autonomous: content is form. Even for Kant, though aesthetic experience may be logically different from historical experience, it exists within it. His theory of the sublime is nothing if not an account of the way in which, as finite beings, we struggle to articulate our sense of situation in a world which we may never fully grasp but whose infinity we glimpse in that very recognition. Through this essentially aesthetic experience, we come to intuit our own power to frame ideas which cannot be sensuously embodied but which confer upon us a magnitude and sense of our own sublimity as human beings in the world (see chapter 2). If such experiences are aesthetic in that they cannot be reduced to pre-existing concepts, it does not follow from this that the autonomy of art is a radical form of non-referentiality where to be is not to mean and therefore not to have ethical implications for the way in which we live our lives.

Romanticism and Postmodernism both articulate a critique of Enlightenment faith in the purely rational. In each there is a recognition of the aesthetic as a mode which can create new realities by circumventing the conceptual in an attempt to integrate body with intellect. Art is autonomous only in the sense that it is a different kind of discourse from the ratiocinative, involving body as well as intellect. However, if it is thus 'world creating', it is not necessarily, therefore, entirely outside the demesne of 'problem solving'.[8] If postmodernist aestheticism carries the logic of Wordsworth's 'man talking to men' further than Wordsworth ever intended, it does not contradict that logic. For some critics, this is seen as the 'commodification' of art or is a dangerous displacement of the cognitive and the moral by the aesthetic. Equally, though, it could be seen as an extension and democratisation of the aesthetic, an attempt to integrate it into life as a mode of imaginative realisation and empathy which can widen our human sympathies and help more diverse groups of people than those traditionally addressed by 'bourgeois' art to shape a more humane world.

---

[8] These are distinctions used by Jürgen Habermas (see *The Philosophical Discourses of Modernity*, 1987) to designate fundamental differences between the discourses of the aesthetic and those of philosophy. Art is a 'world creating' discourse, philosophy, a 'problem solving' one. He is critical of Postmodernism and of deconstructionists like Derrida for attempting to over-extend the aesthetic and to confuse the boundaries of these orders of discourse (see 'Excursus on Levelling the Genre Distinction between Philosophy and Literature in *PDM*, pp 185–210').

IV
Romanticism to Postmodernism
Radical Fictionality and Being There

In this section, I wish to illustrate my earlier point that within this more general ongoing mode of the aesthetic there are two basic orientations which can be traced through Romanticism and Modernism to Postmodernism. They can be understood respectively through the thought of Heidegger on the one hand and Nietzsche on the other (both have been seen individually as either precursors of Postmodernism or as heirs of Romanticism).[9] Given the limitation of space, I can only indicate a trajectory rather than explore it in detail. So far, I have seen Romantic and postmodern thought as modes which, in different ways, privilege art and give it a central place in the organisation of human experience. One can see two broad tendencies in the postmodern critique of grand narratives and subversion of the purely rational: both emphasise art as a form of bodily experience, but one emphasising the situation of body in the world, the other emphasising body as the source of potential transformation of that world. The first is expressed in the postmodern criticism of Susan Sontag, Charles Olson or Ihab Hassan. It often draws its philosophical justification from the Heideggerian notion of radical situatedness, though sometimes transferring this concept to an emphasis on bodily experience. Often accompanying this is a concern with the recovery of intensity through aesthetic experiences which collapse the mind/body distinction. It appears in Olson's poetic of objectivity as humility, a 'getting rid of the lyrical interference of the individual as ego, of the "subject" and his soul, that peculiar presumption by which Western man has interposed himself between what he is as a creature of nature . . . and those other creatures of nature which we may, with no derogation, call objects'. Here it provides a radical critique of the supremacy of science and a call for a recognition of a Heideggerian condition of temporality, for end is 'never more than this instant, than you in this instant, than you, fighting it out, and acting, so. If there is any absolute, it is never more than this one, you, this instant, in action'.[10] This notion of situatedness, as we shall see later, connects the hermeneutics of a theorist like Gadamer to the aestheticised consensus of Rorty and the notion of tradition developed in the criticism of T. S. Eliot. I shall argue that the orientation of the Romantic connection here can be broadly conceived as Wordsworthian. As it moves towards the postmodern, there is an increased emphasis on situatedness in language.

[9]   Key texts relevant to this discussion are: Nietzsche's *Beyond Good and Evil*, *The Will To Power* and *Ecce Homo* and Heidegger's *Being and Time*, *Poetry, Language, Thought* and *The Question Concerning Technology*.

[10]   Important essays by Olson are 'Projective Verse' and 'Human Universe' which clearly develop Heidegger's notion of Being-in-the-World as the basis of a new poetic. The essays are collected in *The Poetics of the New American Poetry*, ed. Donald M. Allen and Warren Tallman (pp147–58 and 161–74).

The other tendency is towards a projective, radical fictionality, where the self exists in its ability to work with the fragments available to it and from them to project on to the world new fictions by which to live. In its postmodern version, it is no longer an Idealist self but an instinctual, bodily driven, precariously held equilibrium. Again, however, the fragments with which it works are often words. This version is explored by a range of writers from Donald Barthelme to Thomas Pynchon. (Pynchon most often presents the negative underside of this position: the paranoia which is the inverse of its potentiality solipsistic narcissism. In *The Crying of Lot 49* (1966), Oedipa's fear that the hierophanic possibilities she reads around her are signs less of a glimpse into the sacred than a recognition that she is the victim of her own uncontrolled and unself-conscious fictionality: that her revelation will be of her own condition of insanity.) Deriving from a notion of the Imagination developed by Coleridge and other Romantic writers, this mode is extended in Nietzsche. His work can be seen as the basis for those postmodern theories of desire (Kristeva's, for example), which view imagination no longer as mediator between human, divine and nature, but as an impulse projected from the drives of the body, shaped by culture, but seeking expression through the reformulation of that culture. Similarly, it has inspired those theories which view the idea of self-conscious fictionality as an impulse of the human rage for order. The idea is developed in Kermode's reading of Wallace Stevens, or in Lyotard's call for the recognition of the importance of 'little narratives' in the organisa-tion of social life. These are versions of the philosophy of 'as if' expressed thus in Lyotard:

> History is made of clouds of narratives, narratives reported, invented, heard and played out; that people does not exist as a subject, that it is a heap of billions of little futile and serious stories, which sometimes get attracted into constituting large narratives, sometimes disperse into fanciful wanderings, but which in general just about hold together, forming what's called the culture of civil society (Bennington, 1988, p114).

As Coleridge attempted to break free of Hartley's associationism, he moved towards a broadly Kantian concept of the imagination as a bridge between the world of the senses and that of the understanding. In the famous thirteenth chapter of his *Biographia Literaria*, Coleridge identified the imagination as firstly the prime agent of human perception, 'a repetition in the finite mind of the eternal act of creation in the infinite I AM' and secondarily, as an echo of this, a mode which unifies and 'dissolves, diffuses, dissipates, in order to recreate' (1956, p167). Poetic value is created through this decreative and combinatory power of the subjective imagination, organic unity in the work of art produced through an act of secondary imagination which echoes that of divine creation. The theory depends upon an acceptance of a fundamental correspondence between mind and world, grounded in a metaphysical framework, where if reason cannot logically prove such correspondence, then Imagination can intuit it. For Coleridge, such intuitions could be expressed only through non-conceptual forms such as those of the aesthetic. Later in the *Biographia Literaria*, he asserts that the imagination is both a mediating and reconciling power, synthetic and magical (a Kantian conception). He berates poets who become too concerned with 'matter-of-factness' as a 'laborious minuteness and fidelity in the representation of objects' (p251), and sees this as 'contravening the essence of poetry' which is to humanise nature through the power of the imagination to infuse in it human fictions and passions. Images simply arising out of nature, 'however beautiful ... faithfully copied' are only of aesthetic value when 'modified by a predominant passion' (p177). The initial structure of value for Coleridge (as for Kant) is in the subjective mind. However, once mind ceases to exist within the *metaphysical* frame of Romantic thought, once correspondence comes under strain, the subjectivist orientation of the theory develops into the modes of late Symbolist aestheticism and finally into a Nietzschean radical fictionality (arising out of the body) in its postmodern form. If the 'I am' is cut loose from the divine 'I AM', then divinity has to be relocated in a self which must aesthetically construct its own ground in a transformation of the body through the body. This is what happens in Nietzsche. The potential for such loss of foundation lurks throughout Coleridge's writing, however, as an inevitable destination should the internal coherence of art seem to fail to correspond with an order outside of itself. When religion and metaphysics appear to fail we cannot live without their consolation, warns Nietzsche, so we must go one step further: 'love yourself through Grace; then you are no longer in need of your God, and the whole drama of fall and redemption is acted out in yourself' (Russell, 1961, p719). This may seem a long way from Coleridge's thought and yet in the famous passage in his notebooks dated 14 April, 1805, he writes that as he looks at the objects of Nature 'I seem rather to be seeking, as it were, asking, a symbolic language for something within me that already and forever exists, than observing anything new' (1957, no. 2546). Remove the forever and there is the spectre of solipsism; remove the inner self as a stable entity which can be looked into and there is Nietzschen bodily driven aesthetic self-overcoming.

For Nietzsche, this is the state of affairs we must embrace, renouncing the nostalgia for correspondence or reconciliation, recognising all facts to be interpretations, trying to free ourselves from those conceptual abstractions which are the fictional projections of others. In the 1873 essay 'On Truth and Lie in an Extramoral Sense', he argues that every concept is necessarily a falsification of what it purports to represent, for the world is radically fragmentary, contingent, and the only authentic reconciliation is not that which claims to reunite us with the world at some higher level of spirit, but that aesthetic shaping which knows itself, self-consciously, to be a provisional fiction. Nietzsche recognises our longing for immediacy. He views the aesthetic as a mode of experience which in escaping the conceptual allows us the biological delight of experiencing the ultimate impulse of the will to power as chaos coming into form: Dionysian fragmentation of energy willing itself into coherence. The Nietzschean subject must create its own order out of itself, for there is no Divine I AM, no blueprint to be discovered. The gods have fled and as the metaphysical base of Romanticism disintegrates, Nietzsche turns to the aesthetic itself as an impulse arising out of bodily desire to supply that foundation. Life itself is now the supreme artistic challenge and the human body both the material to be shaped and the source of shaping energy. The self is always a creation out of available materials, never an archaelogical discovery at a fixed point of origin. It is Coleridge's ourobouros breaking out of its own closed circle to recognise that one never arrives at selfhood, but is constantly engaged in endless reinterpretation of each new fragment: a postmodern self which for all the proclaimed absence of metaphysical ground is still recognisably Romantic in its form.

For Coleridge, the form of the divine is to be discovered in the human mind itself. Once cut loose from its Idealist moorings, however, this subjectivism develops in Nietzsche's writing into a mode of *radical fictionality* which actually both affirms and destroys subjectivity. This shift establishes the orientation for a dominant mode of the postmodern. In Wordsworth's writing, however, the view is offered that we can detect that form situated in nature, a blessing in the gentle breeze which actually blows upon us to meet a corresponding breeze within. Although in many respects Wordsworth's poetics were close to those of Coleridge, this different orientation produces an aesthetic of (what I shall call) *radical situatedness*: a mode taken up in the post-Heideggerin versions of the postmodern. Wordsworth's sense of radical situatedness is expressed through the idea that we grow out of and are part of a nature which is always in motion, which lives in us as we live in it, and is killed if split off as an inert object upon which we gaze in order to experience its 'picturesque' qualities. For Wordsworth, we live not primarily in subjective mind, but in 'the world/Of all of us, – the place in which, in the end,/We find our happiness, or not at all!' (*The Prelude* (1805–6), 1971, X, 726). Throughout this and other poems, metaphor continuously speaks mind through landscape in an immanent teleology where mind comes to itself through *loss* of itself as subjective possession and recovery through being in the world. Unlike in the Coleridgean mode, here the plastic power of the imagination is 'subservient strictly to the external things/With which it commun'd (11, 386). From the moment when the babe of *The Prelude* first enters the world in his mother's arms, he grows into a self through taking in that love which, projectively and introjectively, and inextricably, is part of what he is and what is in the world outside. He literally grows out of world as a tree grows out of earth and, paradoxically, is most free when he recognises this and can throw off those modes of ratiocinative thought which divide him from it and are an extension of experiencing world through the distance of eye alone. To see nature as a picture is to die in his own nature. It is expressed in the despair which the poet suffers in the account of his response to the failure of the rationalised logic of the Revolution. During the Mount Snowdon episode, he recovers through listening to the 'blind', subterranean stream, for in order to listen the external eye must ever be made quiet, so that the impress of those things situated, like himself, in the temporal flow of world, may flash themselves upon the inward eye. Then heart may dance with nature and dancer become, indeed, inseparable from dance. Thus we sink into world as world sinks into us (the poetry is full of such images), giving what is received, the 'gravitation and the filial bond' (11, 263).

Any reader familiar with the philsophical writings of Heidegger will recognise similar elements central to his thought: the idea of world as a texture through which we come to be; the critique of the privileging of vision in Western thought as the foundation for a Cartesian concept of knowledge which radically splits us away from world and leads us to assume the detached superiority of the scientist in relation to an inert object of investigation; the sense of aesthetic language as an alternative to that conceptualisation which divides us from world by allowing a radically ontogenetic 'showing forth', a form of authentic dwelling as disclosing (revelation and concealment). The main argument of Heidegger's work is summed up in his declaration:

> In clarifying being-in-the-world we have shown that a bare subject without a world never . . . is . . . given. And so . . . an isolated 'I' without others is just as far from being proximally given. (Heidegger, 1962, p152).

Heidegger's modernity is more advanced than Wordsworth's, but they are still recognisably connected. For Heidegger, modernity is a condition defined by a characteristic denial or disavowal of being-in-the-world. A detached subjectivity has come to stand over an inert nature, looking, speculating, judging and manipulating it for its own ends. It is the full flowering of that instrumental rationalism viewed in *The Prelude* as the imperialism of the eye. Behind it is an empty subjectivity swallowed up in calculative thinking, radically disembedded from a home it can no longer find, a Being-in-the-world founded on the denial of that world through its subjugation to a technological will. It is this situatedness in a world which pre-exists us (and which cannot be conceptualised through an overlay of rationalism) and through which we come into our own being as it 'worlds' through us, which Heidegger, like Wordsworth before him, calls us to recognise. To accept this is a form of humble acknowledgement that we can only come to presence within the world and through a texture of understanding provided in it. Yet we can take up possibilities which may allow us to retrieve what is as yet unsaid by recognising that Cartesian 'presence' is only one form of relationship: to listen to the 'still, sad, music of humanity' means an openness to as many of the horizons of world as are available to us at any one moment. We must listen and hear rather than look and judge. Language is central to Heideggerian situatedness, just as it is to later postmodern theories like those of Richard Rorty or Michel Foucault's notion of discursive formations. In 'Building Dwelling Thinking', Heidegger argues that 'man acts as though he were the shaper and master of language, while in fact, language remains the master of man. Perhaps it is above all else man's subversion of this relation of dominance that drives his nature into alienation' (Heidegger, 1975, p46). Instead, Heidegger recommends that 'man speaks in that he responds to language. This responding is a hearing. It hears because it listens to the command of stillness' (p210).

If the purely Heideggerian seems inevitably to lead to an ethics of passivity and acceptance, the Nietzschean may destroy both self and other in its imperialistic violence. The aesthetic and political dangers of both modes are obvious. But they are powerful post-Romantic currents in

Postmodernism, reshaped within new historical contexts, and it may be that in re-examining modern and postmodern texts, we can discover in them some modified form or dialectic of these impulses which offers not only a different way of reading but of *being* in that text which is world.

2

THE POETICS
OF THE SUBLIME

Presenting the Unpresentable

This section will engage closely with a central text of postmodern theory which, in drawing on the concept of the sublime, implicitly asks us to think about the relations between Romantic and postmodern aesthetics. Lyotard's essay, 'Answering the Question: What is Postmodernism?'[11], is a useful place to begin an investigation of Postmodernism because it illustrates very well the variety of definitions of and positions on it and the way in which they are bound up with assumptions about Modernism and Romanticism.

I
New Contexts for Lyotard's Postmodernism

Lyotard's essay characteristically concludes with the self-referential assertion that Postmodernism is the essay form itself. What does Lyotard mean by this teasing synechdochal displacement? He uses the mode of synechdoche, however, substituting part for whole, in a postmodern shift of emphasis where whole is an ever ongoing incompleted *process*. He wishes to resist the sort of organicist contextualisation which offers completion through explaining the part as *representative* of the whole. So the essay form can be seen to offer opinions like a speaker in a conversation; the essayist does not set out to offer total explanations (though this is not necessarily to deny that there may be a totality beyond explanation). Lyotard sets

---

[11] The essay appeared as a postscript to the later English translation of *The Postmodern Condition*.

Postmodernism as 'essay' against Modernism as 'fragment': more teasing definitions which seem to deny the possibility of definition? In drawing this distinction, Lyotard implicitly calls upon the Romantic notion of the fragment as a part which impels that representational act of Imagination in search of origins which can totalise and discover a whole through a mental projection uniting inner and outer forms. He sees a nostalgia for such organicism in Modernism, but turns the premises of Kant's concept of the sublime against itself to argue for a postmodern version which is free of such nostalgia in its full recognition that the sublime is the unpresentable in presentation itself and should be respected as such. Political terror is one consequence of attempting to ignore this.

Despite the modernist acknowledgement of contingency, Lyotard implies that its representation of experience as a discontinuous, non-rationalisable flux is always set off against a concern with abstraction as the possibility of creating a coherent autonomous aesthetic form which may yet discover some mode of correspondence with an Order of the Real outside its own constructions. In this essay, at least, Lyotard seems to acknowledge that there may indeed be such a space, an 'outside', or 'real', which is not dependent upon our construction of it, but this space will have to remain 'sublime'. In using this term, he invokes and extends as central to his definition of the postmodern, the Kantian notion of the sublime as confirming the ultimate incommensurability of reality as pure Idea to concept as tool of human understanding. This is in contradistinction to the beautiful which has the effect of seeming to affirm a realisable correspondence between internal and external orders. Kant outlined his theory of the sublime in the Third Critique (*Critique of Judgement*) where he divides the human mind into three faculties: understanding, reason and judgement. He calls the a priori laws of the understanding, the categories, and they are the laws which, of necessity, we impose upon our phenomenal experience of the world. All knowledge is determined by the concepts formed by means of the understanding which is applied to the sensory world through the imagination in its capacity to form images. Set against the concept is the 'idea', the product of the highest faculty of mind, reason, but so far removed from the phenomenal world that it cannot find conceptual or sensory embodiment in it. Instead, it serves as an ideal which we can never experience let alone conceptualise. The sublime is connected to the sphere of pure ideas as the beautiful is to the sphere of understanding.

Sublimity, for Kant, is that experience of an object which invokes an idea of reason, but one which is necessarily radically indeterminate. We cannot formulate, know or judge it:

We observe that whereas natural beauty conveys a finality in its form, making the object appear as it were pre-adapted to our power of judgement, so that it thus forms of itself an object of delight, that which on the other hand in our apprehension of it excites the feeling of the sublime may appear in point of form to contravene the ends of our power of judgement, to be ill-adapted to our faculty of presentation, and to be, as it were, an outrage on the imagination, and yet it is judged all the more sublime on that account (Kant, 1952, p245).

In other words, Kant is saying that the imagination can excite in us ideas which cannot be realised or represented in sensory form. The experience may cause us to feel pain but also to experience a sense of elevation as imaginatively we aspire to the realisation of a power within us which, paradoxically, our imagination is incapable of understanding or conceptualising. The experience is simultaneously one of a glimpsed plenitude and liberation and of a recognition of finite limits and loss or deprivation. The notion appears later in several postmodern psychoanalytic accounts of desire: Lacan's space of the imaginary or Kristeva's maternal body, for example, and articulates that familiar Romantic dialectic of impulse toward a plenitudinous transcendence and recognition, explicit or implicit, of ironic finitude which propels the postmodern modes of self-reflexive fictionality and parody. The sublime transcends every faculty of sense, taunts us with a glimpse of inaccessible plenitude and leaves us with the impossible self-conscious wrestle with words in the hopeless struggle to embody it.

For Lyotard, in a period of what he calls 'slackening' (here again he seems to draw upon Kant's idea of laziness as a cowardly form of tutelage to the conventional and pre-given), of unthinking conformism ruled by money and ready-made conceptual categories, the only authentic Postmodernism is that, in art and philosophy, which asserts the 'unpresentable in presentation itself'. In other words the only authentic mode of expression now is that of the sublime. It is to be a self-conscious postmodern sublime, however, which has renounced all nostalgic yearning for correspondence between our constructions and the world. Existing as a form of radical subjective fictionality, an aesthetic which refuses mimesis, organic unity, consensus, it offers multiple perspectives which ostentatiously and dramatically refuse to coalesce or resolve into some transcendent or more profound whole. In this sense he sees the writing of James Joyce as *post*-modern, for his work alludes to 'something which does not allow itself to be made present' (Lyotard, 1986, p80). He sees in Joyce precisely a self-conscious 'excess of the book', a kaleidoscopic parody of literary styles which flaunts 'literature' as a formal ritual enactment of a substance which cannot be known and which therefore contents itself with a self-reflexive play with its own condition of materiality.

In the same essay, Lyotard dismisses those postmodernisms which offer themselves as populist democratisations of the aesthetic, works which embrace their implication in consumer society. He rejects their theorisation as artefacts which subvert the Romantic legacy which views the aesthetic in broadly Kantian terms as an autonomous sphere of non-utilitarian value. He views such works as naively or duplicitously complicit with the pluralistic free-market values of consumer capitalism, a 'postmodernism' which is indistinguishable from 'kitsch':

> Eclecticism is the degree zero of contemporary general culture: one listens to reggae, watches a Western, eats McDonald's food for lunch and local cuisine for dinner, wears Paris perfume in Tokyo and 'retro clothes' in Hong Kong; knowledge is a matter for T.V. games. It is easy to find a public for eclectic works. By becoming kitsch art panders to the confusion which reigns in the 'taste' of the patrons. Artists, gallery owners, critics and public wallow together in the 'anything goes', and the epoch is one of slackening (ibid., p76).

Paradoxically, Lyotard refers to *this* Postmodernism as a 'realism', a realism of money: a reflectionist aesthetic which in pandering to all needs and tastes simply affirms the capitalist accommodation of all human impulses which are produced within and reciprocally propel the market.

Why does Lyotard wish to define the postmodern as a mode of the sublime, existing in authentic form as a counterforce to the commodifying tendencies of modern capitalist societies? For those readers unfamiliar with the postmodern debate, Lyotard's essay may appear to be a dauntingly difficult place to begin to try to understand it. His invocation of the sublime as definitive of an authentic Postmodernism seems to reinvent the post-modern as a new Romanticism and to demote the more familiar versions of it as the acknowledgement of complicity with mass culture to the status of a spurious cultural legitimation of cheap kitsch. Moreover, the concept of the sublime in Kant is bound to a view of subjective autonomy against which everything in Postmodernism seems to stand. In order to under-stand this, we need to examine the other hidden subtext of the essay: its implicit dialogue with the thought of Jürgen Habermas. There is a passing general reference to Habermas on the second page, but in fact, Lyotard clearly *specifically* invokes the argument of Habermas's 1980 essay 'Mod-ernity versus Postmodernity', originally his 1980 Frankfurt address on receiving the Adorno prize. Lyotard's essay can be seen as an elaborate response to Habermas in a further meditation on this relationship in which Lyotard develops an essentially *Romantic* concept of the aesthetic in order to offer a critique of Habermas's support for a modified continuation of Enlightenment. (However, Lyotard develops a Kantian concept of the necessary separation of the categories of the moral, scientific and aesthetic in an argument which is by no means straightforwardly counter-Enlightenment. Habermas's own subtext was supplied by the immediate occasion of his lecture: Adorno's sustained critique of Enlightenment reason as a form of instrumental, rationalist domination of inner and outer nature which had paved the way for totalitarian regimes of rationalist efficiency serving utterly irrationalist ends. Habermas's project is to reinvent reason in order to complete Enlightenment. Lyotard is opposed to *any* foundationalism.)

II
Enlightenment
Exhausted or Incomplete?

The crux of all these arguments, and of the postmodern debate in general, is the question of the role of art and the aesthetic in relation to the contemporary state of knowledge. In his talk, Habermas wished to claim that the Enlightenment project, what he calls the 'project of modernity', is not exhausted (a position he identifies with Derrida, Foucault and others like Daniel Bell whom he regards as 'neo-conservatives'), but unfinished.

Because reason in the form identified by Adorno and others as purposive or instrumental rationalism (based on a radical Cartesian separation which sets autonomous Subject over inert object), may be seen to have failed, and with it the progressivist and emancipatory ideals of the Enlightenment, this does not mean we should abandon reason altogether as the possibility of epistemological critique in order to embrace various 'postmodern' (often in fact pre-modern) alternatives as evidenced by religious revivalism, post-structuralist celebrations of the jouissance of the freeplay of the signifier or fashionable and hedonistic philosophies of 'desire'. Instead, we need to look again at our concepts of reason. For Habermas also, it is here that a shift in our relation to art and the aesthetic may be of great benefit to us.

For Habermas, the Enlightenment project is incomplete rather than exhausted because its belief in the centrality of human reason as the key to human liberation has been compromised by an accommodation with modern capitalist forces of efficiency which define reason increasingly in terms of a narrow and specialised expertise (Habermas, 1987). Like Heidegger, Habermas is critical both of the domination of a narrow, instrumental concept of reason and of subject-centred philosophies of consciousness which perpetuate this restrictive conceptualisation. He is critical too of 'expert cultures' producing interpretative frameworks as functional ideologies which fragment the lifeworld by divorcing knowledge from context and reproducing it in impoverished forms of abstraction. However, he parts company both with the Heideggerian sense of situatedness as a recognition of the fundamentally ontogenetic power of aesthetic language, and with the post-Nietzschean sense, expressed in Foucault's later work, for example, of *techne* as an aesthetics of existence focused on the body (Foucault, 1988). For Habermas, modernity has become impoverished through overvaluing the cognitive at the expense of the practical and the aesthetic: we need a new balance of these categories. What we do not need, and what he sees as advocated in Postmodernism, is a new hegemony of the aesthetic involving a relegation of the cognitive (scientific) and practical (ethical). For Habermas, the aesthetic, in its distinctive forms, can enhance life by making us aware of the pre-reflective and bodily aspects of experience, but only as one aspect of the expansion of our concept of reason. Unlike Heidegger, he believes that we can know in ways which can (intersubjectively and consciously) be reformulated through *rational* public conversation. Art can facilitate this process: it must not subsume it.

Harbermas is hardly the first to articulate such a position. Though he is anxious to refute postmodern aestheticism, his critique of the dominance of narrow expertise and the fragmentation of human powers, actually borrows from a Romantic critique of industrialisation developed from the writing of Rousseau and Schiller. If he shares their diagnosis of aetiology, however, he disagrees with their proposed cure. And in this he separates himself from Postmodernism too. Lyotard summarises his position thus:

> Habermas . . . thinks that if modernity has failed, it is in allowing the totality of life to be splintered into independent specialities which are left to the narrow

competence of experts, while the concrete individual experiences 'desublimated meaning' and 'destructured form', not as a liberation but in the mode of that immense ennui which Baudelaire described over a century ago (ibid., p72).

In his 1980 talk, Habermas had argued that if the aesthetic (in its characteristic embodied and non-abstract form) could be freed from its imprisonment within the institutional parameters of the expert's critical judgements of taste, it might then enter into the arenas of knowledge and morality while retaining its own distinctive logic and remaining subservient to them and outside of 'truth value' as such. If the 'lifeworld' has been colonised by functional abstractions so that experience is splintered into independent specialities watched over by 'experts' unable to communicate across disciplinary and categorical boundaries, the aesthetic may be a means of facilitating the production of sociocultural unity if its qualities can be released from the grip of the language games of those new arbiters of taste: the institutionalised, professional critics.

III

Terror and the Sublime

The Art of the Unpresentable

Probably the most famous postmodern slogan of all comes at the end of Lyotard's essay. In order to begin to understand the connection between his definition of Postmodernism as an aesthetics of the sublime and his attack on Habermas's particular call for an integration of the aesthetic into the 'lifeworld', it requires quotation in full:

> The nineteenth and twentieth centuries have given us as much terror as we can take. We have paid a high enough price for the nostalgia of the whole and the one, for the reconciliation of the concept and the sensible, of the transparent and the communicable experience. Under the general demand for slackening and for appeasement, we can hear the mutterings of the desire for a return of terror, for the realisation of the fantasy to seize reality. The answer is: Let us wage a war on totality; let us be witnesses to the unpresentable; let us activate the differences and save the honour of the name (ibid., p82).

Lyotard may share some of Habermas's sense of what constitutes 'postmodernity', but as far as he is concerned, in an age where consensus is breaking down and the very foundations of knowledge are being challenged, it is highly dangerous to pursue an ideal of social integration which draws in the aesthetic as a facilitating vehicle. In this context, he prefers to revert to a notion of the value of the aesthetic as a form of non-utilitarian autonomy, a mode which is resistant to any form of conceptualisation and is therefore unpresentable: a particular reading of the Kantian sublime. For Lyotard, an authentic Postmodernism, a form of cultural expression which can resist the commodifying effects of postmodernity as consumer culture, must remain, in effect, in some equivalent form of the Kantian realm of pure reason. In exceeding all that can be presented, in becoming fully an aesthetics of silence or negation, the art of the sublime must remain in a sphere resistant to conceptual understanding. It must remain radically separate not only in order to resist commodification, but also to prevent that attempt to graft the ideal onto the real, in a coercive attempt to produce cultural unity, which for Lyotard has produced the most barbaric moments in history.

Throughout the essay, not only is there an overt identification of authentic Postmodernism with an aesthetic of the sublime, there is, in my view, a similar but covert identification of political conformism, realism in literature, the conventional in art, the aesthetic in Habermas, with Kant's concept of the beautiful. Lyotard implicitly represents the impulse towards the 'beautiful' as co-extensive with a lazy desire for an easy consensus, a therapeutic use of art to reconcile us to the mundane and the apparently given. His example of inauthentic Postmodernism as kitsch suggests that in such contemporary spurious modes (retro chic, Dandyism, purely playful mixing of modes and genres), Postmodernism itself is simply another conformism echoing the surfaces of Late Capitalist consumerism.

Kant had argued that the beautiful induces in us an harmonious feeling, a sense of the connection between aesthetic experience and the understanding of the sensus communis, the shared political world of human values. Although Lyotard does not say as much, he clearly connects Habermas's attack on Postmodernism and defence of the values of the Enlightenment with an understanding of the aesthetic formulated entirely in terms of the beautiful. In the contemporary period this can only represent an unthinking conformism. In Kant's view, when we look at the beautiful, it gives us pleasure and our common response confirms a sense of the shared basis of human understanding and the existence of harmonious, intersubjective experiences of value. To experience the sublime, however, is to recognise the inadequacy of the values produced in conceptual thought or experienced through sensory modes, to be disturbed into an acknowledgement of the existence of that which cannot be thought, analysed, presented through any determinate form. For Kant, this is to recognise those Ideas of Reason which may never be embodied or incarnated in human history.

Lyotard sees in the postmodern, as in the Romantic, expression of the sublime, a form of resistance to the banal and automatising effects of modern life. To attempt to *realise* the sublime as a blueprint for political or historical action would, however, dangerously conflate the different language games of the spheres of the speculative or ideal and those of the cognitive and practical. Existence may be aestheticised, but the aesthetic must not be used to underpin political ideologies which set out to produce new cultures through rationalised ideal frameworks. The language games of the aesthetic are valuable as models of *dissensus*, motivating us with a desire to pass beyond the analytic and the conceptual, offering a continuing sense of the 'as if'. For Lyotard, however, this can only be valuable if the sublime remains a never to be realised *beyond*. So here is a typical paradox of Postmodernism: Lyotard, generally regarded as the leading apologist for Postmodernism defines it, in effect, in terms most obviously derived from a Romantic theory of autonomy which has been most often used to define Modernism; Habermas, leading spokesperson for the continuation of Enlightenment modernity and chief critic of Postmodernism, here appears actually closer to an 'aestheticist' position which has been viewed in popular terms as definitive of postmodern theory.

In a sense, Lyotard's authentic Postmodernism is an ultra-Modernism and a Romanticism, resisting any pressure to embrace the belief that the forms of the aesthetic correspond to or can be translated into the forms and concepts of the historical world. Art must be ultra-autonomous to be genuine. It is a version of Schiller's defence of the aesthetic. And yet most popular accounts of Postmodernism see it as an aesthetic or theoretical mode which fully acknowledges its implication in the consumer world, totally eschewing the Romantic-Modernist belief in the idea of art as a radically autonomous sphere of non-utilitarian value which can therefore oppose the functionalism and instrumentalism of a world given over increasingly to commercial efficiency.

Clearly, a Habermasian response to this might be to argue that in attempting to protect art with theories of a separate aesthetic realm of play or non-utilitarian value, aestheticians from Schiller to Lyotard himself can be seen to intensify the very social effects they set out to remedy in their proclamations about art. They too can be seen to facilitate the process whereby art, like everything else, is sealed off into a realm constituted through and protected by institutional experts: literary critics and connoisseurs. The alternative for Habermas is not to treat life as a work of art in some Nietzschean mode of self-overcoming which simply continues to operate covertly with an inadequate concept of the subject as radically autonomous, but to move towards a model of what he calls 'communicative rationality' where the self is realised through intersubjective conversation which allows some integration of the aesthetic into the spheres of the cognitive and the ethical, but does not, in so doing, displace them or rub out their distinctive modes or identities. Clearly, though, there is a 'modern' slant to Lyotard's Postmodernism and a 'postmodern' slant to Habermas's Modernism.

IV
The Concept Versus the Luminous Detail
Against Totality

As soon as one starts to talk about Postmodernism, its associations and implications are so slippery and elastic that some commentators feel that as a theoretical label, or an aesthetic, or a period concept, it has already exhausted its usefulness. In fact, most of its theorists have been unable, on the whole, to live with the very indeterminacies, paradoxes, refusals of metanarratives, anti-foundationalisms, that they have endorsed as its distinguishing characteristics. To live in a state of 'hesitation', irresolution or paradox, is, indeed, intensely difficult. It is, as Freud argued, indicative of a hard-won maturity. Postmodernists proclaim, for a variety of reasons, the need to wage war on totality, but it is not clear that they always achieve it themselves. Often, as here, Postmodernism is 'totalised' through a concept like the sublime which can itself be used to stand for non-totalisation. Here lies the paradox and in effect the performative self-contradiction of Postmodernism. When Lyotard so strenuously defends the sublime as an autonomous realm of the aesthetic which cannot be integrated into available concepts, as radically heterogeneous, non-harmonious and discontinuous, he intends the elaboration of a philo-sophical position which implicitly refuses available paradigms within the tradition of analytical philosophy. It is a position broadly shared by writers and theorists as diverse as Richard Rorty, Jean Baudrillard, Michel Foucault, Gilles Deleuze and Stanley Fish. All refuse to acknowledge any limits to the realm of imaginary representation, whether it is viewed as radically autonomous from, or fully integrated with, the world of historical experience. Each, in different ways, provides a critique of any claim to a perspective or vantage point which is transcendent, outside of its modes or objects of critique. The position is easy to turn back on itself: is 'the postmodern condition' itself simply a totalisation, an invention of theory as it denies the possibility of theory in a contemporary version of the ancient Liar Paradox? No wonder its modes are those of irony, parody, infinite regress and nested representation. The aesthetic becomes the most authen-tic form of representation because even if it pretends to universal truth, it does so in a non-conceptual mode which must, ironically, always undo its own assertion of universality.

In these terms, to attempt to offer a rational account of human experi-ence through Enlightenment universal categories is to 'totalise'. The first lesson of Postmodernism is that it is impossible to step outside that which one contests, that one is always implicated in the values one chooses to challenge. Even if other values exist (the sublime), they cannot be trans-lated into available historical forms of representation nor function as the basis for epistemological critique. Any theoretical system is simply a provisional working fiction to be used pragmatically and abandoned when no longer useful. As the narrator in Salman Rushdie's *Shame* puts it: 'I myself manage to hold large numbers of wholly irreconcilable views simultaneously, without the least difficulty. I do not think others are less versatile' (Rushdie, 1983, p227). What is valid in one context or 'just' or 'true' may not be so in another: the universal gives way to the local, to a recognition of *situatedness* or of a *radically fictional* sense of truth. The notion of autonomy in any *practical* sense becomes redundant. In neither mode can philosophy or art stand outside or refuse implication in the very economic and ideological dominants of the historical moment in which they exist. To offer critique can only be to challenge from within through rhetorical or narrative disruption. Parodic forms are foregrounded for parody implicitly acknowledges its parasitic dependence on a pre-existing rhetorical mode.

For postmodernists of whatever persuasion, systematic theories which claim to account for all features of human societies or behaviours are always disguised enactments of a will to power which functions through unjust or even violent and dangerous exclusions. This is why Lyotard sees all attempts to translate the sublime into the political as productive of terror. In his later work *The Differend* (1988), he even refuses the notion of community. It is seen as a construction which victimises minorities who can only be identified within the terms of the community but from which they actually differ in ways not able to be articulated under its rules of knowledge. If this is 'postmodern', again I would argue that it is a development of an essentially Romantic preoccupation with the paradoxes of articulating 'inside' and 'outside'. Nathaniel Hawthorne, for example, had presented such paradoxes in his fictional Romance, *The Scarlet Letter*. Here, the basis of Law for the Puritan community is shown to involve a conflation of sin as moral transgression with crime as legal transgression. Law is thus identified in opposition to desire, but where each functions as a construct of the other. The identity of Law is created and maintained through the projection of that desire which it cannot acknowledge within its own boundaries, onto what is thus constituted as its 'outside'. So Pearl, Hester's illegitimate daughter, is of the forest, not to be contained within but actually constructed through and constructive of the world of Law or Custom. Pearl is the wilderness. She is an embodiment of that non-identity of her mother as adulterous transgressor, which is so necessary to the preservation of identity of the boundaries of the Puritan community itself. Hester, meanwhile, can only exist in her own body as the bearer of the scarlet letter which speaks her 'otherness' in the eyes of the community, though she draws on the aesthetic in her art of needlework in a parodic (silently transgressive) mode, fantastically dressing the letter and thus theatrically flaunting her identity as non-identity. The letter presents the unpresentable which is Hester's sexual body. First character in the alphabet and the colour of blood, it signals identity as entry into language and representation, the border between inside and outside as that which is the unpresentable in presentation itself.

Totalising systems create the 'same', the universal, through exclusion of the 'other'. Postmodernism has been referred to as a romance of the marginal or the other. However, all theories function by creating or perceiving similarities and thus producing unities of some kind. Indeed, as Nietzsche argued, concepts are thus, in effect, theories, but we certainly could not function in the world without them. To experience the world as a continuous flux of radically contingent detail (as Borges' protagonist in the story 'The Mind of the Mnemonist' in *Labyrinths* (1964)) would be to capitulate to chaos and disintegration (no sense of continuity in time, no sense of agency, that state of schizophrenia which Jameson, in fact, sees as characteristic of postmodernity in its loss of metanarratives). Alternatively, Postmodernism could be seen as the recognition of the necessity for, but the provisionality and proliferation of, little and grand narratives. In many ways, it simply develops to a more heightened degree of self-awareness that abiding *modern* concern with the relations between contingency and abstraction which arises as the Idealist metaphysical framework of Romanticism comes under increasing strain. The concern is apparent throughout the writing of Eliot, Pound, Joyce, as well as that of philosophers such as Bergson, Bradley and William James.

As early as 1904, in fact, William James expressed what may seem a very 'postmodern' sense of things:

> Up to about 1850 almost everyone believed that science expressed truths that were exact copies of a definite code of non-human realities. But the enormously rapid multiplication of theories in these latter days has well-nigh upset the notion of any one of them being a more literally objective kind of thing than another . . . the notion that even the truest formula may be a human device and not a literal transcript has dawned upon us (1975, p40).

James begins to articulate a conventionalist position, viewing rational constructs as neither the representation of external reality nor forms through which the mind necessarily organises experience. They are simply useful fictions: tools which help us to order experience. Nietzsche went much further than this, of course, to argue that even the most elementary concept is a human fiction, a pragmatic tool, and to attack the Platonic idea that abstractions correspond to underlying and essential realities. His best known representation of this is again in the essay entitled 'On Truth and Lies in a Non-Moral sense', where he discusses concepts as forms of metaphor, ways of connecting disparate experiences so as to confer some general order upon things and to give the impression of a correspondence existing between the abstractions of thought and the sensuous materiality of the world. Thus he argues:

> Every concept arises from the equation of unequal things. Just as it is certain that one leaf is never totally the same as another, so it is certain that the concept 'leaf' is formed by arbitrarily discarding these individual differences and by forgetting the distinguishing aspects. This awakens the idea that, in addition to the leaves, there exists in nature the 'leaf': the original model according to which all the leaves were perhaps woven, sketched, measured, coloured, curled, and painted-out by incompetent hands, so that no specimen has turned out to be a correct, trustworthy and faithful likeness of the original model . . . We obtain the concept, as we do the form, by overlooking what is individual and actual: whereas nature is acquainted with forms and no concepts, and likewise with no species, but only with an X which remains inaccessible and undefinable for us (1979, p83).

This notion of the relationship of concept to metaphor provides one of the starting points, in my view, both for the postmodern shift of emphasis from the autonomy of art to the pervasiveness of the aesthetic and to its critique of the dangers of totalising theory associated with Enlightenment thought. What Nietzsche suggests, is that concepts are not reflections of essences in reality, but disguised or 'dead' metaphors used to organise that chaos of sensation which is experience. We tend to assume, however, that they are transcripts of reality itself. For Nietzsche, art is more authentic than Platonic forms of philosophy because, unlike theirs, its condition of fictionality is not hidden. Postmodern art, in its 'sublime' form, is most authentic for Lyotard precisely because it positively flaunts its condition of fictionality. So too, some postmodern writers like Richard Brautigan develop series of metaphorical constructions where vehicle and tenor are so exaggeratedly disparate that the comically incongruous effect insistently reminds the reader that any perceived order can only be an arbitrary construction of the human mind. In Joyce's *Ulysses* also, the basic metaphorical structure of the novel which draws together the disparate worlds of heroic Greece and less-than-heroic turn of the century middle-class Dublin, in itself, insistently reminds us of its departed creator, a modern radical fictionaliser, supposedly paring his fingernails in the background. It is, amongst other things, a metaphor of the ontogenetic potential of metaphor, *and* a recognition that however much language reproduces world, world also remains outside of language. What we shall need to examine next is whether Postmodernism itself exists outside of the language of its theorists. In its own terms, of course, we simply cannot know.

3

PERIODISING
THE
POSTMODERN

Ism as Fiery Particle

I
Introduction
Constructing the Dominant

'**W**orking with theory', as I have suggested, should not be a matter of the mechanistic imposition onto decontextualised literary texts of remote intellectual paradigms: working with Postmodernism, in particular, has to involve a dialectic of text and context. Because self-consciousness about the concept of periodisation is central to the construction of Postmodernism as a period term, an examination of some of the ways in which this has been defined may illuminate more general issues about the function of *literary*, as well as historical, notions of epoch. The seemingly unavoidable performative self-contradiction of Postmodernism: that it is itself a 'totality' even as it denies the possibility of totality, suggests, in fact, not only that we need generalisation to organise experience, but in so generalising, we preserve a major function of human agency despite all the proclamations about the end of the self-determining subject. General theories are not, of course, total theories, though they may become naturalised to the extent that they begin to function in this way. General theories offer accounts of particular tendencies in experience but do not claim to account for everything. They can be enabling in that their frameworks can allow one to perceive new relationships within different Gestalts, but they may produce blindness if they become 'totalising' in the sense of hardening into exclusive dogmas which shut out alternative perspectives. Frank Kermode has noted that 'ism is indeed a fiery particle; it can add or take away value ... period descriptions have the same ambivalent quality, quite often starting life as sneer words and being converted by their users into eulogisms' (1988, p119). To encircle a period of time with an 'ism' is to organise it according to one or more perceived 'dominants', though as Postmodernism has shown us, what is regarded as dominant will, in part, be a function of one's current and particular situation. Postmodernism is certainly the 'dominant' for a large number of contemporary intellectuals (though, as we shall see, that dominant is constructed in different ways), but it is less clear that it has the same organising power for those outside the academy. Postmodernism, of course, acknowledges this. From Foucault's notion of history as a plurality of discourses with no epochs except those constructed discursively, to Lyotard's concept of 'language games', it both asserts and undermines its own power as a periodising term.

Setting aside, for a moment, the issue of the extent to which Postmodernism is a construct projected onto the social or cultural world and thus enabling the theorist to find there whatever he or she desires, we need, first of all, to look at the concept of a 'dominant'. It has been used in relation both to works of art and cultural epochs. Roman Jakobson originally drew on the concept in a specifically *aesthetic* context, defining it as the 'focusing component of a work of art', which 'rules, determines and transforms the remaining components'. He goes on to suggest that in 'the evolution of poetic form it is not so much a question of the disappearance of certain elements and the emergence of others as it is the question of shifts in the mutual relationship among the diverse components of the system, in other words, a question of the shifting dominant' (Matejka and Pomorska, 1971, p105, 108). Jakobson is talking about formal features in the work; his positivism is echoed in a historical version of the same idea developed from Raymond Williams' concept of dominant, residual and emergent ideologies by Fredric Jameson:

> Radical breaks between periods do not generally involve complete changes of content but rather the restructuration of a certain number of elements already given: features that in an earlier period or system were subordinate now become dominant, and features that had been dominant again become secondary (postword, Kellner, 1989b, p357).

All accounts of Postmodernism work with a particular 'dominant', which may be derived from aesthetics, economics, or the history of ideas, and is often a confusing amalgam of aspects of each of these. Such dominants tend to function hermeneutically, as all period concepts, so that a 'fore-understanding' of history enables one to enter it as an object of study and then closely to examine the features one discovers there without, however, fully being able to conceptualise the extent to which one discovers them *because* of one's preliminary framework. Postmodernism, in particular, shows us that periods make history manageable, but they inevitably raise questions of genealogy, value and power. All who use the term are aware of its self-cancelling reference to its own status as a provisional concept, aware too that *every* 'now' of history, even if modernity is more self-conscious of the process, has wanted to see itself as distinctive by redrawing its relation to the past. Freud famously, of course, said that hysterics suffer mainly from reminiscences (1895, p7) – those unsure of the boundaries of their identity are uncontrollably haunted by the past until they can rewrite it in terms which meaningfully connect with the present. Working with war-traumatised soldiers in 1919, he recognised that in order to gain control over the threat of disintegration and chaos we are compelled to repeat. Just as his shell-shocked soldiers relived their traumas night after night in their dreams – forcing Freud to revise his earlier theories about the pleasure principle (Freud, 1920) – so too, one can see the obsessive concern with the concept of 'post', of transition, of being after but not free of, which defines the parameters of the postmodern, as an expression of an urgent need to be both free of but to define one's relation to the past in order to experience some purchase on the present. Postmodernism is used more often as a period term by those who have good reason to use it in order to recover history and to discover their possible modes of agency in a world which increasingly undermines that power: those whose social function has been a critical one and who now confront a world where critique becomes increasingly difficult to formulate and sustain.

Thus the dominant of Postmodernism is always constructed around a particular interpretation of that of the preceding period and by what is therefore implied by the 'post'. We shall examine some views of modernity and Modernism later in this book and an adequate sense of postmodernity can only emerge in relation to historical definitions of the modern. Here we will concentrate on the implications of the prefix 'post'. The cultural critic Daniel Bell and the literary critic Frank Kermode noted the mood of 'sense of an ending' before the postmodern manifestos began to appear, Bell viewing this as the impetus behind the designation of 'post' 'to define, as a combined form, the age into which we are moving' (Bell, 1974 p54). He listed by way of illustration: post-capitalist, post-Christian, post-industrial, post-liberal, post-Marxist, post-Protestant and many more. The list has since been vastly extended. In each case, the present is hermeneutically constructed in dialogic relation with a perceived dominant characteristic of the past (capitalism, liberalism, Marxism, industrialism, Modernism). Again the problem is to decide the status of this dominant: whether it is a useful conceptualisation of history in that it seems to reflect, as far as one can ever know, the facts that we have about the past, or whether it is being used as a generalisation or 'totalisation' based on little more than a polemical need to establish a contrastive mode of relationality with whatever is to be defined as the present. However, the reiteration of 'post' in relation to so many perceived historical dominants does suggest, if nothing more, that the current epoch is, indeed, characterised by an intense proliferation of value systems whose relativising effect on each other is bound to produce some crisis of legitimation, some sense that the 'master narratives' if not dead, are considerably weakened or in need of intellectual rejuvenation.

We need, briefly, to examine some of the ways in which the historical dominant of Postmodernism has been constructed by critics engaged in the current debate. Lyotard's discussion of the sublime has been criticised by Marxists such as Eagleton for dehistoricising Postmodernism by defining it in purely aesthetic terms. As my own presentation of the postmodern has so far concentrated on the aesthetic, it must now turn to some of the historical accounts of it. Eagleton's own is a good place to start because it illustrates the tendency of its critics to conflate Postmodernism as a cultural and aesthetic practice with the negative values of postmodernity as an economically defined epoch. As a period term, Postmodernism is often used as an uneasy amalgam of the two, a term 'awkward and faintly epigonic' (Barth, 1980, p66). Clearly, Lyotard's notion of the sublime sets out to retain for postmodern art the possibility of opposition and distinct cultural identity, but for Eagleton, Lyotard's Postmodernism is an aspect of a naive post-structuralist embrace of 'desire' as that which can explode out of history in order to deny its own historicity (but, as I have already tried to show, this impulse itself has a much longer history than that of post-structuralism). He suggests that in Lyotard's account:

> The 'modern' is less a particular cultural practice or historical period, which may then suffer defeat or incorporation, than a kind of permanent ontological possibility of disrupting all such historical periodisation, an essentially timeless gesture which cannot be recited or reckoned up within historical narrative because it is no more than an atemporal force which gives the lie to all such linear categorisation (Eagleton, 1986, p135).

This is Lyotard's Postmodernism as the disruptive element in Modernism: Eagleton sees it as typical of a cultural practice which denies history, depth, opposition, and is simply co-extensive with the commodification of all life in consumer capitalism. This is Eagleton's (economic) dominant. In a commercially aestheticised world, art is simply an aesthetic reflection of already aestheticised images. If art in modernist culture was fetishised in order to retain its autonomy in a world of mass culture, postmodern art is simply another depthless surface mirroring the unreality of the images which construct similar depthless surfaces of a consumer society where all commodities are packaged fetishes. Postmodernism is a debased pastiche of the avant-garde, flaunting its commodity status to become 'aesthetically what it is economically' (p141). Every original move it claims is seen to be another reflection of its cultural complicity. Its deconstructive aesthetics or politics of desire simply reinforces by reproducing a subject *already* 'dispersed, decentred network of libidinal attachments' (p145): its commodity form within consumer capitalism. Eagleton reiterates the usual opposition of modernist autonomy and postmodern aestheticism, viewing the modernist artwork as a 'mysteriously autotelic object', having no truck with the real, and the postmodern as a collapse of art into world through a common commercialisation. I will not comment for the moment on this thesis, except to point out that Eagleton's aesthetic categories are entirely theoretical constructs and he offers no examples or discussions of actual works of art. What I shall try to do later in this book is to show how this distinction between Modernism and Postmodernism starts to break down as soon as we examine actual works of art. The aim will be to try to understand, therefore, how it arises as a critical construct and why it is unquestioningly accepted by commentators across the political and theoretical spectrum. If 'working with Postmodernism' can throw light on this critical history, then the postmodern can be seen to play at least some facilitating role in the production of critical knowledge.

II
The Cultural Logic of Jameson's Postmodernism

If Eagleton supports the idea of Postmodernism as the cultural logic of Late Capitalism, it was Fredric Jameson who first produced it. I will examine his position through a close contextualised reading of a central text, 'Periodising the Sixties' (Jameson, 1989) which surveys historical trends characteristic of Postmodernism and then offers an economic analysis of them in terms of Ernst Mandel's categories articulated in his book *Late Capitalism* (1978). As in the seminal essay 'Postmodernism or the Consumer Logic of Late Capitalism' (1984), Jameson here puts forward the view that it is impossible simply to define a position for or against Postmodernism for, 'the point is we are within the culture of postmodernism to the point where its facile repudiation is as impossible as any equally facile celebration of it is complacent and corrupt' (1990, 2, piii). For Jameson, as Eagleton, Postmodernism is co-extensive with the culture of Late Capitalism, emerging in the sixties, and distinctive in its invasion of all remaining, potentially oppositional spaces: Nature, the 'third world' and the unconscious. Jameson's earlier work had made the Hegelian assumption that there *are* spaces outside the logic of capitalism even in its consumerist forms; structures to be inhabited beneath its depthless surfaces; metanarratives such as Marxism which occupy positions of truth and can, therefore, offer opposition and critique. In his more recent discussions of Postmodernism, however, all theories, including Marxism, become problematic because they can only conduct their critique from the very metaposition which Postmodernism as the cultural logic of Late capitalism has abolished.

With this in mind, commentators like Callinicos (1990) and Anderson (1984), have argued that Marxist intellectuals like Jameson have been fatally attracted to a quietist position where Postmodernism can only function as a weakened, necessarily internal critique of Western instrumentalism in the aftermath of the failure of radical political hopes for revolutionary change after 1968. There have been a number of historical events, even before the most recent upheavals in Eastern Europe, which are cited as contributing to an intellectual drift towards forms of postmodern thought. The Marxist labour-capital matrix has been challenged not only through the failure of working class revolution, but also, for example, as a consequence of the shift towards new forms of production and consumption; the challenge to class analysis from new social movements representing concerns of race, gender and eco-politics; the rise of new technologies and new relations between work and leisure. It is not surprising that the efficacy of unified social or political theories may appear to have collapsed and to have bought down their own axiomatic categories of class, history, the subject, Art.

In this particular essay, Jameson suggests that none of these changes, in itself, is radically new. Although Postmodernism may be the cultural dominant of the period we are living through, its characteristics are seen to have accumulated gradually with the continuity of the economic base of capitalism. He outlines dominant features of Modernism: the concern with the autonomy of language, the 'play of the signifier' which undermines the referent, and the idea of depth as meaningful. These are now seen, however, to be 'reaching a certain threshold of excess' which 'in its prolongation now produces qualitatively distinct effects and seems to generate a whole new system' (p200). Like Eagleton, he emphasises the collapse of the autonomy of art: culture becomes 'coterminous with social life in general; now all levels become acculturated, and in the society of the spectacle, the image, or the simulacrum, everything has at length become cultural, from the superstructures down into the mechanisms of the infrastructure itself' (p201). We can no longer talk about 'culture' because its artefacts have become the random experiences of daily life itself. Jameson basically reproduces features of Baudrillard's analysis of the contemporary epoch as a 'media society' or new universe of simulacra, a 'hyperreal' where image can no longer be separated from real in a Beckettian scenario where the qualities previously attributed to subjects are now transferred to a world of objects: commodities which call to us, seduce us and define us. Jameson does not, however, share Baudrillard's technological determinism nor his purely reproductive economy of the sign. Jameson situates himself still within a theory of political economy. But with stresses and strains.

Even as early as *Marxism and Form* (1971), however, Jameson had begun to develop the idea that what characterises the contemporary period in all its forms is loss of depth. The notion of modernity as a particular relation of surface and depth has been a powerful presupposition of much modern thought. In *The Order of Things*, Michel Foucault argued that this concern is the *defining* characteristic of the modern period and though Postmodernism may believe it has moved into a new paradigm we are, in fact, still bound up with this basic dialectic of modernity. For Foucault, the shift from classical to modern was one involving a loss of faith in the possibility of the perfect and transparent representation of truth and a growing uncertainty about knowledge and its acquisition. This has manifested itself in a self-conscious and self-reflexive concern with language, characteristic of most forms of modernity. Only when the notion of representation has been abandoned altogether (rather than simply problematised) will we have moved beyond the modern episteme. This is what Foucault has to say about the issue of depth:

> It is clear that this 'return' of language is not a sudden interruption in our culture; it is not the irruptive discovery of some long-buried evidence; it does not indicate a folding back of thought upon itself, in the movement by which it emancipates itself from all content, or a narcissism occurring within a literature freeing itself at last from what it has to say in order to speak henceforth only about the fact that it is language stripped naked. It is, in fact, the strict unfolding of Western culture in accordance with the necessity it imposed upon itself at the beginning of the nineteenth century. It would be false to see in this general indication of our experience, which may be termed 'formalism', the sign of a drying up, of a rarefaction of thought losing its capacity for re-apprehending the plentitude of contents; it would be no less false to place it from the outset upon some new horizon of thought or new knowledge. It is within the very tight-knit, very coherent outlines of the modern episteme that

this contemporary experience found its possibility; it is even that episteme which, by its logic, gave rise to such an experience, constituted it through and through, and made it impossible for it not to exist ... all that still forms the immediate space of our reflection. We think in that area (Foucault, 1974, p384).

Despite his proclamation that we are in the postmodern condition, so does Jameson. In fact, in this essay, he not only 'totalises' the period according to a depth-surface model drawn from the history of ideas, he also provides an economic base for the entire explanation by drawing on Mandel's analysis. Jameson begins by cataloguing apparently random historical and political events which arose during the sixties and have come to frame our sense of the contemporary period: the crisis of the New Left; the withdrawal from Vietnam; the development of the idea of a culture of narcissism; the growth of multinational corporations; decolonisation and neocolonialism; the breakdown of postwar consensus in Western democracies; the new rhetorics of youth, feminism, ecology, counterculture. However, even before he invokes Mandel's economic historical categories, key post-structuralist concepts begin to emerge as a means of organising this apparently random and disparate material. He lists the features of Postmodernism in these terms: the death of the subject; the culture of the simulacrum; the proliferation of trompe l'oeil art; copies without originals; textuality; loss of historicity (as a sense of teleological linear time); pastiche. All of these categories are attempts to deny depth and to embrace surface, but Jameson uses them as a framework supplying precisely that depth without which he could not theoretically contextualise his random list of historical events.

Jameson effectively shares the view of the postmodern as a response to the exhaustion of the Romantic/Modernist claim to aesthetic autonomy and to the realist notion of art mirroring a world outside the text. Postmodernism is a crisis in the belief in the possibility of authentic self-expression or objective representation. It is a cultural embodiment of post-structuralism (which provides Jameson's own first layer of ideological depth). But Jameson, further subverting his own definition, wants to go deeper still and see both it and post-structuralism as expressions of an underlying economic model. Strictly speaking, of course, his own arguments about the total invasion of the logic of Late Capitalism contradict the attempt to offer a systematic explanation in the terms of a 'total' economic analysis. He offers an analysis of the sixties in the Foucauldian terms of a view of power as a multiplicity of contradictory relations immanent in all cultural forms, constituting identity and thus defying any total resistance and given no foundation in economics. Contradictorily, however, he then proceeds to give his analysis a foundation in a total economic theory.

He manoeuvres round the difficulty by arguing that if Postmodernism is the cultural logic of Late Capitalism, then Late Capitalism is a totality which cannot be thought. In its fragmentariness and depthless surfaces, it can only be grasped within the logic of its own terms: those of poststructuralist absence. We cannot think the impossible global totality of the third and last phase of capitalism because it has determined a cultural mode resistant to totalising thought. This does not necessarily mean that there is no totality: simply that we cannot represent it (a view we saw expressed in Lyotard's notion of the sublime). So, he refuses those period conceptualisations like 'disorganised capital' which refuse totality at any level, because he believes capital is always organised and always systematic in its effects. Mandel, in fact, saw Late Capitalism not as a form of post-industrialisation but as one of *universal* industrialisation penetrating the sphere of the aesthetic and, through neo-colonialism, the 'third world'. The last vestiges of pre-capitalist culture disappear (so the unconscious, for example is no longer to be seen as the site of potential liberation as in Marcusean and countercultural idealism). In effect, all culture is seen to be mass culture, a culture of commodification. In this view, the 'situatedness' of post-Heideggerian Postmodernism is simply an acceptance that there is no way out and the Nietzschean mode simply a reproduction of aestheticist consumer play. How can the 'logic' of Jameson's own argument be resisted?

Firstly, even at the level of experiential fact, it is apparent that Jameson uses vast generalisations. The obvious fact that Mandel dated the rise of Late Capitalism around 1945 rather than 1960 is ignored. We see the problem of setting up a dominant on the basis of partial evidence and then generalising from it across the entire social scene. Jameson ignores the very obvious continuation of modernist and premodernist forms of culture in both the West and certainly elsewhere in the world. He similarly ignores the Bakhtinian insight into the multiaccentual nature of cultural symbols which suggest that no economic mode can in fact ever entirely colonise meaning and value. Perhaps Jameson has overgeneralised from his own sense of the loss of the individual vision of the moderns and the weakening of the grand narratives embedded in his own Hegelian thought. By a process of projective identification, he may have come to see his *own* nostalgia as symptomatic of the postmodern condition itself.

I have attempted to offer a critique of Jameson's essay by working from within his argument. Before moving completely outside to examine alternative conceptualisations of the cultural dominant of the period, it may be worth considering how one could accept the basic 'commodification thesis' as a construction of the postmodern but arrive at a different evaluation of it. The strongest *defence* of the implications of the collapse of high art into commercial mass culture has come from architecture and, in particular, from two practitioners who had previously identified themselves as modernist. By the seventies and for a variety of reasons, each had shifted to seeing cultural Postmodernism as a viable and positive alternative. Paolo Portoghesi's book *After Modern Architecture* (1983) and Charles Jencks' *The Language of Post-Modern Architecture* (1977), both attempt a defence of postmodern art in relation to an analysis of social change not incompatible in many respects with Jameson's own. Recognising that modern capitalism and technology have produced a world which is more like a 'global village' but also composed of what he calls 'small-taste cultures', Jencks uses a model taken from communication theory, that of 'double-coding', to describe Postmodernism. In so doing, he attempts to convert the commodification argument into positive terms:

Since there is an unbridgeable gap between the elite and popular codes, the professional and the popular values, the modern and vernacular language, and since there is no way to abolish this gap without a drastic curtailment in possibilities, a totalitarian manoeuvre, it seems desirable that architects recognise the schizophrenia and code their buildings on two levels ... the double-coding will be eclectic and subject to the heterogeneity that makes up any large city ... Radical eclecticism ... starts design from the tastes and languages prevailing in any one place and overcodes architecture (with many redundant clues) so that it can be understood and enjoyed by different taste cultures – both the inhabitants and the elite. Although it starts from these codes, it doesn't necessarily use them to send the expected messages, or ones which simply confirm the existing values. In this sense it is both contextual and dialectical, attempting to set up a discourse between different and often opposed taste cultures (Jencks, 1987, pp131–2).

Unlike Jameson, Jencks views cultural signs as multi-accentual, always involved in the struggles of different interest groups for definition. He is not claiming that the values of 'mass-society' have colonised the entire cultural world, but neither is he saying that the values of High Art define the universal good. Cultural values are seen to represent the interests of different groups: context and situation are taken into account; strategies like parody, allusion, quotation, borrowing of styles, become ways of freeing cultural forms from earlier identities and investing them with new possibilities of meaning. The picture is generally more optimistic than Jameson's, more cognisant of the post-Heideggerian and post-Nietzschean accounts of the aesthetic appearing in the writing of Foucault or Lyotard. For Jencks, it was the obsession with universalisation, the fetishisation of form as space, the indifference to specific contexts and needs, which led to the demise of modernist architecture. The alternative to its 'universal grammar' is postmodern 'neo-vernacular': buildings developed with *local* participation within specific cultures or groups. This offers the possibility of moving beyond what he sees as a central contradiction of Modernism: an unresolvable tension between an essentially Romantic concept of personal expression (what Jameson calls individual voice) and the notion of a universal grammar, a pure language which can mirror the deep structure of reality itself. It is bound up again with issues about autonomy and aestheticism which can only be resolved when we come on to read some of the texts of Modernism in the light of these theoretical positions.

Later commentators such as Huyssen (1988) have extended Jencks' argument that Postmodernism operates in a new field of tension between high and mass art, but where the former is not necessarily, and certainly not *universally*, privileged over the latter. For Jameson, the radical eclecticism of the postmodern is co-extensive with the commodified surfaces, the pragmatist ethics, performative values and, apparently diverse but underlyingly conformist, aesthetic conventions of Late Capitalism. Yet for Jencks, it represents a genuine democratisation of art and a new historicisation of the aesthetic. What is interesting is that both share an essentially similar view of the parameters and historical determinants of the contemporary period: they talk of the same postmodernisms, in effect, but one evaluated in the terms of a cultural pessimism which can be traced back through Adorno, Eliot and Leavis, the other in terms of the liberatory possibilities of a shift from the autonomy of art to the aestheticisation of everyday life. It is becoming clear how often the postmodern debate returns to this central opposition and why, in my view, it must be situated in a broader historical tradition of aestheticist thought examined in relation to cultural artefacts themselves.

If Jencks broadly accepts the dominant which Jameson uses to describe Postmodernism but offers an alternative evaluation of it, others have perceived the dominant itself in different terms. A literary critic such as Brian McHale (1987) is more concerned to construct a purely cultural dominant and to leave economic and political issues to theorists working in these areas. But Postmodernism is clearly not simply a literary phenomenon even if it is theorised as a condition of universal aestheticisation. In fact, McHale's own categorisation of Modernism as an aesthetic concerned with problems of epistemological uncertainty, and Postmodernism as one concerned with ontological doubt, does accord implicitly with Jameson's account of the effects of late Capitalism or of Lyotard's analysis of the condition of knowledge. Like many literary critics who have entered the postmodern debate, McHale offers a descriptive aesthetics which engages with artefacts but not with broader issues of cultural value. The aim of this book is to attempt to remedy this deficiency.

Of the commentators who, like Jameson, offer analyses of Postmodernism in the terms of cultural value, the differences between them may lie in the selection or construction of a different dominant from within the same category. After Late Capitalism, the favourite economic concept is probably post-industrialisation or its derivatives: post-Fordism or disorganised capital. The work of Daniel Bell is central to theories of postindustrialisation. Basic to these is the view that societies are moving away from economies almost entirely organised around the production of goods to those in which knowledge becomes the key commodity. For Bell, in particular, 'the axial principle of postindustrial society . . . (is) the centrality of theoretical knowledge . . .' (Poster, 1990, p23). One effect of the development of information technology, in particular, is a reorganisation of the 'real' so that things are subordinated to theory and nature to the informational categories produced by the theorist. Again one senses the intrusion of that discursive circularity which impossibly and inextricably conflates the theory with its object. As with Jameson's argument, the entire social world and all its products are seen as uniformly and homogeneously determined by the technologies of mass culture.

Knowledge now determines the shape of the world; knowledge is the key commodity displacing categories like capital and labour. The production, distribution and consumption of knowledge now organises the world and, unlike material goods, it cannot be used up and exhausted: it is infinitely reproducible, without origin, unstable and indeterminate in its effects. The position is close to Jameson's in terms of its view of cultural *effects*, for it shares his sense that 'no society has ever been quite so mystified in quite so many ways as our own, saturated as it is with messages and information, the very vehicle of mystification' (Jameson,

1981, pp60–1). The concept is again weakened, however, if tested against a wider range of empirical evidence. Obviously since the 1960s, the economy of the West has shifted towards a greater emphasis on information and services, but to isolate this as definitive of the period in all its aspects is clearly reductive. Yet the broad concept appears in many versions of Postmodernism: in that political philosophy concerned with the breakdown of consensus or legitimation (because of the instability of knowledge); in the poststructuralist concern with the freeplay of signs and in the aestheticist concern with knowledge as rhetorical performance. The problem of circularity arises again. Whatever the evidence in the world for Bell's thesis, it is obvious that for those engaged in the production of critical knowledge, the possibility that knowledge may become wholly functional, simply another commodity, is likely to loom large in their own analysis of contemporary culture. We are back with the problem 'of what is given and what is received'.

This can teach us lessons, however, about the use of period concepts in literary criticism. It can alert us to the insidious ways in which socio-economic categories are conflated with cultural ones, motivate us to think about the complex ways in which we construct or accept paradigms which organise our lives in terms of everyday experience and how these interact with cultural and theoretical paradigms to shape our understanding of the world. Clearly, with any use of period concepts, the greater the degree of generality, the easier it is to say whatever you want about the nature of historical experience. Postmodernism's obsession with this problem even as it 'totalises' the contemporary period, again has the paradoxical effect of giving greater weight to the significance of *literature* (even as it announces the end of Art). For literature exists as a pattern of particularities rather than generalities. The aesthetic exists not as a network of concepts but as particular details, an apparently sensuous surface, embodiment. The postmodern consideration of period again foregrounds the complicated relationship of knowledge and experience. Period terms cannot be thought through in the pure language of empiricism (the notion that knowledge of reality is derived through sensory experience) nor that of rationalism (the notion that reality can only be known through the formulation of rational theoretical constructs). Neither one's own immediate experience nor the generalities of theory can adequately formulate a 'period' or even its dominant characteristics. As René Wellek argued in 1963, period concepts 'will be combined with different traits, survivals from the past, anticipations of the future and quite individual peculiarities' (Wellek, 1963, p252). Even in purely literary terms there cannot be a simply linear progression. Postmodernism helps to focus on this as a critical problem, because it spills outside the boundaries of the aesthetic in ways which challenge traditional explanations of the relationship between art and society. To work with Postmodernism is to begin to be aware of the way in which our preconceptions about the aesthetic, including concepts like period, shape what we see in individual texts. To read a work as 'modernist', for example, is to read it in relation to particular expectations constructed through dominant paradigms. To recognise that 'Modernism' is itself a particular kind of construction, is to facilitate the modification or suspension of those expectations and to extend the potential of one's reading experience. Postmodernism suggests new ways of reading Modernism. The next chapter will examine some postmodern *aesthetic* forms and techniques in relation to the various constructions of Postmodernism as a period concept.

4

POSTMODERNISM
AS AESTHETIC TECHNIQUE

A View from Theory

I
Introduction

The last chapter examined the periodisation of Postmodernism largely through variations on what I have called the 'commodification' thesis. This tends to present postmodern art as one which pilfers the techniques of the avant-garde, but in the form of pastiche which eschews the latter's serious political and ethical commitment. The postmodern attempt to overcome modernist autonomy and to return art to a form of praxis in life is viewed by critics like Eagleton as straightforward complicity with the values of consumer culture. This chapter will attempt to describe some of the preoccupations and formal characteristics of postmodern literature, both as a way of more comprehensively engaging with Postmodernism as a body of thought, and in order to re-examine the issue of its cultural value from other perspectives. It is evident that if we are, indeed, in the postmodern condition, then its aesthetic forms (parody, irony, self-reflexivity, playfulness) are themselves subject to a pervasive crisis of legitimation. There can be no straightforward relation of form to value. Like postmodern theory, postmodern art tends to mediate a sense of multiplicity, fragmentation, instability of meaning, dissensus, the breakdown of grand theories as either narratives of emancipation or speculation. As we have seen, Eagleton views this as a shameful accommodation to consumer culture and freemarket pluralism in an anti-foundationalist hyper-relativisation which negates the possibility of stable value and thus of any oppositional critique of Late Capitalism.

However, other commentators on postmodern literature have seen it as a formal mode which problematises dominant values by contesting their codes of representation from within, acknowledging an unavoidable implication (situatedness) in the culture of Late Capitalism, but finding ways to reformulate and therefore contest its discursive premises (fictionality). Linda Hutcheon, for example, extends an earlier non-political interest in modern uses of self-reflexive forms such as parody to a defence of its political potential. She believes that parody is a 'perfect postmodern form . . . for it paradoxically both incorporates and challenges that which it parodies . . . (and) forces a reconsideration of the idea of origin or originality that is compatible with other postmodernist interrogations of liberal humanist assumptions' (1990, p11). The view of parody espoused here (though similar to her earlier articulation of it as repetition with critical distance which allows an ironic signalling of difference at the heart of similarity) is broadened in her recent work into a defence of Postmodernism as a mode of intertextual, 'self-reflexive discourse', 'always inextricably bound to social discourse'. In effect, she views it in positive terms as a continuation of the earlier twentieth-century historical avant-garde. However, it has reached a mature recognition of the inescapability of institutionalisation without rejecting the possibility of disruption from within.

What is new is the *comprehensive* nature of postmodern intertextuality: the recognition that we live in a world constituted through multiple kinds of discourse or language games that contradict and contest each other even as they complement and are constructed out of each other. Literary texts cannot be 'autonomous' in these terms, nor can 'theory' be seen to occupy a radically different order of discourse from that of 'fiction'. Postmodern theory and literature are thus seen to be caught up in a web of intertextual overlap, neither (to use Habermas's terminology) being purely 'world disclosing' nor 'problem solving', because both are seen to be part of a world in which such rigid distinctions have broken down. For Eagleton, this is a negative consequence of commodification, for others, like Foucault, it is simply the logic of Enlightenment rationalism subverting its own contradictory foundations. Paul de Man's *Blindness and Insight* was one of the first extensive explorations of the implications of such 'textualism':

> We are entitled to generalise in working our way towards a definition by giving Rousseau exemplary value and calling 'literary' in the full sense of the term any text that implicitly or explicitly signifies its own rhetorical mode and prefigures its own misunderstanding as the correlative of its rhetorical nature; that is, of its rhetoricity. It can do this by declarative statement or by poetic inference. . . . A discursive, critical, or philosophic text that does this by means of statements is not therefore more or less literary than a poetic text that would avoid direct statement . . . The criterion of literary specificity does not depend on the greater or lesser discursiveness of the mode but on the degree of consistent 'rhetoricity' of the language. (1971, pp136–7).

In this sense, to read postmodern literature is, in itself, to work with theory. I would argue that given the aestheticist orientation of the theory, it is, indeed, vital to consider it in relation to postmodern artefacts. Not to do so would be another performative self-contradiction. Paul de Man's argument represents a deconstructive extension of Romantic irony from literature (or world-disclosing discourse) to criticism (as problem solving discourse), extending its aestheticising tendencies in a movement towards a full postmodern position.

All postmodern fiction foregrounds this dimension of critical self-reflexivity in a highly self-conscious fashion. A novel like Julian Barnes' *Flaubert's Parrot* (1984) utterly collapses the distinction between novel, criticism and autobiography, revealing that in the condition of language, however obsessively we search for 'truth', all must be fictional. He reiterates the Romantic Ironist sense that: 'Language is like a cracked kettle on which we beat out tunes for bears to dance to, while all the time we long to move the stars to pity' (p19). That 'on est parlé', as he goes on to suggest, may seem to displace the possibility of human agency entirely with a sense, not simply that one is radically *situated* in a linguistic culture, but that one is entirely *constructed* through it. This is the effect generated in many postmodern fictions and presumably informing Jameson's sense that Postmodernism is a condition where the possibility of human agency has disappeared. So, in the fiction of the American writer Donald Barthelme, for example, abstract nouns and passive constructions almost entirely replace personal assertion or human agency. The story 'Brain Damage' (1971) begins: 'At the restaurant, sadness was expressed'; moods are reflexes of disembodied signifiers rather than of personal feeling. Endless lists, catalogues, insistent stylisation, flaunt the materiality of writing as depthlessness, seem to present a self-conscious articulation of the rules of selection and combination in grammar, an endless play of linguistic substitution for its own sake; metaphors proliferate, syntax continuously breaks down. The reader is offered sentences such as: 'The world is sagging, snagging, scaling, spalling, pulling, pitting, warping, checking, fading, chipping, cracking, yellowing, leaking, staling, shrinking and in dynamic unbalance' (1974, p6). Certainly this sentence is, for as the material world shrinks, the linguistic one expands, and it is the materiality of language again, what Jameson has characterised as the schizophrenic present of Postmodernism, which seems obsessively to be foregrounded. Barthelme parades the mimeticist fallacy and parodies the realist attempt to make language reflect the world. Both the form of the sentence and the semantic associations of the word attempt to embody entropy, but if world substantially drains away, it is simultaneously being replenished with word. Just as text is world, so too is world becoming text. The Romantic impulse towards plenitude is, comically and self-consciously, punctured by an ironic reminder of the frustrations and compensations of the linguistic condition.

Just as Barthelme sets out to flaunt the hidden processes of artistic production, what the Russian Formalists had called 'baring the device', so too, postmodernist theory proceeds by exposing the concealed rhetorical mechanisms which both produce and subvert conceptual meaning. Just as this quotation undermines 'reflectionist' or realist conventions of literary form (where consciousness of its own linguistic status is not obtruded into the text), postmodern theories also set out to subvert any account of knowledge as 'mirror' or 'reflection' of a truth which precedes it and determines the form of its representation. Postmodern literary, as theoretical, discourse is 'grounded', in effect, in the epistemological problematisation of grounding itself, of the idea of identity as absolute or truth as essential. Fictionality is central in both. Just as theorists like Lyotard refer to knowledge as 'just gaming', so writers like John Barth and Robert Coover foreground epistemological and ontological questions about the construction of the 'real' or the 'self' by playing metafictionally on the textual and phenomenological paradox of the book as material object in 'external' space and as imaginary world in 'inner space'. Others, such as Salman Rushdie, John Fowles or John Barth, foreground the paradox of history as both a series of events which happened and also the imposition of a retrospective, paradigmatic and provisional linguistic structure which is itself the product of its own historical situation conceived of as an interplay of textual paradigms . . . ad infinitum.

II

The Question of Value

Salman Rushdie's Shame

It is easy enough to isolate and describe such strategies and fairly obvious how they reiterate the preoccupation of postmodern theory with incredulity towards metanarratives and the aestheticisation of the real. What is far more problematic, as I have suggested, is how to evaluate them in either aesthetic or political terms. If we pause for a moment to examine Rushdie's novel *Shame* (1984), some of the difficulties about evaluation become instantly apparent. Rushdie self-consciously likens his fictional construction of Pakistan and its presentation of the family squabble between Iskander Harappa and Raza Hyder, to the regimes of power which have constructed the actual nation. For Rushdie, a British citizen of Indian origin, to write in English is to be aware that to construct his own textual Pakistan entirely through the monologic voice of the coloniser is stylistically to repeat Imperialist history. But he acknowledges that:

> History is natural selection. Mutant versions of the past struggle for dominance; new species of fact arise, and old, saurian truths go to the wall, blindfolded and smoking last cigarettes. Only the mutations of the strong survive. The weak, the anonymous, the defeated leave few marks . . . history loves only those who dominate her: it is a relationship of mutual enslavement (p124).

Pakistan itself, however, is like a palimpsest, built by obscuring Indian history, rewriting a past that was already rewritten. The violence is perpetrated through language:

> So-called Islamic 'fundamentalism' does not spring, in Pakistan, from the people. It is imposed on them from above. Autocratic regimes find it useful to espouse the rhetoric of faith, because people respect that language, are reluctant to oppose it. This is how religions shore up dictators; by encircling them with words of power, words which the people are reluctant to see discredited, disenfranchised, mocked (p251).

Although he recognises that it is the 'desire of every artist to impose his or her vision on the world' (p87), he is also conscious that the monologic production of another mythical Pakistan would simply constitute a further act of Imperial violence, another coercive manufacture of illusory community. So he disrupts the narrative with parodies of sacred texts (recognising how nationalism depends upon religious vocabularies), Indian legends, motifs from popular cinema, a jostling of voices which attempts to speak his own condition of migrancy and of those, like the women, whose voices have been muted by Imperialist hegemony and who 'marched in from the peripheries of the story to demand the inclusion of their own tragedies, histories and comedies' (p173). These alternative voices produce alternative histories or facilitate the intermeshing of fragments of old stories to produce new and as yet unthought of possibilities. Authentic Postmodernism is here a condition of migrancy, of refusing to inhabit or to impose on another any one fixed discourse, of recognising that colonialism lives on in language but parodying, fragmenting, mixing and meshing its possibilities to produce new, provisional identities. *Shame* can thus be seen as a critique of regimes of power which set themselves up through the production of totalising discourses which, in suppressing other voices, establish their own as exclusive dogma.

Now one could argue that as a strategy for dismantling oppressive hegemonies, such narrative perspectivism is highly effective. However, in a text where *all* positions seem to relativise each other and where *everything* is seen to be an effect of rhetoric, then the possibility of occupying an oppositional space from which to speak in the name of some greater justice is itself abolished. Rushdie has said that the 'triple disruption of reality' experienced by migrants, teaches that 'reality is an artefact, that it does not exist until it is made and that, like any other artefact, it can also be made well or badly and that it can also, of course, be unmade' (Grass, 1984, pxiii). It is a statement of the positive as well as negative implications for post-colonial people of an aesthetics and politics of postmodern fictionality. Because it offers no stable condition of identity, however, not even one of critique, it may therefore amount to no more than another demonstration of the postmodern capitulation to performative pragmatism and the easy (freemarket) pluralism of Late Capitalism. It may represent a negative or passive nihilism as much as a positive or active one.

What these two radically opposed evaluations reveal, of course, is the way in which conceptual or theoretical presuppositions shape what we see, in part construct the object of critique, and certainly reveal how values themselves shift across different contexts and situations. In this, as in any postmodern fiction, the pervasive use of parodic forms makes it impossible to disentangle complicity from critique. For some critics, therefore, Postmodernism represents an irresponsible ethical relativism, for others, an open-minded refusal to impose exclusive dogmas or espouse a naive rhetoric of liberation. It is possible to offer a negative evaluation of the celebration of artifice, pluralistic narrative voices, self-reflexive narcissism, viewing them as the endorsement of a rapacious capitalism and as another manifestation of the culture of the simulacrum. Alternatively, one could view the postmodern emphasis on the power of language and signs to construct the real, as a positive image of the potential capacity of the human imagination to reshape the ostensibly fixed material world of history in order to reformulate and produce new and more humane identities for the human beings in it. Postmodernism, on the one hand, represents a transformation of the Romantic faith in imagination, and on the other, exists as an ideological weapon of capitalism inuring us to a tawdry world of commercial image.

III
Representation and Postmodern Anti-Foundationalism

What are the narrative and rhetorical strategies of postmodern fictions? (see McHale, 1987, Waugh, 1984). Here are a few of the most frequently used techniques: insertion of the situation of writing itself into the text in order to evoke the image of a space outside the text (self-cancelling, of course, because the assertion of the situation can exist only within the text); reminders that the narrative is an imposition of the order of a writer but that the writer is also constituted through the conventions of the narrative; structures of infinite regress which undermine the possibility of ground or foundation; dissolution of typographic, conventional or generic boundaries. As we have seen in the example from Donald Barthelme, a range of forms of stylisation flaunt the materiality of writing itself by foregrounding the equivalence of sound at the expense of semantic coherence. Lists, for example, take words out of context and make the reader think about other qualities aside from semantic ones: here meaning is continuously deferred as a condition of decontextualisation. Brian McHale (1987) has argued that what is common to all of these strategies is a characteristic mode of ontological problematisation which distinguishes postmodern techniques from the epistemologically questioning strategies of Modernism. Whereas modernist techniques foreground questions like 'How do I interpret this world?', postmodern ones raise questions like 'which world is this?', leading to meditations upon the possible existence of multiple worlds.

Although McHale does not presume to comment on the wider implications of the postmodern condition, he broadly shares the theoretical position of Lyotard and others that Postmodernism expresses a crisis about the legitimation of modern forms of knowledge. At the end of this book, he suggests that the postmodern text's concern with levels of ontological transgression has the moral effect of allowing us to imagine our own non-existence and thus provides us with a new, badly needed *ars moriendi*. In effect, he suggests that, in the midst of our post-Enlightenment concern with controlling and dissecting the world we inhabit, postmodern fictionality can lead us to that recognition of common human situatedness upon which humility and acceptance are founded. Despite the effects of Enlightenment, we are still only able to control our own mortality through imaginative acceptance of its inevitability. With this in mind, it is interesting to think about how often the techniques which McHale designates as postmodern, in fact, appeared extensively in pre-Enlightenment literature and art: techniques such as mise-en-abyme or allegory, reflecting uncertainties about the status of forms of human representation in a pre-Cartesian age [12]. One could cite here examples such as the worlds within worlds in the poetry of Spenser, the extensive similies which generate ontological complexities in *Paradise Lost*, the kaleidoscopic confrontation of levels of artifice in the courtly masque or Restoration comedy, the play within a play in *Hamlet*. In post-Enlightenment literature, in the nineteenth-century novel, for example, such forms as mise-en-abyme often appear (where a nested representation reminds us of the condition of fictionality), but tend ultimately to reinforce the reader's sense of a shared social world of which the fiction is an imaginative extension or reflection. Thus, in the fiction of Jane Austen (*Mansfield Park*) or Charlotte Brontë (*Jane Eyre*), they are often used as temporarily disruptive learning experiences, soon reintegrated into the basic realistic frame in their function as correctives of the heroine's previous misapprehension of the real.

In postmodern texts, such strategies problematise, rather than confirm, a sense of the real. One could cite a whole range of techniques which have this effect. In *Shame*, not only are fictional and historical characters indiscriminately mixed, so too are levels of discourse. Metaphors, for example, may be confusingly and surrealistically literalised. The condition of 'shaman', for which there is no equivalent English word, materialises in a human body as a literal enactment of the effects of cultural repression in a form taken from the popular cinematic werewolf genre. Sufiya's condition defies human laws of space and time and cannot be recuperated realistically through a psychoanalytic account of somatisation, but only through a notion of supernatural demonic possession which splits open the ontological coherence of the historical narrative by obtruding into it a distinctly other world. Such contradictory frames challenge us to reconsider the processes of rational thought whereby we confer coherence on structures of experience and to question the foundational premises of such thinking.

Another way of referring to the effects of such problematisation is the term 'possible worlds'. Again, though, it is not in itself a radically new idea. William James, for example, in *The Varieties of Religious Experience* (1902) wrote this:

> Our normal waking consciousness, rational consciousness as we call it, is but one special type of consciousness, whilst all about it, parted from it by the filmiest of screens, there lie potential forms of consciousness entirely different. We may go through life without suspecting their existence, but apply the requisite stimulus, and at a touch they are there in all their completeness, definite types of mentality which probably somewhere have their field of

---

[12] It is perhaps not surprising that writers critical of modernity should often draw on models from pre-modernity. Thus Foucault returns to a Greek model of self-mastery, Heidegger to the Greek concept of 'techne' and 'alathaeia', Deleuze and Guattari use the image of the 'nomad' to imagine a liberatory order, Alisdair MacIntyre draws on a notion of 'virtue' derived from Aristotle in order to offer a critique of Enlightenment universalism and contemporary ethical relativism and emotivism.

application and adaptation . . . they all converge towards a kind of insight to which I cannot help ascribing some metaphysical significance. The keynote of it is invariably a reconciliation. It is as if the opposites of the world, whose contradictoriness and conflict make all our difficulties and troubles were melted into unity. Not only do they, as contrasted species, belong to one and the same genus, but one of the species, the nobler and better one, is itself the genus and so soaks up and absorbs its opposite into itself (1985, p388).

The idea of such shifts of experience occurs throughout postmodern writing as a fictional version of Lyotard's concept of language games. If we look at an example of one of these, however, it will become apparent how the postmodern version has shifted out of the previous Idealist framework of assertion. In Donald Barthelme's novel, *Snow White* (1967), the character Jane writes a letter to Mr. Quistgaard:

You and I, Mr. Quistgaard, are not in the same universe of discourse. You may not have been aware of it previously, but the fact of the matter is, that we are not. We exist in different universes of discourse . . . It may never have crossed your mind to think that other universes of discourse distinct from your own existed, with people in them, discoursing. You may have, in a commonsense way, regarded your own u. of d. as a plenum, filled to the brim with discourse. You may have felt that what already existed was a sufficiency. People like you often do. At any moment I can pierce your plenum with a single telephone call, simply by dialling 989-7777. You are correct, Mr. Quistgaard, in seeing this as a threatening situation. The moment I inject discourse from my u. of d. into your u. of d., the yourness of yours is diluted. The more I inject, the more you dilute. Soon you will be presiding over an empty plenum, or rather, since that is a contradiction in terms, over a former plenum, in terms of yourness. You are, essentially, in my power. I suggest an unlisted number. (pp45–6).

How do these assertions of 'possible worlds' differ from each other? Most fundamentally, the first is articulated through a post-Hegelian language of consciousness where possible worlds are effectively varieties of states of mind resolvable into a metaphysical transcendent whole. The experience of multiplicity is simply a consciousness of the diverse forms of this whole expressed in an organicist metaphor derived from Coleridgean thought with its Idealist framework intact. The passage from James can be read as an attempt to reconcile the non-rationalist concept of intuition with the empirical language of sensory experience: 'stimulus' and 'touch' connect us to this metaphysical realm. It is the language of Romantic correspondence. Rhetorically, its most complete form of expression would be in metaphor, reconciling the apparently dissimilar through the consciousness of a more profound possibility of connectedness where the abstract finds expression in the concrete and where the point of correspondence hovers somewhere between mind and world.

In the second passage, possible worlds are no longer states of consciousness but 'universes of discourse', fragile in their coherence, dependent for it on the worldly acquisition of power, and liable to the hypodermic 'injection' from other universes. These discourses enter the body via skin (hypodermic): they are expressed through the language of materialism. According to the quasi-physical law offered, they will necessarily 'dilute' pre-existing orders: 'The more I inject, the more you dilute'. Here, universes are not corresponding reflections in consciousness of an intuitive perception of non-rationalisable transcendent unities, but provisional material constructions which may not reflect anything other than the exercise of power as rhetorical performance: linguistic pragmatism. Foucault called this concept of radically incommensurable worlds of discourse, a heterotopia (1970). It is a commonly produced effect in postmodernist fiction, frustrating the reader in his or her attempts to project any unified realm of the imaginary, conveying the counter-modern belief of Barthelme that fragments are the only forms he trusts. The 'plenum' we all desire is simply the construction of those with power or the experience of those who complacently accept what Nietzsche called the 'herd' mentality. As with all postmodern writing, however, the ironies are far from stable. If Barthelme presents this as simply the way of the postmodern world, his vocabulary need not imply endorsement of the situation. Both the references to technological determinism: 'At any moment I can pierce your plenum with a single telephone call, simply by dialling 989-7777' and the idea of 'injection' with its association of control through drugs, produce a typically postmodernist fictional ambivalence. The recognition of alternative 'universes of discourse', non-resolvable into a monological whole, may promise the possibility of a genuine recognition of otherness, a non-egotistic awareness of our tendency to incorporate the worlds and experiences of others into our own. Equally, however, it may reflect a situation of competing language games where performance establishes validity and where the strongest win and gain temporary legitimation through the persuasiveness of their particular discursive formation. In this sense we all preside over empty plenums: assemblies filled with projections of our own desire. In James, the 'as if' impulse, the fictionalising imagination, is still a reflection of absolute Mind; in Barthelme it is thoroughly a pragmatic tool. In both, however, ultimately non-rationalisable impulses of desire (even in the form of power) propel the aesthetic impulse to shape: plenitude still seduces us.

In its anti-foundationalism, postmodern theory always involves a critique of philosophical 'mirror' theories of truth. One can see postmodern literature engaged in the same process through its refutation or at least re-examination of the epistemological grounds of Realism and its linguistic forms. This is another way of perceiving the connections between postmodern theory and literature and of approaching the complex issue of value. Realism in literature is normally understood as the expression of a belief in a commonly experienced phenomenological world. In a realist fiction, a variety of points of view may be expressed, but as part of a controlled pluralism where no single voice is allowed to challenge the authority of omniscience recognised as the voice of commonsense or of the 'sensus communis'. What seems to follow from this presupposition is that the language of Realism must therefore appear 'transparent', a window onto a reality it simply reflects. Contradictory voices must be suppressed or found accommodation within the greater whole. The conventionality of narrative must be disguised so that the *projected* world appears to be a *reflected* world, an extension of the commonly experienced world outside the text. Language here functions simply as a medium through which reality can be transcribed and re-presented in aesthetic form, and reality, even if only apprehensible in the deep structures of world, transcends any verbal formulation of it.

This theoretisation of Realism is often presented in highly generalised terms by critics wishing to defend postmodern modes. Again, what one sees is a tendency to totalisation for polemical purposes. Just as Eagleton ignores the specific strategies of postmodern artefacts in order to proclaim a generalised condemnation of Postmodernism as the logic of commodification, so too its defenders often set Postmodernism against some other generalisation in order to show its greater authenticity. In my view this is where theory can learn from literature, for just as many postmodern artefacts can be shown to bear little resemblance to Eagleton's generalised categorisation of them, most realist novels involve modes of irony and linguistic playfulness which are ignored in many of the theoretical formulations of Realism. Engaging with postmodern theory should make us conscious of the way in which those fictions which we call generalisations are used pragmatically by all of us as strategies of power in the mode of polemic. The defence of Postmodernism often involves a negative evaluation of Realism, though this may be disguised as objective description. Usually it is developed through an extension of post-Saussurean linguistics which sets up humanism as an ideology grounded in the assumption that experience exists prior to language which is viewed simply as a tool expressing the essential way in which the world is sensorily and reflectively processed. Realism is the logical expression of this ideology. It is therefore founded on the necessity for suppression of its own linguistic conventionality. The real must not be experienced as a rhetorical effect, but as a pre-existing condition which can be faithfully transcribed through language.

Postmodernism in literature can be, and has been understood as a refutation of the epistemological grounds of Realism thus understood. Certainly, much postmodernist fiction ostentatiously explores the limits of realist convention. In so doing, it may expose some of the contradictions of humanism. So, for example, the implicit patriarchal bias in some uses of omniscience is explored in texts by Muriel Spark and John Fowles (see Waugh, 1984), or its implicit authoritarianism is contested in a rumination in Barth's *Lost in the Funhouse* on the Flaubertian analogy between the authorial self and the God of creation:

> Inasmuch as the old analogy between Author and God, novel and world, can no longer be employed unless deliberately as a false analogy, certain things follow: 1) fiction must acknowledge its fictitiousness and metaphoric invalidity or 2) choose to ignore the question or deny its relevance or 3) establish some other, acceptable, relation between itself, its author, its reader (1969, p128).

In generalising the relations between Realism and humanism in the above manner, however, defenders as well as detractors of Postmodernism are equally guilty of reductive totalisation for polemical purposes. In 1977, David Lodge wrote that he could not accept that Realism is a totally relativistic concept because the 'norms of the historical description of reality have remained remarkably stable for at least the last two or three hundred years' (p46). Many postmodernists would claim that these norms have now qualitatively shifted, that we are experiencing a radical break in history. Post-Saussurean and anti-humanist accounts of postmodern literature tend to support this reading of the situation. I have already claimed that one can trace many of the assumptions of Postmodernism back to Romantic aesthetics, and similarly I would like to argue for a more complex sense of relationship here. In claiming a radical break, of course, postmodernists nearly always undo their own argument because they are forced to 'totalise' what has come before in order to see it as bygone history. In my view, it is most fruitful to see Postmodernism in its literary modes not dissolving but rescuing the possibility of coherent subjectivity, historical significance and ethical stability by re-examining rather than refuting their foundations in modern thought and representation. By exposing the contradictions of humanism, for example, Postmodernism can be seen to make its premises available for re-consideration: literature can only examine an ideology by embodying it (even if in an ironic mode), so that if theorists can operate through reductive totalisations, fictional texts by their very nature have an inbuilt resistance to this. If Postmodernism is a validation of aestheticism in whatever form, then any consideration of it which ignores a close engagement with actual works of art is incomplete.

Perhaps this is why many literary commentators on Postmodernism have often been drawn to the work of Mikhail Bakhtin rather than Baudrillard. Bakhtin's dialogism sees knowledge of world, self and other, as always historically situated, relational, open-ended and perspectival, a process shifting through time and space. None of these categories is a self-sufficient construct, but a relational process anchored in provisional and continuous 'authorships'. Although Bakhtin is probably best known for his work on carnival and his concept of 'heteroglossia', it is in his lesser known essay on the chronotope (1981) where he most fully articulates this position in a way which seems most relevant to the postmodern debate. The essay draws its idea of dialogism from the perspectivist implications of Einstein's theory of relativity. Einstein had challenged Newtonian science by introducing an inevitable perspectivism and thus a question of responsibility of choice and value into the perception of space and time. Similarly, Nietzsche had introduced a similar perspectivism as part of his critique of the Cartesian transcendental ego (the idea one can transcend the particularities of situation and offer a 'view from nowhere'). Bakhtin's aesthetics also arise out of a commitment to perspectivism and relationship. Reality here is always an experience of exchange, fluidity and process, which calls for a situated and particular response from each individual in it, a responsibility for recognising that although self and identity are experienced as open-ended and other as consummated, each is always what George Eliot described as an equivalent centre of self. One should strive to experience other as well as self as a fluid and relational process requiring constant redefinition and an ever-open semanticity. Returning to the postmodern construction of Realism, one can see that in order to identify the postmodern as fluidity, open-endedness, particularity, situatedness, its theoretical defenders have often offered a 'consummated' view of Realism. Even as an object of critique, however, in the embodiment of the *artistic* text, Realism cannot be consummated in this fashion and is inevitably drawn into the fluid and processional. By looking at some further fictional examples, we can begin to develop an alternative way of approaching Postmodernism, avoiding the reductiveness of both its detractors and defenders, but using Bakhtinian insights to show how consideration of the literary text may modify one's reading of theory: just as theoretical awareness may modify one's aesthetic experience.

Detractors of Postmodernism see it as a narcissistic and ethically insouciant expression of a commodified culture. Defenders view it as an authentic exposure of the illusions of preceding systems of knowledge and representation. If we think in Bakhtinian terms, however, we can try to imagine the 'post' as an engagement with, and modification rather than refutation of, the 'modern', which involves a reciprocal openness. How might one begin to rethink such relations? Clearly, postmodern fictions, like its theories, do play with fictionality in ways which challenge onto-logical and epistemological certainty. A realist text such as Jane Austen's novel *Emma*, for example, clearly does not. Austen's textual manipulation which plays off the perspectivism of free indirect discourse against the 'objectivity' of dramatic scene and dialogue, exposes Emma's ethical and perceptual limitations by establishing a secure foundation from which to judge her behaviour. Throughout the novel, Austen is preoccupied with issues about the difficulty of interpretation and critical judgement; the nature of the connection between social manners and ethical foundations; the social determinants of class, gender, urban and rural values. And no character sees whole – even Mr. Knightly is prejudiced by feeling and limitations of situation. But *Emma* is clearly not postmodern: there *is* a correct way of seeing; manners appear at times provisional, but are actually the social expression of permanent and lasting values; consistency of character is not only desirable as the basis of moral action, but actually attainable if one works for it through extension of sympathies and resistance to the attraction of arrogant social presumption. It would be difficult, if not impossible, to read *Emma* as a postmodern fiction. In this sense, Lodge is right to see Realism as a concept which is not entirely elastic.

It does not follow from this, however, that Postmodernism is necessarily an expression of the total exhaustion of such values, giving itself up instead to an irresponsible carnival of jokes and linguistic games for their own sake as yet another symptom of that cultural decline which has displaced truth and value with rhetoric and performance. Certainly, it would be difficult to find a character with the moral authority of a Mr. Knightly in a postmodern novel (and what self-respecting contemporary woman would bow to his patriarchal assumptions anyway?). It would even be difficult to find a narrative voice which could manipulate distance and remain relatively stable in its ironic implications. But is Vonnegut's parodic examination of the economic, social and psychological roots of war in *Slaughterhouse 5* (1969), or Salman Rushdie's presentation of the instrumental uses of fundamentalist literalism to produce the fictional reality of nation in the novel *Shame*, any less serious or less engaged with history? Have these novels, in fact, abandoned the norms of the historical description of reality? Could it not be argued equally that they have simply challenged the restrictive and reductive representational forms which these norms *can take* within specific discursive formations in order to effect a type of conceptual liberation which has *always* been a function of art and continues to be so even in this age of so-called universal 'commodification'? If Rushdie incorporates motifs from the popular cinematic genre of horror, or Vonnegut from the genre of science fiction; if both redefine 'history' by assaulting the Hegelian foundations of it as a dialectical movement underwritten by metaphysical causality or necessity, why should this, in itself, be sufficient grounds for seeing their work as capitulating to the market or to a nihilistic linguistic constructionism where the only reality is text. Why does the postmodern debate, ironically, so often fall into rigidly polarised positions? Instead of defending Postmodernism as an authentic response to the exhaustion of other modes of art or knowledge or attacking it as an inauthentic capitulation to commercial culture, why not see it as an attempt to *modify* the past through reformulation of its modes in the light of a present in which recognition of the pervasiveness of consumer culture is not, necessarily, total capitulation to it.

III

History and Subjectivity in the Aesthetic Mode of the Postmodern

Reading Alice Walker's The Color Purple

This chapter will conclude with some fictional examples which show ways in which one can see Postmodernism as a mode of fictional expression which exists in dialogue (in the Bakhtinian sense) with other dominant literary modes and which offers re-examination rather than outright refutation of the so-called 'humanist' concerns of realist fiction. Although apparently more 'realist' in form than Rushdie's *Shame*, a novel such as Alice Walker's *The Color Purple* (1983), both engages with, and can be read through, the concerns of the postmodern. The novel uses intertextual displacements extensively to challenge the normative sense of History as the public acts of Great Men. Only by offering alternative 'universes of discourse' can the monologic discursive identity of History so conceived be exposed. Celie's letters (written initially to herself, but there being no available concept of self to ground the process of introspection, actually addressed to God as an impersonal and Authoritative being) offer such an alternative 'universe of discourse'. It is her voicing of a rural, uneducated vernacular (not subsumed into or interpreted by an omniscient, authoritatively middle class, implicitly masculine, Western narrative voice), which articulates, from within its own situatedness, the consciousness of both racial and sexual oppression. In this process an alternative model of history is offered to the normative one enunciated in the letters of Nettie who, educated by white missionaries, achieves a stylistic perfection which embodies an internalisation of white middle class culture. *The Color Purple* is a dialogic reconstruction of American history through the intertextual relationship of these universes of discourse.

Why can one see this as postmodern? It is postmodern in its recognition of implication as a condition of historical situatedness, but of freedom as one involving the aesthetic manipulation of voice and discourse in order to contest and disrupt from within. Alice Walker is aware of the dualities of her own position as a woman Afro-American writer unable to stand entirely outside the values of white middle class American culture: its notion of the aesthetic; its individualistic, rationalistic and implicitly masculine concept of subjective identity; its view of history as competitive progression. But she can contest these from within. Even the embedded representations of art in the novel contribute to this effect. As Celie, Shug and Sophie stitch, quilt, cook and garden, they produce a communal art which, in its 'functionalism', is devalued according to the ideology of the aesthetic as autonomous splendid isolation. But this art can and does contest the values of commercial culture and in fact suggests that the individualistic basis of the aesthetic ideal of autonomy may be caught up in the very values it seeks to challenge. 'Cultural heritage' is thus re-established as a living connectedness linked neither to profit nor 'individual talent', but to the collective human need for warmth, food, beauty, relationship: the significant values which Celie comes to recognise as her denied history as a black woman living in a racist and sexist society. Throughout, the novel examines as problematic for black women, tradition-bound myths of origin as enshrined in religious, political and legal discourses: Christianity, with its anthropomorphised white-haired old Man; the founding of American ideals of democracy and equality through the liberal establishment of rights which denied political identity to blacks and effectively sanctioned slavery; the institutionalisation of marriage as the place where ownership of women confirms the 'freedom' of men. It accomplishes this critique through the characteristically postmodern use of parody. The actual structure of the novel parodies the forms of the early eighteenth-century European bourgeois novel: the uncertainties of epistolary communication; missing letters; fears of incest; mistaken identities, coincidences of plot used as a simulacrum of the mysterious workings of Providence. Thus, Walker can both acknowledge the weight of a literary heritage which has, in part, made her own writing possible, but uses the contestatory modes of parody and stylisation to signal her distance, as an Afro-American woman, from its ideological implications.

Throughout, conventional political and literary discourses are seen to be inscribed with, and constructive of, relations of patriarchal and racial power. Such assumptions are buried deep in the stylistic elegance of Nettie's prose, which is set against the confessional vernacular of Celie's. This voice eschews modes of ratiocination or even correct syntax and instead builds indirect emotional and symbolic resonances through reconstructions of the sensory experiences of everyday life and its domestic objects. Even official history itself is subjected to this discursive mode:

> The way you know who discover America, Nettie say, is think about cucumbers. That what Columbus sound like. I learned all bout Columbus in first grade, but look like he the first thing I forgot. She say Columbus come here in boats called the Neater, the Peter, and the Santomareater. Indians so nice to him he force a bunch of 'em back home with him to wait on the Queen.

However, the Janus-faced nature of the postmodern is apparent. The vernacular voice may distance, by rendering absurd, the official heroic version of the founding of America, but her domestication of it also allows Celie an identification with and internalisation of its ideologies. Thus has she come to conceive of herself as sharing this heritage with the 'people of America'. In doing so, of course, she also negates her own particular history as a black woman. But this can only be recovered through the very vernacular mode which has facilitated her identity in the terms of the 'official history'. Her identity is founded on relations of negation (her writing begins with the words 'I am' crossed out). The novel explores the process of coming to identity in positive and authentic terms and recognises the way in which the same words or discourses can come to take on different meanings and values in different contexts and situations. As Celie learns to use her vernacular to explore the possibilities of asserting her own sense of agency and personal memory, the very same discourse which had functioned as the vehicle of oppression facilitates her liberation. She begins to recognise the importance of the aesthetic in political reconstruction for, at the very least, what is familiar may need to be defamiliarised before it can become a vehicle of consciousness for the oppressed. Celie begins to perceive what official history writes out in its legitimation of a particular set of power relations as 'truth': class relations filtered through racial victimisation and sexual relations determined by economic domination. She begins imaginatively to build upon the things about her through an identification with objects in the world of nature uncontaminated by the subjective definitions of white men and learns 'that feeling of being part of everything, not separate at all. I knew that if I cut a tree, my arm would bleed' (p167). Trees are objects in their own right in the world of nature, objects of beauty in the world of human meaning, and also, for the Olinka, Divine in their provision of that basic shelter which is a fundamental human need. Celie's sense of radical situatedness, of identity as a stripling tree growing out of the soil of a culture, is modified by her developing awareness of an aesthetic power in herself which can imaginatively reformulate the conditions of that situatedness. Thus the aesthetic may facilitate the reformulation of the ethical and cognitive.

This insight, though central to postmodern theory, does not necessarily involve an abandonment of traditional forms of thought or aesthetic expression. In *The Color Purple*, there are no holes in pages, no fundamental disruptions of the physical laws of nature, there is no ludic or self-reflexive authorial voice. But the novel is clearly informed by the mood of the postmodern and uses contestatory voices and parodic modes to challenge political consensus, expand concepts of history and personal identity, expose the machinations of the process of legal legitimation. The representational norms of the description of history are not abandoned, but neither are they reproduced in unmodified form.

IV

Raising the Dead

Bringing Back The Author

It would be possible to take any of the terms of accusation levelled at Postmodernism and to re-evaluate them in the light of a detailed reading of imaginative literature. I have tended to focus above on the accusation that Postmodernism is ahistorical, concerned only with the present materiality of writing or that it is simply complicit with the ideological norms of consumer culture. There is not space to examine the entire vocabulary of critique, but I will finish by glancing briefly at the idea that in its textual narcissism, Postmodernism represents the dissolution of the self into language. Again, if we examine fictional writing, what we tend to see rather is a problematisation of available concepts of subjectivity. Postmodernism is often seen as an accomplice to the murder of the Author. What does this mean? In his essay 'From Work to Text', Roland Barthes speaks of this new understanding of authorship:

> It is not that the Author may not 'come back' in the Text, in his text, but he then does so as a 'guest'. If he is a novelist, he is inscribed in the novel like one of his characters, figured in the carpet; no longer privileged, paternal, aletheological, his inscription is ludic. He becomes, as it were, a paper-author: his life is no longer the origin of his fictions but a fiction contributing to his work . . . and the I which writes the text, it too, is never more than a paper I (Barthes, 1977, p161).

Jorge Luis Borges explores this dilemma in many of his fictions, explicitly in 'Borges and I' (1957), where he recognises that the more one tries to fix oneself in writing, the more one is forced to recognise that in converting oneself into a linguistic category, a sign, one can in fact never be present to oneself. Narrative is retrospective, even if, as Georges Poulet has argued, 'to feel oneself live is to feel oneself leave behind in every instant of time an instant which was the self' (Poulet, 1956, p16). The problem is another extension of the Romantic struggle between irony and plenitude. The postmodern response is often to explore the possibility that if writing, as an attempt to articulate subjectivity, divides up the continuum of experience into the discrete and public orders of grammar, then maybe an exaggeration, a flaunting of the 'now', of the situation of writing itself, can capture identity in some more intuitive but absolute way. Here self-conscious fictionality is explored as a means through to immediacy. Again the strategy has a long aesthetic history. It informs every page of that essentially romantically ironic novel, *Tristram Shandy* (1760–1).

The eponymous hero of this fiction, in attempting to fix himself, to catch up with the present of autobiographical endeavour, presents a random succession of sensations as they occur in the 'now' of writing. He hopes that he may come to recognise sequence in the immanent experience of temporality itself. His desire is to capture identity as a primordial time-forming activity of consciousness. In order to achieve this, consciousness must be freed from the spatialising and abstracting logic imposed through the conceptual retrospection of history as 'sense of an ending'. The desire is to find some way of gathering the self as a continuum through time into the 'now' of writing without imposing a pattern of retrospective causality. Fluidity is all. But it cannot, of course, lead in itself to the desired state of plenitude or moment of full self-possession even though it may expose the limitations of Cartesian rationalist introspection. Postmodern fictions similarly play on this necessary gap between the linguistic pronoun 'I' (a universal grammatical category only ever personally fixed in specific context) and the existential 'I'. Writing cannot represent a pre-existent self so much as reveal its impossibility. 'I' is always fixed as a relation with 'you', and in the condition of writing, 'you' is an entirely anonymous entity, a mysterious 'Dear Reader'. The recognition may produce the tortured soliloquies of Beckett's *Trilogy* or the comic attempts to identify Gustave Flaubert (or is it really Geoffrey Braithwaite or possibly Julian Barnes) in the novel *Flaubert's Parrot*.

Such postmodern texts do not annihilate subjectivity unless one is working with a reduced and restrictive concept of it (a common polemical device, as I have argued above). They do, however, persuade us to think about it in ways which may disrupt or extend conventional boundaries. To conceive of subjectivity as contextual, fluid, relational, constituted and annihilated through language, is to recognise that as one writes the self one's self is similarly also written. In popular versions, whether critical of or proselytising for Postmodernism, this may be translated into the idea that the self is simply a bundle of competing language games, utterly constructed through language and totally devoid of agency. Postmodernism is not simply a problematisation of humanism. It is an assault on human beings. And so the contemporary battlelines of Ancients and Moderns are redrawn, each consummating the other through caricature and reserving the dignity of openness and complexity for itself. This is a depressing lesson to be learnt from 'working with theory'. Its implications though are clear. Like much in the postmodern debate, they are not simply about how to read literary texts: if I am caricatured in my efforts to understand through the imposition on me of ready-made and reductive concepts then I must endeavour not to impose similarly reductive labels on others and to resist their effects on myself. As Doris Lessing said in the preface to *The Golden Notebook*:

> Handing the manuscript to publisher and friends, I learned that I had written a tract about the sex war, and fast discovered that nothing I said then could change that diagnosis. Yet the essence of the book, the organisation of it, everything in it, says implicitly or explicitly, that we must not divide things off, must not compartmentalise. Bound. Free. Good. Bad. Yes. No. Capitalism. Socialism. Sex. Love. (1973, p10).

It is time to look more closely at the theoretical postmodern critique of such forms of conceptualisation and to consider further the identity and perceived role of the aesthetic within this third and final frame: Postmodernism as critique of Enlightenment.

5

THE VIOLENCE
OF BEING MODERN

Postmodernism as Critique of Enlightenment

I

Introduction

Kant and Enlightenment

This chapter will focus on Postmodernism as a body of thought presenting itself as a critique of Enlightenment. The radical break view has been particularly prominent in this area, but I would still maintain the argument that if we situate this variety of Postmodernism in a predominantly *aesthetic* context, it makes much more sense to see it, like the other modes, as a culmination of a gathering critique of Western cultural forms of representation. This critique has a long and significant history within aesthetic thought, if a less prominent one in political, sociological and analytic philosophical thinking. If one can talk of a break in this area, it would also seem to be a consequence of the recent way in which aesthetic formulations have more pervasively entered the processes of what were formerly considered to be purely ethical or practical, and purely cognitive or scientific, modes of representation. Distinctions between these categories have become unprecedentedly blurred.

For many commentators, Postmodernism is a term synonymous with that current of contemporary theoretical debate whose main focus is the representation and analysis of a perceived breakdown in the universalising and rationalist metanarratives of the Enlightenment: those grand theories which have grounded modern Western politics, knowledge, art and ethics, for the last two hundred and fifty years. The rationalist claims of Enlightenment thought were amazingly ambitious and so too, as we shall see, are its aestheticist postmodern refutations.

In an essay entitled 'An Answer to the Question: What is Enlightenment?' (1784), Kant wrote that, 'Enlightenment is man's release from his self-incurred tutelage' (Kant, 1984, p30). The major presupposition behind this assertion is that there is a stable entity called a self which has access to inner states and the outer world. Through the application of its faculties, this self is able to arrive at knowledge of both these states and can therefore rise above their 'tutelage', achieving a condition of freedom. Kant's essay castigates those lazy people who will not think for themselves. For Enlightenment can only begin with individual self-will, but thus established, it exerts a centrifugal force to become a social dynamic. However, it is the duty of all citizens to promote its public forms, for Enlightenment is a 'sacred right' of all. Fundamental to it is not so much a method of thought as the existence of the conditions for *freedom* of thought. Only if human thought can be spontaneously self-determining, freeing itself from emotional determinants within and institutional pressures without, can it be truly critical and therefore truly enlightened.

Like all Enlightenment thought, Kant's philosophy is dependent upon the acceptance of certain a priori and irrefutable grounds or foundations. As we have seen, for postmodernists, there can be no such foundation in Reason or, arguably, in anything else. In Kant's system of 'transcendental idealism', such foundations are provided by the 'categories' which determine the nature of truth, justice and freedom. Accordingly, the mind can discover correspondences between the a priori forms of thought and the structure of world. As long as we can think or reason, in the right kind of way, then we can know world and self and achieve inner harmony through transcendence of the irrational forces within and the prejudices and superstitions which exert pressure on us from outside:

> Emancipation from superstition is called enlightenment, for although this term applies also to emancipation from prejudices generally, still superstition deserves pre-eminently (in sensu eminenti) to be called a prejudice. For the condition of blindness into which superstition puts one, which is as much as demands from one as an obligation, makes the need of being led by others, and consequently the passive state of the reason, pre-eminently conspicuous. . . . But the question here is not one of the faculty of cognition, but of the mental habit of making a final use of it. This, however small the range and degree to which a man's natural endowments extend, still indicates a man of enlarged mind: if he detaches himself from the subjective personal conditions of his judgement, which cramp the minds of so many others, and reflects upon his own judgement from a universal standpoint (which he can only determine by shifting his ground to the standpoint of others). (Kant in Simpson, 1988, p113).

Reason must never be passive. It must always transcend personal situation and prejudice, otherwise it cannot be consistent and no universal system of truth or ethics can be established. Looking into ourselves, if we are to discover what Kant calls the categorical imperative, the one correct principle, then we must discard all distractions from it, all irrational and contingent desires or 'empirical conditions', and arrive at a point outside personal experience which would apply to all rational beings and thus constitute a universal law. Enlightenment is the state of believing that human beings are collectively engaged in a progressive movement towards moral and intellectual self-realisation through the application to their situation of a *universal rational faculty*. The notion of personal autonomy is central to this: precisely defined as the condition of being free from servitude to irrational forces within or without. It is an ideal which has informed not only political theories of democracy, but specifically modern movements in thought such as psychoanalysis. Indeed, it has permeated most of the ways in which modern human beings have thought about, and represented, themselves and their world.

The very large claim of postmodern theory is that the foundational premises of these assumptions of Enlightenment thought are now clearly shown to be untenable. The institutions built upon them are exhausted. A weaker version is that these premises are not necessarily untenable *per se*, but will need substantial redefinition if they are to be of beneficial force in the contemporary Western world. Although Freud saw himself as an Enlightenment thinker, arguing 'where id was, there shall ego be', he was also instrumental in subverting the confident rationalism of Kantian thought, showing reason to be a product of desire and the unconscious to be structured through the social pressure to conform. Thus, for many people living in a post-Freudian age, it seems difficult to imagine the possibility of coming anywhere near to the condition Kant sees as 'enlightened': free of emotional impingements on rational consciousness, above prejudice, unswayed by the contingencies of everyday historical life. Few, perhaps, still believe in the possibility of achieving such a consistent, universal, transcendental position, except in particular contexts such as scientific research. But many would wish to maintain Kant's position as an *ideal* informing our activities: ethical, political, aesthetic. The most radical mode of postmodern thought is that which rejects Kantian reason and autonomy, even as an ideal. Yet, again I would argue that this position is not radically new. It has a long history within *aesthetic* thought. Even in its most radical form (which claims that Enlightenment-style reason can be seen to be complicit with an authoritarian rationalism producing terror in place of emancipation and disguising its will to power as a disinterested and scientific desire for truth), its roots can be traced back to Romantic aesthetics: to the Wordsworthian critique of rationalising logic, for example, which we examined in the opening chapter. If it is more thorough-going and more apocalyptic in its postmodern forms, this is because modernity has fully revealed itself, in the meantime, in all its most rapacious and dangerous aspects. For postmodernists, as the logic of late capitalist expansion penetrates ever further and deeper, the entire life-world seems to have been subjugated to the rationalising logic of efficiency: the harnessing of time for profit and, therefore, for no conceivably rational end.

In its weaker form, Postmodernism would view Enlightenment thought as exhausted because inappropriate to the latest phase of consumer capitalism. A common argument here is that global monetary expansion has collapsed the secure containment of boundaries like 'nation' and with it, the political economies and systems of law founded on such premises. In this area, many of the period concepts examined earlier provide the frame for the perception of Postmodernism as a critique of Enlightenment. Thus, some commentators may choose to emphasise the effects of the technological changes of the 'information age'. All postmodernists believe that we are living through a legitimation crisis. Contestatory theories and models have exploded upon us: incommensurable ethical positions, competing language games. In this view, Enlightenment thought is the latest victim of modernity as it moves into a phase of self-destruction. In its stronger form, however, Postmodernism views Enlightenment thought itself as the main source of the terrors and disorder of the modern world. In this version, the distorted embodiment of the Kantian ideal of Reason must bear much of the responsibility for placing us in the iron grip of forms of oppression, external and internalised, which though more invisible, are more insidiously powerful than pre-modern forms of control.[13]

In what sense can one think of Enlightenment reason producing terror? Its language sometimes, and paradoxically, has a feeling of violence about it, expressing an overwhelming desire for a rationalist dream of a world where we might all be freed from the importunate gnawings of feeling and superstition. Here is the eighteenth-century philosopher D'Alembert expressing his hopes for the new age:

> The discovery and application of a new method of philosophising, the kind of enthusiasm accompanying discoveries, a certain exaltation of ideas which the spectacle of the universe produces in us – all these causes have brought about a lively fermentation of minds. Spreading through nature in all directions like a river which has burst its dams, this fermentation has swept with a sort of violence everything along with it which stood in its way ... Thus from the principles of the secular sciences to the foundations of religious revelation, from metaphysics to matters of taste, from the scholastic disputes of theologians to matters of trade ... everything has been discussed and analysed (Cassirer, 1951, p4).

One senses a violent, dynamic impulse pressing forward, and a countercurrent, seeking containment and stasis, pressing back. The source of both is the newly discovered powers of the human mind itself, the excitement and terror of the experience of being 'Faust at the mirror of Narcissus' (Berman, 1982). For those caught up in the tremendous pace and change of modern life, the possibility of a still point of pure knowledge hinges upon the discovery of that contemplative space which will allow one to look inside and know. For Kant, such a possibility arose out of modernity, but in achieving universal knowledge, would transcend it. He does not fear that Faust may turn into Narcissus: knowledge turns out to be merely the solipsistic projection of one's own irrational desire, one's self-love, upon

---

[13] Foucault's interests have been consistently focussed in this area. In *Language, Counter-Memory, Practice* he argues that: 'Humanity does not gradually progress from combat to combat until it arrives at universal reciprocity, where the rule of law finally replaces warfare; humanity installs each of its violences in a system of rules and thus proceeds from domination to domination' (1977, p151). Critics such as Habermas have argues that Foucault wilfully ignores progressive aspects of modernity in seeing it as an increasingly sophisticated refinement of forms of discipline and domination. Others have pointed out that in his development of a pervasive Nietzschean will-to-power, he ignores macrological forces such as the state or the persistence of class and capitalist economic expansion. This is an argument which could apply across the range of postmodern thought. Indeed, it is a criticism which could be levelled at the entire aestheticist tradition from Schiller onwards: chapter nine examines its ramifications in the criticism of T. S. Eliot.

the world. But once the metaphysical frame of Kantian Idealism starts to weaken, its introspective method may open, not onto universal ground, but to the sound of that key, turning at nightfall, which confirms the prison of solipsism. The fear that haunts Modernism. However, the spectre which hovers over Modernism has come to terrorise Postmodernism: for if one begins to doubt the Kantian synthesis of rationalism and empiricism (the idea that structures of mind correspond to structures of nature and that in using reason to gain self-understanding we can simultaneously gain knowledge of world), from whence is one to derive universal foundations of thought in a secular culture? And without foundations, how will the edifices of this modern world remain standing? Eliot's *The Wasteland* foresaw precisely the 'postmodern condition': its apocalypticism *and* its focus on the aesthetic as the possible site of redemption; its 'Cracks and reforms and bursts in the violet air/Falling towers/Jerusalem Athens Alexandria/Vienna London/Unreal' (p72).

Kant is often seen as the perfect embodiment of a belief in reason as the basis of emancipation and the means of discovering the categorical imperative. Yet he is also a harbinger of Modernism, exposing the frailties of Enlightenment. Clement Greenberg, the great advocate of American Modernism, was one of the first to suggest this:

> I identify modernism with the intensification, almost the self-critical tendency which began with the philosopher Kant. Because he was the first to criticise the means itself of criticism, I conceive of Kant as the first real modernist ... The Enlightenment criticised from the outside, the way criticism in its more accepted sense does; modernism criticises from the inside, through the procedures themselves of that which is being criticised (Greenberg, 1973, p67).

Greenberg is drawing attention here to the self-reflexive concern of modernist art with its own formal nature. Kant showed that truth could only be discovered through a self-reflexive awareness of the tools and methods of thought used in its investigation. So too, the formal properties of modernist art define the mode and nature of its autonomous aesthetic truth: content is form. Art discovers the pure essence of its own condition through formal self-reflexivity. It is an extension into art of Kant's concept of self-criticism as the discovery of the universal form of truth and morality. In effect, Greenberg suggests that modernist art must now take on the burden of Kantian autonomy. If one can no longer view autonomy as the possibility of existential self-determination in the world, then the concept may be rescued by transferring it entirely into the space of art. Here are the roots of that autonomy construction of Modernism which we will need to trace more carefully later in this book. Postmodernism provides us with the tools to challenge it. Greenberg's comments, however, suggest the beginnings of an intuition of that unresolvable tension in Kant's notion of reason which makes its full dramatic entrance in Postmodernism. The Kantian concept of self-determination, in fact, set up impossible problems about self-grounding and self-legitimation which can be seen to surface acutely in the self-referential obsessions of much modern art. Similar concerns were soon to enter modern science. Philosophy too, was to become obsessed with epistemological issues about the extent to which one's instruments of knowledge shape or construct what one sees, so that investigation must begin with the instruments themselves: language, materials, concepts, one's own position in space and time.

The postmodern critique of Enlightenment can thus be seen as an extension of insights provided by a philosopher generally regarded as its fullest embodiment. In this form too, Postmodernism is as much a development of existing tendencies in Western thought, as a break with and refutation of them. Postmodernism effectively extends the formal self-reflexivity of Kantian idealism to a limit where there can be *no* position outside the instruments of knowledge with which to offer a critique of them. How can one analyse a set of linguistic relationships which construct 'knowledge' when the tools of one's analysis will be another set of linguistic relationships with no more claim to authority than the first. This is the point from which postmodernists tend to offer their critique of Enlightenment 'grand narratives' by showing that the concept of a trans-cendent 'metanarrative' is a convenient fiction which, as it topples under its own internal strain, brings the entire Enlightenment edifice down with it to its very foundations, and not before time. The will to truth which has propelled the mythologisation of such fictions is a disguised form of that will to power which has trapped us in the iron cage of a rationalising efficiency whose exclusions and repressions have produced the violences of modern life. Whatever functions as origin or source of knowledge – Pure Reason, for example – is now shown to be a category produced through a particular and provisional set of institutional discourses rather than being the origin of them. Such discourses are the expression of forms of desire as much as those of reason.

II
Is Deconstruction a Postmodernism?

The idea of the impossibility of a metacritical position is central to deconstruction as well as Postmodernism. Although the two modes overlap in many areas, it is worth trying to sort out the distinctions between them. The term deconstruction is normally used to refer to a set of strategies whose operations expose and subvert the unarticulated presuppositions of metaphysical thought which, in remaining unexposed, maintain dominance within Western culture. As a strategy, it has much in common with Postmodernism, and could be seen as a manifestation of postmodernity in any of the epochal senses discussed earlier. Rhetoric is basically used to subvert logic rather than to support it. Favourite techniques are: reversal of binary oppositions which appear equal but where one term has a negative or secondary relation to the first; displacement, which renders the first term dependent on the second; parody, which subverts the myth of pure origin; forms of repetition with difference, which have a similar effect; and the demonstration that truth is always a metaphor. Deconstruction is a form of ruthless exposure from within; all things undo themselves. Gayatri Spivak describes it thus in her introduction to Derrida's *Of Grammatology*:

> If in the process of deciphering a text in the traditional way we come across a word that seems to harbour an unresolvable contradiction, and by virtue of being one word is made sometimes to work in one way and sometimes in another and thus is made to point away from the absence of a unified meaning, we shall catch at that word. If a metaphor seems to suppress its implications, we shall catch at that metaphor. We shall follow its adventures through the text coming undone as a structure of concealment, revealing its self-transgression, its undecidability. (1976, 1, xxv).

It is difficult to say where deconstruction ends and Postmodernism begins, particularly if the latter is thought of as a philosophical 'mood' rather than aesthetic mode or cultural epoch. The two are, indeed, often conflated. However, apologists for deconstruction tend to see it as a mode of writing which, unlike Postmodernism, retains a realistic recognition that we cannot, ultimately, think without metaphysical concepts and for this reason it is pointless to imagine Enlightenment to be exhausted. Derrida is often quoted to support this position. Yet Derrida's work is also used to support arguments which clearly go beyond this. A recent study of Postmodernism, for example, includes him in an account of the current attempt to undo the violence of metaphysical thought by freeing writing *entirely* from the obligation of representation and meaning so that the 'Real' is preserved as infinitely open, fluid, non-commensurable with the categories of conceptual thought (Flax, 1991). If Derrida's work is described in these terms, it is difficult to see how it can be distinguished from Lyotard's postmodern sublime. However, in Christopher Norris's view, if the central doctrine of the Kantian Enlightenment is the idea that knowledge is achieved through the exercise of reason in acts of independent critical reflection, then even if Derrida sees this as non-achievable, he is not a postmodernist in that he believes we should continue to aspire towards it *as an ideal* (Norris, 1990). Derrida knows it is impossible to go beyond metaphysics, that one will inevitably and unconsciously be naming grounds, whether new or old, for systems of thought, and that one's language will always be complicit with the language one seeks to deconstruct in ways one simply cannot see. His deconstructive thrust is simply to look for moments in a text which threaten to collapse its coherence as a conceptual system. He achieves this by revealing that the apparent founding premises or origins of its argument are in fact not reflections of stable categories outside, but metaphors within the text for unrepresentable concepts outside the text which are already metaphors themselves. The heady belief of D'Alembert, that human reason can bring all under its purview, has disappeared. According to Norris, however, this does not entail that we see Derrida as a thoroughgoing textualist. In essays such as 'Structure, Sign and Play in the Human Sciences' (1966), he does appear to assert a postmodern fictionality in arguing that all language is dependent upon rhetorical tropes and that philosophy is therefore a branch of literature. In his series of lectures, *The Philosophical Discourses of Modernity* (1987), Habermas reads Derrida almost entirely in such terms. For Norris, this is a misreading based on Hàbermas's own desire to discredit *any* system of thought which could imply that all forms of reason are forms of instrumental violence. How are we to sort out these positions? Again, the difficulty in assessing these arguments is in determining the extent to which polemical intent shapes the categories which are the object of critique. To turn Norris's defence of deconstruction against itself, one could point out the obvious fact that Postmodernism is degraded and reduced to textualism or dangerous aestheticism by defining it entirely through a discussion of those works by Lyotard, Rorty, Fish and Baudrillard which mostly lend themselves to this sort of interpretation. In this view, Postmodernism is simply an extension of that tendency in structuralist thought which sees the 'real' as purely a construct of intra-linguistic processes which confine one forever to the prisonhouse of language. Worse still, postmodernists are 'lost in the funhouse' of art. This is certainly one way of reading postmodern theory, but it arrives at an assessment of Postmodernism as a mode of over-aestheticisation without taking account at all of postmodern works of art. Similarly, it ignores alternative evaluations of the aesthetic as a shaping power in the world which might allow one to view Postmodernism, as I have done here, as the culmination of a way of seeing with its roots in Romanticism. From this perspective, it may be seen to carry beneficial insights as well as dangerous tendencies.

III
Modernity and the Critique of Instrumental Reason

Habermas is suspicious of Postmodernism because he views it as a theoretical position which over-generalises the *instrumental* element in Enlightenment reason. This is only one of the possible modes of reason, and in his own work he develops an alternative to it with the idea of *communicative* reason. In this section, we will need to look at the concept of instrumental reason, and its relation to theories of modernity, in order to understand the focus of the postmodern critique. What Habermas broadly shares with Postmodernism is a sense that, as capitalism develops and Western societies become increasingly concerned with the efficient rationalisation of the lifeworld, modes of relationship which are not conducive to efficiency become either devalued or split off into private spaces. We have seen how this critique arose with Romanticism, and in its emphasis on the aesthetic as a possible solution, Postmodernism can be seen as the heir of this earlier movement. Romanticism, however, tended to imagine redemptive moments out of time, a legacy it passes to much modernist writing, whereas in Postmodernism, the aesthetic is extended into theories of the social in an attempt to integrate art into the contingency of temporal experience itself. All three concern themselves with time. In capitalist societies, time is the most valuable commodity: to make it new is to break with the past and to innovate, but to make profit is to be able to convert one's innovations into mass-produced objects for consumption.

The constant search for new forms and new markets produces the unstable, crisis-prone dynamism of capitalism but the need for efficiency produces an adherence to or creation of structures which allow human behaviour to be predicted. In a secular world where 'all that is solid melts into air, all that is holy is profaned' (Marx and Engels, 1975, p487), both processes are regulated according to a mode of rationalisation which can harness time to the ends of profit. The idea of 'instrumental rationalism' arose in Weberian social theory as a means of explaining this process whereby modern societies were progressively 'disenchanted', divested of traditional structures and brought under a bureaucratic 'iron cage' of reason whose only end is efficiency. The Romantic critique of industrialisation asserted the importance of art as a disinterested activity outside such purposive logic: Postmodernism pursues the possibility of seeing the aesthetic as an impulse which can disrupt it from within.

If modernity is viewed as a process of disenchantment from traditional structures of belief, Postmodernism can be seen as an attempt to disenchant us from modernity. Instead of emphasising the positive aspects of modernity: its release of new and productive energies, its fostering of the belief in the capacity of human beings to improve continuously their conditions of existence, Postmodernism tends to focus on the dark side of this process. Enlightenment reason is viewed as complicit with this. Foucault's work has shaped this view. Reason is seen to clarify a world which it has set up in its own terms, in a disguised manifestation of a will to power which secures itself through an insidious exclusion of all that it identifies as non-rational: desire, feeling, sexuality, femininity, art, madness, criminality, non-Caucasian races, particular ethnicities. Reason, even in its Enlightenment mode, is thus seen as part of the impulse to control and subjugate which is the logic of capitalism and which has led to the violent forms of oppression in the modern world: imperialism, colonialism, racism, sexism, destruction of the environment, automatisation of human beings for the purposes of efficiency. Economic affluence in the West is seen to be dependent upon exploitation elsewhere. It is facilitated by a supposedly 'universal' but in fact exclusionary logic of identity which does not include these 'elsewheres' within its terms. Technology is now seen to threaten the planet with annihilation. The mood of disenchantment infects postmodern theory and literature alike. Doris Lessing expresses it thus:

> As for our thoughts, our intellectual apparatus, our rationalisms and our logics and our deductions, and so on, it can be said with absolute certainty that dogs and cats and monkeys cannot make a rocket fly to the moon or weave artificial dress materials out of the by-products of petroleum, but as we sit in the ruins of this variety of intelligence it is hard to give it very much value: I suppose we are undervaluing it now as we overvalued it then. It will have to find its place: I believe a pretty low place at that (1979, p74).

For postmodernists, it is this 'iron cage' of rationalisation without reason which produced Auschwitz. Taking their cue from Foucault, some theorists have referred to this as the violence of the logic of the same, viewing their own activity as an attempt to preserve difference, reject universalisation, praise the local, the particular event, the specificity of the contingent. So, generalising abstractions are viewed in Nietzschean terms as pragmatic and provisional fictions, and events or objects in the world may be viewed in a Heideggerian mode which attempts to respect their own specificity instead of reproducing them instrumentally through the conceptual categories of the subject.

IV
Postmodernity in Modernity
Wasteland

Postmodernism tends to focus almost exclusively on the dark side of Enlightenment reason and to turn to the aesthetic as an alternative way of knowing. I have argued that this is not a radical break with, but the culmination of, tendencies with a long history in modernity itself. Not only Romanticism, but also Modernism, drew on a language of apocalypse and crisis to represent its own condition as a radical break. However, when Virginia Woolf announced that human character had suddenly changed in December 1910, she was actually articulating the sense of a moment where the changes which had been occurring over the last century had seemed to culminate in a decisive turning point in Western culture. These changes were part of what postmodernists see as the logic of modernity: imperial expansion (such that by 1900 the British Empire covered one quarter of the world's surface); increasing tension between capital and labour and fears of social unrest; changes in relations between men and women; changes in the human relation to space and time in the physical world – Einstein had published his general theory of relativity in 1905, Heisenberg his 'uncertainty principle' in the twenties; Freud and Darwin had assaulted traditional psychological and biological views of human beings. That Woolf should have seen these changes as specific experiences of the twentieth-century seems, with hindsight, not an unreasonable assumption for her time. Yet it is clear to us now that much of what seemed dramatically new to make 1910 a turning point in history had actually arisen in the nineteenth century. If we glance at some of these impulses, we can see even more clearly that just as Modernism was a radical break only to those writing from within it, so too, it may be more fruitful to view Postmodernism in such terms.

Wherever we look at the cultural, political or ideological tendencies which helped to shape the modernist response to the twentieth-century world, we can see nineteenth-century roots. Even such an apparently, irrefutably radical new theory of subjectivity as offered in Freudian psychoanalysis (now the source of so many *postmodern* versions of 'decentred consciousness'), clearly extends well-established nineteenth-century scientific assumptions. Frued's theory of the unconscious basically posits the idea that the individual psyche is driven, not by reason, but by the instincts of the id. This pleasure principle, with its own, fundamentally asocial associative logic, is at loggerheads with the social world of the 'reality principle' and yet, in its expression of our most profound desires, fuels the compensatory forms of fantasy which are generated in order to make bearable our existence in the world. One can see here an obvious source for the *postmodern* critique of Kantian reason, but Freud's account of this process was dependent upon a theory of instincts and drives derived from nineteenth-century physical science; he formulated concepts of psychological struggle which drew on the vocabulary of nineteenth-century religion, though shorn of the absolute moral imperatives which would oppose a diabolical desire to an idealised realm of reason. Freud's distinctively 'modernist' breakthrough was, of course, to show how reason is derived from desire, but even here, he inherits a mode of dialectical thought developed by nineteenth-century philosophers such as Hegel.

The same tensions of old and new inform other varieties of knowledge. The main conceptual thrust of the new physics, for example, was the effective denial that human knowledge reflects the essential structure of the world. In this it seemed to challenge not only Platonic and Kantian notions of the real but also nineteenth-century positivist scientific ones. Instead, physicists were suggesting that scientific concepts are simply pragmatic tools, useful instruments with only provisional explanatory power: postmodern fictions, in effect. This seems a long way from Kant's universal categories, yet one can still see in the various cultural expressions of late modernity (including modernist literature), a tension between the new sense of contingency and provisionality and a desire to find some way to retain the notion of universal categories. How else to discover a correspondence between the rational conceptualisations of mind and the essential orders of the world, to use rational means for universal ends? What has come into the foreground of Postmodernism is palpably there, troubling modernists too, and, as I argued earlier, was implicit all along in the Kantian legacy.

What seems to emerge in Postmodernism as a dialectic of situatedness and fictionality can be seen as a continuing logic of modernity as much as a critique of it. Baudelaire was one of the first to articulate this sense of being modern as it reveals itself in aesthetic form: 'beauty is made up on the one hand of an element that is eternal and invariable . . . and, on the other, of a relative, circumstantial element, which we may like to call . . . contemporaneity' (Baudelaire, 1972, p403). In Modernism, this dialectic is culturally expressed as one of abstraction and contingency or, in the terms more familiar to students of literature, of 'form and flux'. On the one hand is the relativism brought into play by the focus on shifting perspectives, Paterian subjective impressionism, and on the other hand, is a search for a principle of order no longer open to ordinary deductive logic (the ratiocinations of the shopkeeper mentality, the average mass-produced mind) but possibly available to the higher reason of art. As we have seen, this tension was implicit in Romanticism, played out in the nineteenth-century mode of the Paterian and Arnoldian, and appears again in the aestheticism of the postmodern. In the latter condition, however, order is already always aesthetically fabricated, never simply discovered as an essential foundation. We are in culture and we cannot simply step out of it. For some modernist writers, though, if order is no longer manifest in that nightmare cry in the street which is post-Hegelian history, there is still a desire to see it as possibly latent and recoverable through modes of expression which resist deductive logic and operate through association, symbol, metaphor. Modernism retains the depth/surface logic of modernity but transfers its faith in the discovery of correspondence from reason to art in an extension of Romantic aesthetics. Postmodernism takes this logic to its conclusion.

Postmodern theory is a continued elaboration of the sense of living in a world whose foundations have been shaken, and where security, or knowledge, or identity, may seem to be available, if at all, through the modes of the aesthetic rather than those of pure or practical reason in their discrete forms. The feeling was given remarkable embodiment in Eliot's *The Waste Land* (1922). If Kant had believed it to be possible to achieve a position of universal disinterestedness through reason alone, Modernism was to initiate an ongoing aesthetic exploration of the ways in which this human reason was in fact confined to limited perspectives or had fallen into complicity with a debased instrumental form whose end is, at best, simply its own enhanced efficiency. The poem is a collage of interpenetrating voices which never lead to a Kantian 'view from nowhere', a transcendental Absolute, but always to another vista in a kaleidoscope of shifting cultural contexts. Most immediately, however, *The Waste Land* conveys a sense of modern urban existence where one's situation is both literally (as a physical viewpoint), and metaphorically (as a world-view), bound to an acutely shifting and partial perspectivism. This is *physically*, in fact, the experience of being on a crowded street: an endless processing of random shocks, gestures, movements, fragments which refuse to cohere, unpredictable contacts, constant bombardment of the senses with no time for that reflective assimilation which allows one to situate one's own bodily self in some meaningful relation to sensation. The nerves are, indeed, as if stretched in patterns across a screen. In *The Waste Land*, there is a pervasive sense of a flowing, larval crowd in which identities surface, for a moment, and then are again submerged into the brown fog of a winter dawn. There are moments of arrest in the flow when an identity, trailing its history like an infernal shadow, is glimpsed, and then lost again. Metonymy, a figure of speech which substitutes part for whole, anatomises human experience so that only a supreme effort of imagination could reconstitute the fragments into some meaningful whole. Eyes and back look upward from the routinised office processes where the rational structures of industrial efficiency are experienced as ends in themselves. Human affection is subjected to the same logic: exploring hands encounter no defence. Afterwards, an automatic hand moves the automatic arm of a music-producing machine, while the body registers only a half-formed sense of relief that the sexual transaction is over once again. She is hardly aware of her departed lover, her brain allowing only one half-formed thought to pass, for the shocks, flashes, gestures, noises, have become the routine surface of the experience of modernity, the random flow traversed by the bureaucratic grid of order. All experience and knowledge is absorbed into the habitual processes of industrial capital. What Marx had called alienation is the normal condition of existence, in which the recommendation to 'only connect' is carried out in the flushed assault of a house agent's clerk as accustomed to the satisfactory discharge of his pecuniary duties as of his biological urges. To hear strains of music upon the water, to engage with the world through the non-instrumental form of the aesthetic, is to glimpse, painfully, a plenitude which may be lost forever, even if its existence was only ever imaginary in the first place.

Eliot tends to dwell in culturally pessimistic fashion on the experience of modernity, but it is not viewed as entirely beyond redemption. Indeed, what emerges is that concern with discovering relations between depths and surfaces which we have already seen to be characteristic of modern expression. Eliot may have abandoned faith in reason as the instrument of knowledge, but he has not necessarily abandoned faith in the possibility of discovering a universal order which implies some meaningful relation between the contingent surfaces of everyday experience and latent structures of truth. Eliot shores his fragments against his ruin, hoping to make them cohere through the discovery of a deep aesthetic logic expressing universal mind in some version of a collective unconscious. The faith is not strong, but the desire is everywhere in evidence. As with most modernist writers, the burden of the task is transferred from reason to the aesthetic, but it is unclear whether art can *reveal* order through its non-conceptual creation or whether it can only construct a coherence which can discover no external correspondence. Famously, he wrote in 1921:

> A poet's mind ... is constantly amalgamating experience; the ordinary man's experience is chaotic, irregular, fragmentary. The latter falls in love, or reads Spinoza, and these two experiences have nothing to do with each other, or with the smell of cooking; in the mind of the poet these experiences are always forming new wholes (*Selected Prose*, 1953, p117).

It is the non-conceptual language of the poet, rather than the rational thought of the philosopher, which takes on a burden beyond the capacities of ordinary men. If redemption is to come through art, only The Artist can discover it: though tending towards the postmodern in transferring the burden of knowledge from the rational to the aesthetic, Eliot's assertion is modernist in its conception of the production of High Art as an experience which is distinctive from that of everyday life. If the lifeworld has, in the meantime, been even more thoroughly instrumentally rationalised, then perhaps it is not surprising that one response (the postmodern) is to become even more thoroughly aesthetic. Even in Eliot's assertion, the relation between the formation of wholes and their discovery has become blurred. For Kant, orders in mind, if understood, revealed forms of correspondence with the world outside the mind. For Eliot, as for most modern writers, and all postmodernists, neither the fact of correspondence nor the means of its achievement seem so clear. Is order simply at a deeper level of mind so that the rational exploration of the relation between surface and depth (the province of analytic philosophy, modern science and the realistic novel) is unable to penetrate it? If truth is bound in some order beyond reason would the suspension of reason allow one to fathom it, but without reason how would one know that one had arrived there? How can one discriminate in the first place between the projected orders of one's own or others' desire and that which lies outside? If the tools of reason are shown to be pragmatic fictions, is art another form of radical fictionality or, in seeking to create new orders, to amalgamate disparate experience, to produce new metaphors of existence, can it thereby in some more authentic way discover existing orders through its own creative fabrications? Michel Foucault's postmodern response to Kant in his essay 'What is Enlightenment?', takes up concerns which more and more insistently informed Modernism. For Foucault, modernity lies not in the sense of discovery of pre-existing truths, but in the fact that their discovery lies always in their creation. The hero of modern life is thus the Dandy who has perceived the fundamental role of style in the creation of the modern. For modern man 'is not the man who goes off to discover himself, his secrets and his hidden truth; he is the man who tries to invent himself. This modernity does not liberate man "in his own being", it compels him to face the task of producing himself' (1986, p42).

The Frankfurt School of Critical Theory analysed cultural Modernism in terms which, more than any other, have carried over into the postmodern debate. Any genealogy of the postmodern would be incomplete without some reference to their work. Thomas Mann's *Dr. Faustus* embodied many elements of Theodor Adorno's aesthetic theory. Leverkühn, Mann's modern Faust (and in part a portrait of the composer Schoenberg), comments on the pervasive self-consciousness of the art of late modernity:

> For a cultural epoch there seems to be a spot too much talk about culture in ours, don't you think? I'd like to know whether epochs that possessed culture knew the word at all, or used it. Naivete, unconsciousness, taken-for granted-ness, seems to me to be the first criterion of the constitution to which we give this name. What we are losing is just this naivete, and this lack, if one may so speak of it, protects us from many a colourful barbarism which altogether perfectly agreed with culture, even with very high culture. I mean: our state is that of civilisation – a very praiseworthy state no doubt, but also neither was there any doubt that we should have to become very much more barbaric to be capable of culture again. Technique and comfort – in that state one talks about culture but one has not got it (1968, p61).

Leverkühn reiterates paradoxes about 'naive' and 'sentimental' art first extensively addressed by Schiller, but exploring in the light of a new modern Terror the possibility that the fall into self-consciousness may turn out to be a fortunate one after all, on one level, if an irreplaceable loss on another. The appearance of self-consciousness as parody in much modern art was central to Adorno's aesthetic discussions. Leverkühn, however, goes on to entertain the possibility that we have arrived at a condition where modernity has so exhausted its possibilities of unself-conscious expression that authentic art can now *only* respond to the modern condition by taking on the forms of that exhaustion itself through the modes of parody and joke. Mann's modern condition seems indistinguishable from the postmodern. In fact, many of Adorno's perceptions of the condition of modernity have become central to the postmodern debate. His hope for redemption through the aesthetic, but fear that this too has become incorporated into the overwhelming logic of instrumental reason, is a feeling that pervades postmodern writing. Adorno too rejected the adequacy of reason to grasp the totality of the real and saw the violence perpetrated in the name of the rational when the real is subdued to the tyranny of the concept. Thus he writes:

> To define identity as the correspondence of the thing-in-itself to its concept is hubris; but the ideal of identity must not simply be discarded. Living in the rebuke that the thing is not identical with the concept is the concept's longing to become identical with the thing. This is how the sense of non-identity contains identity. The supposition of identity is indeed the ideological element of pure thought, all the way through to formal logic; but hidden in it is also the truth moment of ideology, the pledge that there should be no contradiction, no antagonism (Adorno, 1986, p408).

However, Adorno's own anthropomorphisation of the concept, conferring on it the capacity to long, enacts the the essence of his argument: that we cannot, in fact, abandon the cognitive *ideal* of identity without collapsing into irrationalism. This ideal continuously thrusts itself (even at this moment) into our rhetorical forms. Thus art is viewed as a last remaining space where it may be possible for the violence of the concept to be suspended (and with it that instrumental rationalism which seeks the subjugation of object by separate subject), without a fall into irrationalism. For Adorno, however, art can only function in this way if it preserves disinterestedness by withdrawing from any utilitarian engagement with the world. In the condition of late modernity this can only be achieved through: a self-contained and self-conscious reflection upon the processes of its own production as illusion; a commitment to dissonance which refuses easy and comforting resolution; and an abstraction which imitates the petrified and alienated relations of modernity itself. These are arguments we have already considered in relation to Lyotard's concept of the sublime. Art becomes not a mirror, but a negative reflection of the forms of modernity, inverting its values, but through a necessary appropriation of its forms.

Central to both Lyotard's postmodern sublime and Adorno's modernist aesthetic, is a resistance to the notion of a correspondence between concept and the real, because the attempt to materialise such a correspondence produces Terror. Authentic art is that which refuses the nostalgia of correspondence by showing it to be a provisional fiction or by showing that the ground of the 'real' is itself aesthetic. Though Adorno writes in a systematic theoretical mode, like postmodernists later his concern is to refuse the totality of theoretical explanations, to expose the potential violence of rational conceptualisation and to assert the importance of the aesthetic in the preservation of unintelligibility: the mode of the sublime. The difference in the later position is that experience itself, in all its forms, is now seen to be aestheticised, so that the non-conceptually embodied unintelligibility of works of art now becomes the condition of all things whose mystery must be preserved from the violent reductionism of reason itself. And whereas Adorno attacks the dominance of radiocinative thought but preserves a belief in the ideal of reason, postmodernists may throw out reason with the ratiocinative, overvaluing fragmentariness, unmediated desire, the perceived authenticity of the body.

Few postmodern artefacts, in fact, simply celebrate 'desire' in these terms, though many examine the limitations and failures of the Enlightenment project. Perhaps this is because whereas theory inevitably uses a conceptual mode in attempting to vindicate the authenticity of the non-conceptual, works of art can inhabit the position in their irreducible particularity. Postmodern art is less at the mercy of its own performative contradictions than postmodern theory. Again, therefore, I will now pursue this argument through the examination of two *literary* texts, one generally regarded as postmodern and one modernist.

V

The Fictional Critique of Enlightenment

Reading Doris Lessing's Memoirs of a Survivor *(1974)*

A novel such as Lessing's *Memoirs* engages with many of the issues outlined above but, throughout, avoids *conceptual* definition of the condition of late modernity by referring to it as 'it' and by embedding a critique of enlightenment rationalism in a fictional embodiment of the failures of materialist utopian thought. The novel begins with the exposition of a world which is at the point of collapse after a nuclear disaster, and goes on to explore the possibility that salvation can only come through modes of consciousness radically different from those which have structured the politics of the West. Lessing too, suggests ways in which so-called enlightened rational structures may have actually produced that violence which destroys the world in her novel (and by extension, the one outside), collapsing the human into the savagery of the hunted animal.

As the foundations of the material world collapse all around, releasing the anarchic violence of a disintegrating political unconscious, human beings actually take on the attributes of wild animals, scavenging, hunting in packs, while the animal world (represented by the strange beast Hugo) takes on the 'humanist' values of love, loyalty, devotion, dignity. Human systems, political theories, disintegrate. Human beings abandon their useless commodities and gadgets, for the redundancy of these cultural artefacts is now urgently apparent. The narrator and the mysterious others, the 'we' for whom she speaks, attempt, in Kafkaesque style, to continue the application of rational modes and routines in a situation where deductive logic, far from warding off the catastrophe, actually becomes its mode of expression. The reader is informed:

> This is the sort of thing we accepted as normal. Yet for all of us there were moments when the game we were all agreeing to play simply could not stand up to events: we would be gripped by feelings of unreality, like nausea. Perhaps this feeling, that the ground was dissolving under our feet, was the real enemy ... or we believed it to be so. Perhaps our tacit agreement that nothing much, or at least nothing irrecoverable, was happening, was because for us the enemy was Reality, was to allow ourselves to know what was happening (p21).

Not only consensus about authority and right government, but about what *constitutes* the real, is breaking down. The unusual fictional use of 'we' is a desperate strategic attempt to create a consensus in a situation where the possibility of any agreement has become uncertain. Lessing, in effect, projects an intensely apocalyptic futuristic version of the postmodern condition where reason has produced violence; a crisis of political legitimation has led to a total collapse of consensus; and the reversion to archaic modes of tribal behaviour produces the vision of a world very close to that imagined in the sort of theoretically apocalyptic postmodernism which we saw earlier parodied (and therefore both asserted and negated) in Derrida's statement. Here is another (non-parodic?) theoretical account of this version of the postmodern condition:

> A dead space which will be marked by increasing and random outbursts of political violence, schizoid behaviour and the implosion of all signs of communication, as Western culture runs down toward the brilliant illumination of a final burn out (Kroker and Kroker, 1988, pxvii).

This is the condition embodied in Lessing's novel. But the narration is retrospective. The novel begins 'We remember that time' (p7): so there is a beyond, a transition to a different order. Looking back, there is uncertainty about what happened:

> Yet we do tell each other over and over again the particularities of the events we shared, and the repetition, the listening, is as if we are saying: 'It was like that for you, too? then that confirms it, yes, it was so, it must have been, I wasn't imagining things' (p7).

Looking closely at this passage, however, is to see in it an optimism not apparent in Kroker's postmodern. There is a strong sense of the uncertainty of the real, the extent to which it is mythologically or fictionally constructed, but here people are constructing a version of it through communication, listening, sharing, empathising, reassuring each other. Lessing explicitly allows this mode an authenticity not given to the 'official' version of events, the attempts to maintain political authority through the manipulation and distortion of information which is called 'news': 'of course one must have the stamp of the official. . . . But the truth was that every one of us became aware at some point that it was not from official sources we were getting the facts which were building up into a very different picture from the publicised one' (p8). *Listening*, in fact, as a suspension of the conventional expectations and modes of thought of Western political economies, becomes the vehicle through which she explores alternative, aesthetic forms of consciousness to offer an implicit critique of those which are in collapse. As the narrator finds herself able to suspend the dissecting consciousness which sets manipulative subject over inert object, she begins to listen more intently to different sounds:

> I was putting my ear to the wall, as one would to a female egg, listening, waiting . . . and then I was through the wall and I knew what was there. . . . I did not go in, but stood there on the margin between the two worlds . . . I felt the most vivid expectancy, a longing: this place held what I needed, knew was there, had been waiting for . . . all my life. I knew this place, recognised it. The

rooms were empty. To make them habitable work needed to be done (pp15–16).

Set against the disintegrating city (which, as often in Lessing's writing, is a symbol of the alienated modern consciousness) is a room: a space beyond the wall (and the ego or rational consciousness) suggesting containment, shelter, the inner psyche. The hierophanic imagery of transgression, of being on the threshold of a new world, has a long history in Christian mysticism as well as psychoanalysis. It is used here to represent the possibility of crossing from the disintegrating space of the 'Same', of discursive reason, to that of the non-discursive space of difference, in effect, that of 'desire'. Lessing's novel itself sets a 'realist' discursive space against a shadowy symbolic world which cannot easily be assimilated to the premises of realism. Journeying back through reinvoked emotionally charged scenes to her own personal and then collective history as a woman, the narrator discovers in the room not only the psychological and social origins of the repressive forms which reason has taken in her own life, but also the potential for violence which has produced the current apocalypse.

Without recognition of the exhaustion of these forms of reason, any attempt to reform the world outside through new political practices must fail. Gerald and Emily try to rebuild the material world on the basis of an enlightened collectivist politics, only to find themselves burdened with, and frustrated by, the 'old forms': the seemingly inevitable institutional drift towards hierarchy, the unconscious reconstruction of a 'pecking order', the revalidation of racial and gender stereotypes. Above all, they fail to deal with 'it': the nihilistic modern principle of joy-in-destruction personified in the Ryans. But their impulse towards the collective is shown to be structured through their continuing unconscious acceptance of a model of individuation based on notions of autonomy and reason which perpetuate the impulse to own, dominate, and control, others and the world. Attempts to rationalise the political economy are seen to be disguised manifestations of a continuing will to power. Lessing does not imply that we should abandon reason, but she does reveal that the over-generalisation of instrumental forms of it may have produced the very violence and irrationalism against which it was supposed to protect. Lessing, like other postmodernists, searches for a new mode of reason, informed by the aesthetic, involving communication, interdependence, resistance to forms of subjective domination. In an interview earlier, she had said:

> Since writing *The Golden Notebook* I've become less personal. I've floated away from the personal. I've stopped saying, 'This is mine, this is my experience . . .' Now, when I start writing, the first thing I ask is 'who is thinking the same thought?' Where are the other people who are like me? I don't believe anymore that I have a thought. There is a thought around (Raskin, 1970, p173).

If 'desire' explodes in *Memoirs of a Survivor* it is not in some *liberatory* mode of the postmodern, but as a way of expressing that condition of starvation produced when people are fed through an intellectual and utilitarian construction of the 'good society' which is premised on the necessary repression of fundamental needs. To acknowledge the existence of such needs would dangerously challenge the premises of that rational order: the enlightened political economy of the West. Lessing suggests, in a poetic version of the thesis of Adorno and Horkheimer's *Dialectic of Enlightenment* (1972), that Western democracy has been purchased at a price whose exorbitance in terms of its hidden deprivational effects is only now becoming apparent. As outer nature reveals that it cannot be manipulated forever in this way, the crisis in legitimation has produced that crack through which inner nature has begun its revolt.

Emily (the child who appears mysteriously after the narrator has passed through the wall for the first time), with her violent need and hunger, is also the narrator as child and a reminder of the child in all of us. Desire, indeed, 'explodes' in Emily, expressed poetically through images of orality, incorporation, mergence: ingesting, licking, sucking, 'mingling constantly with others, as if some giant rite of place, everyone tasting and licking and regurgitating everyone else' (p78). Emily feeds and feeds, becomes all mouth, 'even the intake of words through her eyes was another form of eating, and her daydreaming a consumption of material which was bloating her as much as her food' (p50). In a reiteration of the imagery of *Alice in Wonderland*, Lessing's narrator revisits the past with the eyes of Emily the child, seeing from her small perspective the large and threatening Victorian world of correct behaviour and emotional repression with its atmosphere of fear and sterility. The famine outside is a product of the famine within and vice versa. Emily experiences only that rage for order symbolised in the obsessive 'hygiene' of her mother. As her arms reach out to meet an absence of comfort, they become, in their turn, 'those great arms that had never been taught tenderness' (p134): the iron grip of modern political economy.

The novel asserts our fundamental need for love, shelter, nurturance, our formation out of an interdependence with other human beings based on such needs. Its apocalypticism reveals how, in rationalising the life-world without due care for the range and complexity of these needs, we may have starved the human race altogether. The most frightening aspect of the projected world of *Memoirs* is that the wild semi-humans born out of upheaval, brutality, the failures of over-rationalised logic, cannot even recognise each other's needs and have, in an awful parody of humanism, fed each other by turning cannibal and are literally consuming each other. Lessing suggests that we may even begin to perceive the violence produced through our misguided rationalism if we start to observe the behaviour of animals, of the instinctual, of those who live without rational theories or ideal categories or utopian blueprints:

> We have been living with them as blundering, blind, callous, cruel murderers and torturers, and they have watched and known us. And this is the reason we refuse to acknowledge the intelligence of the creatures that surround us: the shock to our amour propre would be too much, the judgement we would have to make on ourselves too horrible: it is exactly the same process that can make someone go on and on committing a crime, or a cruelty, knowing it: the stopping and having to see what has been done would be too painful, one cannot face it (p75).

Lessing chastises us into the only mode which she sees capable of saving us: that of humility, and in so doing produces a devastating assault on the complacencies of Western rationalism. In a rather more paradoxical fashion, so had Joseph Conrad's *Heart of Darkness* (1899) some seventy years before in its exploration of the connection between the violences of Imperialism and the instrumentality of the enlightened rationalist discourses of modern liberalism which are used to justify it. I now wish to turn to that novel, for though it is often regarded as a key text for Modernism, we will see again that it engages with precisely those issues which have come to dominate postmodern theoretical debates. A careful examination should suggest the naivete of taking any simple radical break view of Postmodernism: as a critique of Western thought, an aesthetic practice or a cultural epoch. With this in mind, it is time to begin to re-examine modernist writing in the light of the issues raised by the postmodern debate.

Part Two

POSTMODERNISM
READING MODERNISM

Challenging Autonomy

6

MODERNISM
AND ENLIGHTENMENT

Reading
Joseph Conrad's Heart of Darkness

Heart of Darkness is a text much concerned with consciousness. Indeed, in the famous preface to *The Nigger and the 'Narcissus'* (1897), Conrad informs us that self-reflexive introspection is the basis of aesthetic knowing. The artist, 'descends within himself, and in that lonely region of stress and strife, if he be deserving and fortunate, he finds the terms of his appeal'. In the same preface and apparently contradictorily, Conrad asserts that the task of the artist is above all 'to make you see'. Here, in effect, we have a Kantian conception of knowledge: what is outside can only be understood by looking inside. In order to arrive at the meaning of Kurtz, that emissary of light, Marlow must arrive at the meaning of himself. But by the time Marlow embarks upon his retrospective journey, the Enlightenment mind of Europe has succumbed to its own repressed violences. Marlow sets out to try to save it: and himself. He seeks a new model of knowledge which can transcend the potentially violent solipsism of individual consciousness. Indeed, he attempts to recommend forms of knowing where consciousness is suspended: absorption in work, practical immersion in routine, community of effort. Marlow is a narrator, however, who continuously subverts his own recommendations, is at the mercy of an introspective and brooding consciousness which can arrive at no final knowledge at all: a parody of Kantian reason. He struggles with that dialectic, of fictionality as subjective projection and situatedness as immersion in the world, which is Kant's legacy to late modernity. To be conscious is, as the narrator of *The Nigger* suggests, to be over-civilised, even to be rotten. After Enlightenment what forgiveness? Conrad's preoccupations with the limits of rational consciousness are still our own: if the postmodernists are to be believed.

Marlow's difficulty, of course, is that even as he longs to throw off the burdens of consciousness in his critique of its limitations, he is inevitably complicit with its forms. He too, apparently, shares the postmodern condition. Marlow has seen the dark side of Enlightenment but, to map its geography cognitively, he must use its very rhetorical modes. The object of his critique is a corrupt 'enlightened' idealism which actually facilitates Imperialist expansion, but his critique is conducted in the very terms of what it sets out to condemn. He ends, therefore, by participating in the violence of its conceptual imposition. Marlow is no deconstructionist, but Conrad lays before us the very contradictions upon which Postmodernism has come to brood so obsessively. However, Marlow cannot abandon his rhetorical mode, the language of consciousness. To do so might be to open himself to that excess of darkness which is the black hole of nihilism. But equally, in continuing to inhabit its structures, he implicitly condones the very imperialistic behaviour which his narrative has attempted to expose as monstrous.

Postmodernists have been much concerned, as we have seen, with endings. The possibility of order, the perception of causality and thus rational determination, is dependent in narrative on that coherence and significance conferred by retrospection. Even if we give up the Grand Narratives, we need the little ones. If Reason fails us, then the contingency and chaos of experience may be redeemed, perhaps, by the act of aesthetic shaping itself. It is at least consolation. It may be all the order we have. Marlow is looking for a bigger narrative than this though. He chooses to interpret Kurtz's acknowledgement of the horror not in the aesthetic terms of fictionality, but in the categorical terms of Kantian ethics. It is an heroic act. Kurtz is a hero because he is capable of registering a moral response to his capitulation to the powers of darkness: he sees the horror that he has become. He arrives at knowledge of his condition. Such self-knowledge must negate the ascendancy over him of the dark powers. But ironically, of course, one can see in Marlow's eloquence a mirror of Kurtz's own. That consciousness, earlier condemned as corruptive, is now the consciousness which redeems. It is Marlow's too, whether he likes it or not, brooding over the great abyss which it has created. Marlow refuses to acknowledge what Conrad's text makes unavoidably present: that it may simply be his own aesthetic consciousness, his own retrospective narration, which redeems. Rather than the experiential act itself, it may be Marlow's conceptualisation of it which confers moral redemption. And in using the vocabulary of Enlightenment morality, he invokes a heroism whose foundation he has already condemned.

It could be argued that *Heart of Darkness* is modernist rather than postmodernist because the issue is not resolved. We are left hesitating between the possibility that redemption has come experientially, or that it is simply a narrative and textual construction. Here, the argument might be that no such hesitation is possible in the mode of the postmodern. In postmodern texts, the sense of an ending is explicitly posited as something which has to be continuously revised through the endless deferral of repeated narrative reconstruction. Experience becomes text. History is narrative. The End is the insight that there can be no ending, no beginning, no ground, because everything is being endlessly rewritten. No way out of text. In my view, Postmodernism simply makes explicit the fear haunting a text like *Heart of Darkness*. However, if postmodernists seem driven to undermine every foundation, modernists are still keen on conservation. They reformulate the terms of modernity: autonomy, structure, consciousness, ethical universals, rather than abandon them. Conrad, as much as Adorno and Horkheimer later, is conscious of the paradoxes of the 'dialectic of Enlightenment': the knowledge that the capitalist economic relations on which modernity rests both facilitate the development of autonomous identity and personal freedom, and make possible the rise of a philosophical tradition which could ratify this. However, this process also facilitates the colonisation of the social world by an *instrumentalism*, as apparent in the philosophy of consciousness as in the entrepreneurial spirit, which also bureaucratises and fragments world and self. On the one hand, it creates the ground which fertilises the romantic nihilism of Kurtz as one mode of the Imperial will. On the other, it facilitates the meticulous obsessionalism of the accountant, whose methodological attention to detail obscures the ends for which this service is given. One mode exposes the irrational will to power behind the apparently rational will to truth. The other reveals the irrationalism of a rationality whose end is simply its own efficient functioning. As a man of the sea, Marlow is both adventurer and committed to service, romantic explorer and bureaucrat, and thus uniquely positioned in a relationship of complicity and critique with both poles of the dialectic.

We have seen how Enlightenment is founded and flounders upon the concept of self-knowledge. In the current condition of late modernity, the institutional discourse which has made us most aware of these paradoxes, and whose popular appeal is itself a symptom of our 'postmodern condition', is psychoanalysis. It seduces us with the offer of self-knowledge, as it reveals the fraudulence of any such promise. *Heart of Darkness* is interesting in this respect. The confessional narration to the sea-faring audience of 'specialists' gathered in the twilight gloom, with its echoes of modern and archaic worlds and its insistent but protean symbolism, is Marlow's own attempt to find a *talking cure*. The outer narrator tells us that Marlow is a seaman, but a wanderer too, whose mind is not of the 'stay-at-home' order of the average seaman. And Marlow's tale, a confessional narrative which struggles to resolve and name his experience in a way which will make past and present cohere, is not an ordinary seaman's yarn but an attempt to contain an experience which has torn apart the foundations of his sense of identity. And Marlow, indeed, achieves integration. He manages to assimilate Kurtz's actions to his preconceived moral and epistemological categories, manages therefore to assimilate those hitherto unrecognised parts of himself which he discovered in the projective identification with Kurtz. The talking cure restores him to himself. Modern psychotherapy could not have done better. But Conrad is not so complacent. The novel as a whole leaves unresolved a series of cruxes which serve not only to expose the fragile contradictions of Marlow's framework of Enlightenment belief, but actually reveal the complicity of the latter with the violences of Imperialism itself. The postmodern awareness of the problem of linguistic complicity helps to alert us to the way in which Marlow is forced to use the same enlightened vocabulary of idealism to justify Kurtz's actions as he uses to come to terms with his own. It is a vocabulary which he repeatedly condemns as the ideological smokescreen of Imperialism itself.

> The yarns of seamen have a direct simplicity, the whole meaning of which lies within the shell of a cracked nut. But Marlow was not typical (if his propensity to spin yarns be excepted), and to him the meaning of an episode was not inside like the kernel but outside, enveloping the tale which brought it out only as a glow brings out a haze, in the likeness of one of those misty halos that sometimes are made visible by the spectral illumination of moonshine (p8).

The statement could serve as a description of classical Freudian analysis viewed in terms of Freud's own concept of 'Nachtraglichkeit' or deferred action. In the *Interpretation of Dreams* (1900), Freud explained this as that process of secondary revision where the dream is actually produced through the dreamer's retroactive narration of it. It implies that the primal location of any event is always ambiguous: produced as much after the fact of, as during, its occurrence. Only through its later narration can it be recognised for what it is. Marlow embarks upon his 'talking cure' in an attempt to recover the experiential grounds of his journey to Kurtz (his own equally eloquent double). But he is brought up against the possibility that there can be no such personality to recover but only one to fashion, ever anew, through whatever tools are available. Paterian impressionism is one mode of subjective dissolution to which Marlow is heir, but whose legacy he wishes to resist. He has no desire to see his complicity in the culture of Imperialism. In *Plato and Platonism* (1893), Pater had argued that even 'our common ideas are not the consequence, not the products, but the cause of our reason in us: we did not make them, but they make us what we are, as reasonable beings' (1910, p168). When the Intended says to Marlow that she knew Kurtz better than anyone, he has to agree that 'perhaps she did' (p107). If personality is ever a process of reconstruction through available interpretative modes, the Intended has constructed a Kurtz through the mode of Romantic idealism. And Marlow, in effect, belatedly comes to condone the construction as truth. The novel mounts a thoroughgoing critique of idealism in its Romantic heroic modes when founded not upon self-knowledge but upon a self-deluded complicity with corruption. But Marlow finally draws back from his own critique. It would be too dark altogether, because it would signal the death of his belief in Enlightenment. It would be a darkness visible which, in a secular world, could leave him only with that nihilism he cannot endure. He lies to himself as much as to the Intended. For, as her name implies, and as everything about Kurtz has suggested, one arrives not at truth, but only ever at rhetoric. Nothing in the novel is ever finished.

In a letter to R. B. Cunninghame Graham written in 1898, Conrad wrote:

> Faith is a myth and beliefs shift like mists on the shore: thoughts vanish; words, once pronounced, die: and the memory of yesterday is as shadowy as the hope of tomorrow – only the string of my platitudes seems to have no end. As our peasants say: 'Pray, brother, forgive me for the love of God'. And we don't know what forgiveness is, nor what is love, nor where God is. Assez (Conrad, 1969, p65).

The letter expresses doubt about the capacity of language to reflect truth and the difficulty of maintaining faith in what may turn out to be merely empty concepts. In *Heart of Darkness*, Conrad explores the possibility that human knowledge of self and world may indeed turn out to be empty concepts reflecting only their own rhetorical insubstantiality. His narrator, though, draws back from such darkness in an attempt to affirm the classic epistemological framework of Englightenment morality. He fails. But if he is shown as less than the Buddha in wisdom, he avoids seeing Kurtz as a condemned Faust. At the end, as Marlow feels the dusk rising and whispering with the wind a repetition of Kurtz's last words, momentarily, he glimpses again the heart of darkness. But to acknowledge now its continuing presence within or without would be 'too dark altogether' and to preserve the sepulchral whiteness of the Intended's idealism he tells the necessary lie. The lie to the Intended exposes the possibility that his earlier moral formulation of Kurtz was a lie to himself. His own idealism may be as corrupt as Kurtz's own, or simply as misguided as the young Russian's. Only if Kurtz's words were a moral affirmation can there be substance behind the rhetoric. Voice must function as a synechdoche preserving the sublimity of wholeness beyond the corruptions of the body. Marlow cannot sacrifice idealism to rhetoric. Words must signify something beyond themselves.

In fact, throughout, the status of what is heard is as unclear as what is seen. Conrad's text produces an effect of extreme epistemological uncertainty. The conceptual categories of interpretation are cast into doubt in Marlow's account of his voyage; the evidence of his senses cannot be trusted. The landscape through which he journeys is made surreal and fantastic. However, even as Marlow tells us he cannot find an adequate vocabulary with which to narrate his story, he uses language which reproduces a familiar occidental ideology of the oriental as a strange, exotic, sexual, primal and bodily repudiation of the conceptual categories of the West. Nineteenth-century traveller's tales were full of an Africa dangerously and excitingly beyond law or restraint. Here, such images are used by Marlow both to narrate his own experience and to condemn the behaviour of Kurtz. Marlow condemns the construction of a modern Prospero's island where Kurtz wields his technological Western magic to subdue the Calibans around him into worship and acts of deification. But his account of his own experience is formulated through the same vocabulary of the exotic and the primitive.

On one level, of course, Conrad simply uses this continuous narrative and interpretative uncertainty as a technique of retardation for stimulating suspense. But physical descriptions are the vehicles of moral response. Marlow cannot escape consciousness. The landscape is a dark inversion of the Garden of Eden. The river snakes its way forward to that voice apparently beyond good and evil in a primal landscape of dream where moral categories appear to turn on themselves and dissolve before his listeners' eyes. The echoes of the synechdochic voice produce a powerful effect of suspense and the reader too awaits its completion, its reassimilation into a body as the moment when indeterminacies of significance will be resolved. As Marlow himself has done, the reader waits for the visionary revelation from the heart of darkness, desiring not just eloquence and rhetoric but the plenitude of the word made flesh. Conrad's text is caught up, to use Nietzsche's terms, in a modernity not modern enough. Its exploration of the ethics of modernity collapses into the religious structures of a psychodrama involving the struggle of good and evil, the possibility of damnation, the search for redemption (Marlow's narrative act itself). Repeatedly, the discovery is that consciousness is not knowledge; reason fails; words echo only themselves, while the jungle remains mute and dumb. Imperialism was always at the heart of Enlightenment and is its end.

Repeatedly the reader inhabits the perspective of the experiential Marlow who cannot process or adequately reflect upon sensation because his conceptual categories are unable to deal with the situations in which he finds himself. Symbolic and metaphoric associations, particularly of light and dark, and white and black, shift and invert themselves throughout. The city of Brussels, a clean centre of European civilisation, is a whited sepulchre. Classical and Dantesque allusions to hell litter its description, just as they will later convey the conditions of the natives in the Grove of Death. The imagery alone implies how the latter is the product of the former. Similar images of sepulchral whiteness and impenetrable gloom recur during Marlow's visit to the Intended, inexplicably tracing a network of connections linking trade to idealism, capital to Enlightenment. Kurtz's sketch of a shadowy, blindfolded woman, standing with a torch against a black background, is a nested iconic representation associating the traditional Western figure of truth and justice with the rapacity of blind and opportunistic (woman as Roman Fortuna figure?) imperial invasion. Again though, at the very moment of critique, Enlightenment is also reproduced. Throughout the novel, Conrad freezes women into iconic moments where they cease to be individuals. They are reproduced in statuesque form as Woman: bearer of a naive and dangerous, seductive and deadly, idealism. It is viewed as an irrational idealism of desire against which the superior masculine reason can identify itself. It must therefore be protected. So Marlow, too, reproduces this impulse at the end. He must be a gentleman: he must therefore protect the Intended's dreams. He ends in effect by condoning Kurtz's Nietzschean parody of the aristocratic Imperial will (My ivory . . . my woman . . . my Intended), choosing to ignore the racist and sexist assumptions upon which its heroism rests.

Marlow continuously doubts the reliability of his instruments of knowing: senses, moral categories, scientific concepts, language. Throughout the novel, he struggles with an invading sense that the wilderness which confronts him is no longer the safe red part of the map where useful work is being carried on. It is a place so radically alien that his normal linguistic categories seem to dissolve as they are projected onto it in an attempt to discover significance. Marlow is caught between two responses. One is an impulse towards identification: the possibility that in surrendering up his language and culture (in effect, consciousness itself) to it, he might discover some archaic form of mind or nature which would provide an alternative universal foundation. A Darwinian missing link. But equally, there is an impulse towards the absolute retention of his own cultural categories as the only means of protection against the fate of Kurtz. For Marlow informs his listeners that it is Kurtz's soul, not his intellect, that has gone mad. He has not simply surrendered consciousness, but has kicked himself free of earth altogether. The paradox, of course, is that Kurtz's fall is a consequence of too much consciousness, a subjective idealism finally manifesting itself as a naked will to power. And for Marlow, the only solution is that Enlightenment must protect us from a horror which is its own monstrous progeny. Kurtz, indeed, enacts the contradictions of modernity as a Faust at the mirror of Narcissus.

Both the 'unspeakable rites' (cannibalism?) and the sexual relation with the native woman represent for Marlow ways in which Kurtz has literally taken in the wilderness. Enlightenment eloquence collapses into the scream of: 'Exterminate the brutes'. Marlow *is* tempted into the abandonment of his rational commonsensical modes of comprehension: attracted by the huge, still, dumbness of the jungle and its promise of primal immediacy. Attracted, that is, until he witnesses the damnation of a European who seems precisely to have embraced this temptation. Accordingly, he chooses identification with that 'restraint' encoded in the bureaucratic rules of the Imperial authorities of the time: do not be seduced by the alien; above all preserve your superior and civilised ethnocentric perspective. Once Kurtz materialises as a body, in all its horror, Marlow can only save himself and salvage the former's reputation by repudiating his earlier doubt and reaffirming his belief in Enlightenment. Having doubted consciousness, he now asserts that Imperialism, in its Roman form, may be 'robbery with violence', but this is because there is no *idea* to redeem it, only men going at it blind: no vision and no eloquence. The Enlightenment world to which Marlow returns at the end, however, is an irrevocably fallen one. Idealism is inextricably wedded to corruption, or to a dangerous Romantic heroism inimical to real self-knowledge or altruistic behaviour. So, Marlow's own narrative becomes the 'idea' whose function is to redeem but out of a complicity with the corruption it seeks to condemn.

For the 'idea' is unavoidably the ideology which sustains Imperialism. Efficiency and attention to work is itself behaviour necessary to the functioning of capitalism. Marlow has exposed the 'glamorous' Romanticism of the Russian with his need to live dangerously and for the moment: such Nietzschean excess is precisely what capitalism cannot survive. Marlow has looked on the wilderness and its silence and felt himself to be deaf and even blind in his inability to understand. But the wilderness is always represented as a construction of his own consciousness. Imperialism does not allow the slave to speak, nor does patriarchy give a voice to women. (Women occupy a realm which is too beautiful for words, Marlow informs his listeners.) Native and female remain inert and outside the boundaries of reason as constructed through the language of the so-called liberal political economy. The dumb exoticism of the wilderness is not dangerous so long as, in its dumbness and exoticism, it remains outside. The real danger is for it to become indistinguishable from one's own experience of self: for the safety of the Cartesian boundary to dissolve. Marlow's narrative confirms the old boundaries. As a 'talking cure' it works. But it also reveals that the 'talking cure' must always fail if health is truly dependent upon self-knowledge. Health is always self-delusion.

On one level, then, *Heart of Darkness* is a secularised parable of that Fall which is the inevitable outcome of an overweening impulse to know. There seems no possibility of authentic knowledge. Indeed, almost everything in the novel is tainted. Postmodernism will go on, of course, to a full acknowledgement of the inevitability of implication in and complicity with a debased commercial culture. It will deal with this recognition through modes of parody. *Heart of Darkness* contains similar moments. Kurtz is a parody of the aristocratic individualist entrepreneur displaced by the corporate imperialism of the modern state. He is also a modern Faust. Marlow's tale parodies the expectations we have of the seaman's yarn; the corporate language of the company is a travesty of a religious vocabulary. But Conrad's tale cannot fully embrace the catharsis of parody. It is not self-conscious enough. The novel passes an Enlightenment-style judgement on Enlightenment without full self-reflexive awareness of the contradiction involved. It does know, however, that we cannot know. There is no pure, autonomous, Kantian self-determination of self-knowledge – no total emancipation from the irrational forces within and without. In a world where knowledge and reason are harnessed to trade, idealism becomes either corrupt or Romantically dangerous. However, as an aesthetic text, *Heart of Darkness* actually embodies and *enacts* that problematic relationship of knowledge to experience which postmodern theory can only conceptualise. Its very existence makes a claim for the recognition of other ways of knowing. A recognition which will be made entirely explicit in Postmodernism. Let us examine how Conrad's text achieves this.

Marlow's account of his first and subsequent sighting of Kurtz's residence is an excellent example of Conrad's skill in creating a sense of fundamental epistemological doubt. The reader, too, must question the relations of perception to reflection, time to space, normally assumed as a ground of knowledge. Throughout the novel, Conrad manipulates the implicit distance in first person narrative between the 'I' whose perspective on events is constructed retrospectively from the position of narration, and the 'I' who is the character experiencing those events in the imaginary continuous present of the story. The advantage of first person narrative in manipulation of distance for effects of suspense and curiosity, is that it is very easy to slide invisibly from one perspective to the other. Thus at several points during the narrative, Marlow suspends the perspective of retrospection and inhabits the sensational and reflective uncertainty of the experiential self. The effect is to heighten suspense, but also to situate the reader in a perspective which must raise awareness of the inadequacies of our tools of knowledge: the unreliability of the senses; the limitation of our conceptual categories.

This is Marlow's first description to his listeners of the station which houses Kurtz:

> Through my glasses I saw the slope of a hill interspersed with rare trees and perfectly free from undergrowth. A long decaying building on the summit was half buried in the high grass; the large holes in the peaked roof gaped black from afar; the jungle and the woods made a background. There was no

enclosure or fence of any kind; but there had been one apparently, for near the house half-a-dozen slim posts remained in a row, roughly trimmed, and with their upper ends ornamented with round carved balls (pp74–5).

There is no perturbation here. The reader is drawn into the perspective of the experiential Marlow, struggling to orient himself spatially and visually, distinguishing foreground from background, past from present (apparently there had been a fence). Because of the adroit manipulation of perspective within the shared narrative voice, we do not notice the absence of a retrospective view from the *narrating* Marlow. A few pages further on, the station is sighted again and we are made aware of the shift in spatial awareness in the continuous present of story rather than discourse:

> There were no signs of life, but there was the ruined roof, the long mud wall peeping above the grass, with three little square window holes, no two the same size: all this brought within reach of my hand as it were. And then I made a brusque movement, and one of the remaining posts of that vanished fence leapt up in the field of my glass. You remember I told you I had been struck at the distance by certain attempts at ornamentation, rather remarkable in the ruinous aspect of the place. Now I had suddenly a nearer view, and its first result was to make me throw my head back as if before a blow. Then I went carefully from post to post with my glass, and I saw my mistake. These round knobs were not ornamental but symbolic; they were expressive and puzzling, striking and disturbing – food for thought and also for the vultures if there had been any looking down from the sky; but at all events for such ants as were industrious enough to ascend the pole. They would have been more impressive, those heads on the stakes, if their faces had not been turned to the house (p82).

The narrating Marlow, of course, has known all along the identity of the round balls, but has chosen to inhabit the perspective of the experiential character. Reader and listener share his slow approach, with some trepidation and much anticipation, to Kurtz's station, awaiting the first signs of the embodiment of that Voice heard through Marlow's narrative. But authority and control of information are the narrator's privilege. Marlow's eloquence is a match for Kurtz's. He chooses to order his discourse so that we can share the original experience of surprise as the posts leap up in our vision too. Expectation increases with the references to ants and vultures. The final confirmation, cleverly grammatically displaced, is thrown out in nonchalant fashion. These are indeed 'heads on the stakes'. Conrad uses the effects of delay here for a number of reasons. Most obviously, as we have seen earlier, it increases suspense. When the uncertainties clear at a level of sensory impression, however, they are only just beginning at the level of narrative hermeneutic significance. What is Kurtz's relation to the heads? What has Kurtz become? How does this relate to Kurtz as the 'mind of Europe'? If Marlow uses the shift simply as the device of a good storyteller aware of the importance of suspense, Conrad uses it to carry the burden of the novel's investigation of knowledge. Because the reader experiences Marlow's original *sensory* confusion, his current *interpretative* problems appear to be simply one more layer of epistemological uncertainty. The technological equipment of the Imperialist (field glasses) as the symbol of scientific knowledge, as in E. M. Forster's later examination of relations of East and West in *A Passage to India* (1924), may appear to clear up doubt about what is being seen. But not before we have realised the extent to which even the simple physical act of looking is fraught with uncertainty. To look is not necessarily to see. That the interpretative issue of En-light-enment should then remain an irresolvable textual problem is perhaps not so very surprising. If postmodernist theory tells us that we cannot know and why, and reminds us of the dangers of ignoring our limitations, a text like *Heart of Darkness* allows us to participate *experientially* in both the recognition of this and of the fact that at some level we still need to continue to believe that we can know.

7

RECONSTRUCTING MODERNISM

Life as Art

I

Aesthetic Autonomy

From Kant to New Criticism

Postmodernism and postmodernity tend to be understood as continuations of or breaks with whatever is constructed as the dominant of Modernism or modernity. The most consistent 'dominant', appearing throughout the vocabularies of both critics of and proselytisers for Postmodernism, is the concept of autonomy. Postmodernism, for both groups, represents a break with or modification of autonomy theories of art. Critics, however, tend to see this as a consequence of its debased mode of commodification, whereas defenders view it as a democratising liberation of the aesthetic. Neither evaluation fully acknowledges the various and complex meanings of the term autonomy: its literary and philosophical modern roots in Romantic thought and its recent literary history. In my view, this is because the term tends to be restricted to a *formalist* definition, largely established by the New Criticism, and disseminated after the important modernist texts had been published. This definition tends to ignore the wider Post-Kantian implications which I discussed earlier: expressive freedom, subjectivism and self-determination. In the later restrictive terms, Postmodernism is seen to refuse autonomy viewed simply as linguistic autotelism or as aesthetic withdrawal from a debased mass culture. To its defenders, it therefore refuses aesthetic disengagement from the world. It recognises the pervasiveness of the aesthetic in *life* and thus represents a new form of avant-garde praxis, returning art to life. For its critics, however, it is part of a pervasive 'textualism' which, in aestheticising all, destroys the very rationale for art as a special sort of practice. The aesthetic thus loses its distinctiveness.

We have already looked at these debates. The next task will be to extend the discussion begun with the consideration of *Heart of Darkness*. The rest of the book will examine the construction of Modernism in the terms of autonomy, considering the way in which intentionalist statements by modernist writers have been interpreted by New Critics and later formalisms, and challenging this construction through textual interpretations which draw on postmodern insights.

A recent commentator on Postmodernism, Alex Callinicos (1989), has argued that no-one ever really believed the autonomy theory of Modernism, not even modernists themselves. Thus Postmodernism's repudiation of the possibility of internal self-grounding, impersonality, and pure aesthetic language, is simply a repudiation of a construction it has invented itself in order to claim a distinctive identity. There may be some truth in this, but it over-generalises. Certainly within a specifically *aesthetic* context (curiously so often ignored by political commentators), autonomy theory has been extremely powerful. Generations of students grew up learning their Modernism in these terms (including the present writer). And, as we have seen, the term has a much longer history in that philosophical thought which undoubtedly shaped its aesthetic use. If we look at intentional statements of modern writers, it is obvious that the term often appears still attached to a Kantian notion of self-determination which grounds a basically expressive view of art. Even when the term seems to be unquestionably used to designate pure *formal* autonomy, in Eliot's concept of an 'objective correlative' or Pound's theory of the ideogram, there is often a buried expressive aesthetics hidden somewhere. It is as apparent in the early and extreme aggressive individualism of the *Blast* manifesto ('There is one truth, ourselves, and everything is permitted') as in Pound's famous definition of the image as 'that which presents an intellectual and emotional complex in an instant of time' (which he later qualified with the explicit comment that his notion of 'complex' had been derived from the new psychology).[14] Critics such as Hugh Kenner have refused to acknowledge the expressive element in such statements, but it is clear that Pound, like Eliot, continued to see the image as ultimately expressive of the complexity of consciousness or 'feeling' or 'creative emotion'. Later formalist interpretations suppress the latent ambiguity in these famous modernist declarations: the tension between a concept of autonomy attached to linguistic form and the same concept tied to a Kantian sense of self-determination through self-expression. Approached through that dialectic of radical fictionality and situatedness which I have identified as coming to the foreground in Postmodernism, however, one could interpret this modernist ambiguity, the hovering between subject and object, contingency and abstraction, personality and impersonality, in terms which are not only less contradictory but which allow one to think about autonomy in a more flexible way. The Nietzschean notion of radical fictionality and the Heideggerian sense of Being-in-the-world challenge both the concept

---

[14]   See *Blast* 1, June 1914, p148 and the essay 'A Retrospect' in *Literary Essays*, ed. T. S. Eliot, New York, 1968.

of subject as consciously willed ego and that of object as a discrete factual entity whose identity transcends context. Both foreground the aesthetic as an aspect of the existential. I do not believe that modernist writers viewed their activities in terms of an autonomy which divorced their writing from existential contexts. I believe that a reformulation of these issues in the above terms may suggest alternative ways of seeing which respond to contexts of thought ignored in the later formalist construction of modernist aesthetics. First though, we need to examine the historically dominant interpretations. In my view, the formalism of the New Criticism, which has had such a powerful influence on literary studies since 1945, repressed this expressive potential in order to construct a Modernism entirely in the terms of formal self-sufficiency, impersonality, the autotelic art-object. In the first chapter, I drew attention to the ambiguities in Kantian thought and the way in which they intensify as the Idealist framework comes under pressure. The New Critics resolved such ambiguities in the direction of formalist coherence. In doing so, they attempted to transfer to a purely linguistic *aesthetic* context a concept of self-determination which had lost its *existential* security.

In 1977, David Lodge wrote:

> Formalism is the logical aesthetic for modernist art, though not all modernist writers accepted or acknowledged this. From the position that art offers a privileged insight into reality there is a natural progression to the view that art creates its own reality and from there to the position that art is not concerned with reality at all but is an autonomous activity, a superior kind of game (1977, p48).

In this book, Lodge himself writes from the late formalist perspective of a structuralist reading developed from the work of the linguist Roman Jakobson on aphasia. Lodge himself, therefore, clearly works within a critical paradigm which Michel Foucault has seen as characteristically modern. What Lodge recognises is that if autonomy as formal coherence cannot be shown to correspond to an order outside of itself, it may simply be experienced as a self-contained linguistic game. In some ways, Structuralism itself can be seen as a last-ditch formalist attempt to reconcile autonomy with the possibility of correspondence through a depth/surface model which avoids mediation through a personal expressive theory of art. Central to structuralist thought was the idea that meaning exists as a relation of surface to depth where the historical contingency of appearance is always in fact regulated by an essentially unchanging deep structure. Lodge himself effectively analyses modern writing in such terms. Post-modernism is often described as a shift in thought or aesthetics which, in proceeding by dismantling the presuppositions about the relationship of depth to surface characteristic of the modern period, anticipates a new cultural epoch. Postmodernism has rejected the illusion of deep structure and even given up nostalgic longing for it. Or so the popular argument tends to run. Obviously, if this view is accepted, it is easy to see how Postmodernism can be dismissed as a joke or trivial game with words. It is in the interests of its critics to see it, through such reductive reasoning, as a travesty of true autonomy. In fact, like the New Critical use of the term, such arguments manipulate the associations of the concept of autonomy for their own ends. Marxist critics themselves often use the term in ways which ignore its full Kantian implications. Robert Weimann noted in 1976 how often formalist presuppositions are unconsciously reinscribed in new theoretical vocabularies: 'the tradition of formalism was, and is, so deeply ingrained that there are no mature foundations for an alternative paradigm in criticism' (1976, p2). He goes on to argue:

> In mid-twentieth century England and America criticism has all too often provided criteria of reinterpretation that remained influential, not simply because they were predominantly formalist, but because in their formalism they had developed a whole close context of categories and criteria by which their various assumptions and procedures were reciprocally interlocked and hence fortified ... most of these counterproposals were not based on a break with the underlying ideology and cultural assumptions of formalism ... But it was difficult to perceive even the need for such a change. For was not the New Criticism itself preoccupied with a more 'autonomous', and hence more objective, conception of literature as art? And did it not, in contrast with the impressionism and subjectivism of the late romantics, plead for an impersonal, more rational definition of poetry? ... Once the intrinsic conceptions of verbal and semantic autonomy were established, language could be separated from consciousness. Now 'meaning' could be correlated with words, not with an aesthetic mode of Weltanschauung. Most important, 'structure' was divorced from both 'genesis' and 'effect', in other words, from the historical world of both the author and the reader. Since the structure of literature was so rigorously dissociated from its social functions, the whole question of function was reduced to the purity of an intrinsic problem and ceased to be considered as a 'genetic' or an 'affective' one. In sum, each of the terms and concepts became part of a self-contained world of poetics that shut out the world of history and thus became impervious to any objections short of a total critique and systematic refutation of the formalist aesthetic (Weimann, 1976, pp2–4).

Postmodernism is often viewed negatively as an extension of modernist autonomy understood in these terms. We have already examined 'fictionality' and 'situatedness' as alternative ways of understanding the aesthetic in terms which are not self-enclosed but which have far-reaching existential implications. Postmodernism has brought to full consciousness some of these implications. I have argued that they were also the concerns of modernists. In order to understand why this remained obscured for so long, we must look at the way in which the formalist 'autonomy' reading of Modernism so powerfully framed the critical vision of modernist texts. We have used Romantic/modernist concepts to understand Postmodernism, now we must use postmodern insights in order to imagine alternative ways of reading Modernism. The idea of art as an elaborate game is one consequence of approaching it through the frame of theories of formal autonomy. But the attack must necessarily shift its focus if 'game' is understood as *play* in that radical sense which arises with Schiller but is developed in Nietzschean critiques of regimes of truth as aesthetic formations, modes of fictionality.

What is the essence of this view of Modernism? Basically that its experimental forms are developed in harness to an aesthetic commitment to the disruption of mimetic or expressive representational modes in order to assert an absolute sense of the primarily autonomous, self-contained nature of the realm of art. It must be autonomous, however, in order more profoundly (depth again) to reveal the real. Art is about the world through being about the creation of a self-referential, internally coherent aesthetic world which is 'purely' itself. The earliest most explicitly elaborated statement of this was Joseph Frank's 1945 essay, 'Spatial Form in Modern Literature' where he explained the linguistic mode of modernist literature in these terms:

> Since the primary reference of any word group is to something inside the poem itself, language in modern poetry is really reflexive . . . instead of the instinctive and immediate reference of words and word groups to the objects and events they symbolize, and the construction of meaning from the sequence of these references, modern poetry asks its readers to suspend the process of individual reference temporarily until the entire pattern of internal references can be apprehended as a unity (Frank, 1958, p73).

Frank referred to this mode as 'spatial form'. He argued that in a poem like *The Waste Land*, in order to construct a satisfactory interpretation, the reader must follow the complex web of cross-references and linguistic equivalences and repetitions which function independently of, or in addition to, the codes of causality and sequence. 'Meaning' is seen to be constructed primarily through internal linguistic relationships and the poem thus achieves a verbal autonomy, a 'spatial form'. What is so interesting about Frank's essay is the way in which it both uses New Critical notions of the poem as verbal icon and anticipates the structuralist notion of literary texts as structural systems. In so doing, he illustrates precisely what Lodge seems to have in mind when he talks of formalism as the logical aesthetic of Modernism. Modernists themselves, of course, did discuss their writing in similar terms. A famous precursor was Flaubert's expression of the desire to write a 'book about nothing, a book without external attachment which would hold together by itself through the internal force of its style' (Huyssen, 1986, p54). There are numerous weaker versions of this where any relation to the non-aesthetic world is still seen to be negotiated through modes of formal decreation or *distantiation*: Cubist dissolution of the external shape of objects through multiple perspectives and their reformulation through an internally associative form; erosion of the solidity of the specific through forms of displacement such as symbol and metaphor; contestation of causal and deterministic models embodied in conventional plot forms by associative modes based on mythic analogy, leitmotif, attempts to render primary process logic through symbolic association; collapse of narratorial reliability and authority into competing perspectives or a use of free indirect discourse which inextricably conflates the voices of characters and narrators allowing neither a distinctive identity.

In offering broad cultural explanations for such technical shifts, critics tend to perceive them in ethical terms as signifying that breakdown of modes of cultural legitimation which enters a crisis phase in Postmodernism but basically reflects a growing loss of confidence in nineteenth-century 'grand narratives' derived from Kantian thought: the idea that there can be an intrinsic and organic moral relationship between the form and interconnections of the structure and language of the artwork and the actual relations of the world outside the fiction. We have already examined some of these ideas about modernity. Whereas nineteenth-century realism, for example, blended public and private experience through the formal presentation of authorial omniscience and limited point of view to produce the impression of a commonly experienced and ultimately epistemologic-ally stable world, modernist texts tend to be seen as emphasising internal self-referring coherence which foregrounds a loss of established moral connection between what is inside the work of art and what is outside. The formalist construction of Modernism, however, tends to foreground these concerns to the exclusion of other considerations. The preoccupation with internal coherence is seen gradually to displace all concern with external correspondence. The notion of aesthetic autonomy is thus shifted from the idea of the self-grounding of the work of art in linguistic forms which resist incorporation into the routinised discourse of commercial society (evident in the writing of Kant, Schiller, Wilde, Eliot, Leavis) to the idea that art is so entirely ontologically distinct it can only be about itself. In such a view, the realist concern with correspondence through reflection or the Romantic sense of its occurrence through vision ('what we half create and half perceive') is abandoned for the discovery of the impersonal essence of pure form in the work itself.

It would be pointless to try to argue that this construction of Modernism is entirely a fiction projected onto experimental texts of the period 1900–1930 through a post-1945 extension of the formalist premises of the New Criticism. But I believe the hegemony of a certain style of formalist aesthetics developing from the late forties onwards gave a particular inflection to the intentional statements of modernist writers. It suppressed important elements deriving from their specific historical context which connected them to a tradition of European Romantic aesthetics even as they disavowed this connection. A distinctive feature of this construction of Modernism was its American genesis. It emerged in the late forties: the period of the Cold War and the rise to supremacy of the United States as the 'Free Nation' of the world. It was bound up with the designation of Abstract Expressionism in painting as the new indigenous American Modernism. Concurrent with this was the popular dissemination of the New Criticism through a burgeoning academic textbook industry. To academics and intellectuals in England, too, these developments repre-sented an attractive alternative to the parochialisms of the Movement and the Leavisite moral-aesthetic which tended to ignore or disparage the technical experimentation of modernist writing. They also conferred a new power on the specialist literary critic, trained in linguistic analysis and close reading, who could unlock the recalcitrant mysteries of the opaque and recondite modern text. Autonomy, by implication, suggests disengage-ment with historical contexts, so this specialism could be offered as a new democracy of criticism, available to all, requiring no arduous scholarly acquisition of obscure historical detail. So North American critics such as Greenberg and Kenner could be seen to offer a liberation of Modernism from the repressive authoritarianism of European aesthetic tradition. Art would now exist in the freedom of its own pure and specific identity as form. Moreover, if formal autonomy is the product of modern alienation, it is also the antidote to it. Pure form redeems. Greenberg argued that Modernism 'acts upon itself' revealing the possibility of autonomous identity to be the exploration of its own purely formal boundaries. Kantian self-determination is preserved as the ideal of modernity but agency is shifted from the self of the artist to the work itself.[15] Art is thus non-referential, non-conceptualisable, protecting a mode of experience destroyed by commercialisation and industrialisation of the historical world. Art is thus ontologically distinct from that world.

In a world colonised by the 'expert', art must be safely situated in an autonomous sphere. Ironies lurk however. Once situated in such a realm, the *expert* literary critic must then be called in to unlock the mysteries of a text which have become opaque to ordinary *existential* modes of perception. Thus the 'objective' criticism which can unlock the autonomy of the text can be seen as complicit with a mode of rational instrumentalism it is intended to oppose. Autonomy undermines itself. The fundamentally Romantic idea of art as a disinterested activity freed of the will-driven propensity to functional action enters New Criticism, expressed, for example, in Ransom's attack on abstraction or the 'Platonic censor'. But if art is completely autonomous, it can only be returned to the world through the critic trained to unlock its ontologically distinct language. Thus New Criticism is born as a form of that very method it sees as destructive of the world and resisted only through the aesthetic. Its practice effectively dismantles its own theoretical premises. Ransom referred to the aesthetic sign in contradistinction to the scientific one, as 'iconic': in its embodied particularity it creates an object which though ontologically distinct resembles the fullness of an existential object. It thus gives world back to us by creating what is effectively a self-contained simulacrum of it.[16]

New Criticism can be seen as a response to the breakdown of the metaphysical foundation of Romanticism. By transferring the qualities of the transcendent imagination to the formal properties of literary language itself, it tried to preserve a theory of autonomy which threatened to trivialise art into game once the basis for correspondence with world (through Imagination or Nature) came under attack. Critics like Cleanth Brooks (1947) recreate Coleridgean organicism as a property of the distinct ontological linguistic world of the poem rather than as an effect of the poet's mind. If the pure non-conceptual language of literature is opposed to an abstract and rationalising language of science, it is only a short step

---

[15]   Greenberg's key essays 'Avant-Garde and Kitsch' and 'Towards a Newer Laocoon' are reprinted in *Pollock and After: the critical debate*, ed. Francis Frascina, London, 1985.

[16]   The earliest extended discussions of this concept appear in J. C. Ransom *The World's Body* (N.Y., 1938) and in his later book *The New Criticism* (N.Y., 1941). Brooks' and Warren's *Understanding Poetry* (1938) popularised the ideas of the New Criticism and inaugurated a flourishing text book industry. Brooks' *The Well-Wrought Urn* (1947) refined but institutionalised the concept of autonomy as did Wimsatt's *The Verbal Icon* (1954).

away to see literature as being only about itself. It can redeem the world only if it refuses to express ideas about it or to communicate beliefs. The world's body is redeemed through a non-conceptual simulacrum of it. It is not surprising that those technical virtuoso performances, modernist texts, should seem to be the 'logical' embodiment of such an attempt to deal with the contradictory legacy of Kantian aesthetics. But there are other ways of viewing Modernism now that we can see the contradictions of the term 'autonomy'. This is where Postmodernism can begin to read Modernism through different frames.

II
The Core of Darkness
Autonomy Theory and Virginia Woolf

It is time to imagine what a 'postmodern' close reading might look like. Accordingly, this section will offer contextualised readings of a key passage from Woolf's *To the Lighthouse* (1927): firstly through a post-New Critical interpretative frame and then through a 'postmodern' perspective. There have been a number of recent feminist readings of Woolf (including my own: 1989) which attempt to relate her formal aesthetic to her political commitment. Such readings have been powerful in freeing Woolf's writing from earlier interpretations, but they bring with them certain problems of their own which, again, I feel can be usefully addressed through focusing on the issue of autonomy. Woolf's ideas about art were indeed shaped powerfully through the autonomy theories of her day: the writing of G. E. Moore, Roger Fry and Clive Bell (with their objectivist or subjectivist orientations). They were equally shaped by philosophers like Bergson and James whose writings deeply problematise autonomy. But Woolf saw art as engaged with world. A world in which men control and possess women and which she connected to the patriarchal politics of fascism. In her non-fictional writing such views are entirely explicit. *Three Guineas* (1938), for example, suggests that the conversion of women into sexual and reproductive objects within so-called enlightened liberal political econo- mies is an expression of the same instrumental view of human beings which leads to military dictatorships. In this text, she argues that women must not fight men on their own terms but occupy a critical and satirical distance in order to project alternative values which will subvert the public and private worlds which are 'inseparably connected'. She asserts vehe- mently that in such a political economy, poetry must not withdraw into an autonomous realm of the imagination. Equally, however, it should not be used as a direct weapon of political aggression. This would be to comply with the forms of the aggressor. Woolf talked of 'killing' and its consequ- ences for herself, of course, in the famous 'Angel in the House' argument (1931). What is killed here, however, is a myth of patriarchy. An alternative construction must be produced not through the instrumental discourses of political liberalism, but through the 'psychological sentence of the feminine gender'. Only this voice could suspend the frailest particles, envelop the vaguest shapes and stretch to new extremes. Only this voice could begin to break down the boundaries which produce the violence of gender stereotypes and project other possible worlds. Its tones may have been shaped by its development in a particular historical condition, but they can be reformulated to offer a critique of that condition. Woolf's notion of the voice is used to articulate a post-Romantic sense of the capacity of the imagination to recombine elements of the social world to form new and liberatory orders, but her focus is specifically on relations between men and women and she is conscious of the way in which that imagination has itself been socially shaped (1918). It is no longer the supreme point of origin. This is not the sense of her writing one would acquire from reading the key critical accounts of it from 1950 onwards. In the readings by Auerbach, Empson, Daiches, Bradbury and Lodge, *To the Lighthouse* is seen to be fundamentally about itself, resolving its tensions by proclaiming its own autonomy as art. Aesthetic autonomy becomes the only possibility of human significance and order in a world otherwise rendered meaningless by death. Malcolm Bradbury, for example, sees the novel in New Critical-inflected Symbolist terms: 'the repeated hints of a pattern which traces its mystery in the universe, the repeated suggestion that the flux is potentially a world of broken forms mirroring true forms in a world beyond, is the basis of Mrs. Woolf's charged style of discourse' (1973, p129). Undisputably, these are elements evident in the novel, but I would argue that this Symbolist aesthetic is held up to critical gaze: it is overtly parodied in the figure of Augustus Carmichael. A very different matter. Repeatedly, the construction of any purely aesthetic significance is undermined. Woolf's irony constantly reminds us that boots, indeed, may simply be boots. Even so, these readings still exert a powerful influence on students of literature. More often than not, the complex analysis of the Victorian marriage of Mr. and Mrs. Ramsay is reduced to Woolf's recognition of the need for 'fact' to complement 'vision' in art. Similarly, Lily's struggle with her emotional identification with, and sexual desire for, Mrs. Ramsay is reduced solely to aesthetic preoccupations seen to mirror Mrs. Ramsay's and Woolf's own. One can see a number of reasons for the continued adherence to this sort of reading and to the 'autonomy' construction of Modernism in general. An account of art which confers upon it redemptive powers previously reserved for religion, and then confers singularly upon the shamanic critic versed in the specialised vocabulary of New Critical autonomy the power to unlock its mysteries, is bound to remain in some way attractive to those engaged professionally in the reading of literature.

I am not denying that Woolf was influenced by Pater's aestheticist subjective impressionism, nor by Bergson's idea of the aesthetic as offering access to a deep pre-conventional and pre-linguistic order. However, I do believe that later 'autonomy' readings distort the full range of implications of this influence by suppressing their Romantic or Kantian roots. Bradbury, for example, goes on to claim that the vision at the centre of the novel is represented by the 'unified sensibility' of Mrs. Ramsay who becomes a sort of mouthpiece for what is seen as Woolf's own aesthetic ideology of Pure Autonomy. But Mrs. Ramsay is seen as too tied to the human world to express the 'pattern' which must, therefore, be left to Lily, as artist, to translate into Form. So, argues Bradbury, the novel 'ends as composition, entire and of itself; while the flux may be the flux of consciousness, it moves inevitably towards a coherence, not of the human mind of the characters but of the aesthetics of composition' (Bradbury, 1973, p132). Once again a modernist text turns out simply to be about art. Autonomy is over-generalised as the only preoccupation of modernist writers: characters, philosophical, social and political concerns are treated simply as linguistic counters in what turns out to be a treatise on art disguised as a novel. As I have argued elsewhere in a specifically psychoanalytic feminist reading of the novel, Mrs. Ramsay is clearly not the focus of a simple affirmation of aesthetic vision but the object of a critical gaze, largely represented through the ambivalent perspective of Lily as a woman (as well as an artist) who sees the pernicious gender implications of Mrs. Ramsay's self-presentation in these terms. In order to focus on the specific issues of autonomy, however, it will be useful to imagine ways of reading a specific passage. Here is the well-known 'epiphanic' moment where Mrs. Ramsay sits alone after her children have departed to bed:

> It was a relief when they went to bed. For now she need not think about anybody. She could be herself . . . and one shrunk, with a sense of solemnity, to being oneself, a wedge-shaped core of darkness, something invisible to others. . . . Beneath it is all dark, it is all spreading, it is unfathomably deep; but now and again we rise to the surface and that is what you see us by. Her horizon seemed to her limitless. Losing personality, one lost the fret, the hurry, the stir; and there rose to her lips always some exclamation of triumph over life when things came together in this peace, this rest, this eternity; and pausing there she looked out to meet that stroke of the Lighthouse, the long steady stroke, the last of the three, which was her stroke, for watching them there in this mood always at this hour one could not help attaching oneself to one thing especially of the things one saw; and this thing, the long steady stroke, was her stroke. Often she found herself sitting and looking, sitting and looking, with her work in her hands until she became the thing she looked at – that light for example (pp99–101).

In support of a reading from the 'autonomy' position discussed above, one might begin by thinking about voice in this passage. No-one speaks. If the passage is not an expression of personality, it is because it is an expression of itself as aesthetic reality. Such claims have been made about Woolf's tendency to merge indistinguishably the voices of characters and narrators. Some critics have seen this as a mark of Woolf's inability to engage with the 'real world' of history and people: it is the expression of a preference for withdrawal into a closeted aesthetic world. The reason 'no-one speaks', of course, is that Woolf uses free indirect discourse throughout the novel in a manner which often makes it difficult to decide *who* is speaking. Individual subjectivity dissolves into a verbal intersubjectivity. Here, the overt voice is that of the narrator, as indicated through the use of the third person past historic, but the temporally disjunctive adverbs indicate that we are to read this passage as if situated in the ongoing continuous present of Mrs. Ramsay's thoughts and impressions: 'For now she need not think about anybody'. Who then speaks the sentence written in the present tense: 'Beneath it is all dark...'.? If we take it to be Mrs. Ramsay, then it appears to rise out of the experience of the moment, the sudden solitude, the view out to sea, the children asleep in their beds, the steady lighthouse beam: that moment of sinking into oneself which comes after a strenuous day engaged in concern for the welfare of others. If it is the voice of the narrator, however, it takes on greater philosophical weight as an expression of the existence of the self as a deep core distinct from the superficial 'personality' which people see in the world. In Bradbury's version, however, the Bergsonian notion of the aesthetic recovering a primordial flux pre-existing division into subject and object, would be translated into the terms of aesthetic autonomy. Mrs Ramsay's negative capability is the expression of aesthetic withdrawal. The reference to the three strokes of the lighthouse and Mrs. Ramsay's identification with the long last stroke could be seen as her apotheosis of herself as aesthetic artefact. The reference functions as a metalingual gloss on the novel itself: title, plot and three-part structure.

So, Woolf's and Mrs. Ramsay's vision could be seen to be entirely one. The passage would thus be read as reverberating in organicist fashion with echoes from elsewhere in the novel to produce an internally coherent spatial form where the pure pattern which is art is clearly evident beneath the surface flow. Eric Auerbach's *Mimesis* (1953) had established this sort of interpretation. In his reading, Woolf produces her characteristic effect of flow but always reintegrates the apparently discontinuous fragments into some higher unity of the aesthetic through the use of symbol, repetition, analogy and metaphor which gather together the 'orts and fragments' into a totality of what he calls 'symbolic synthesis'. Thus, he argued:

> We are constantly endeavouring to give meaning and order to our lives in the past, the present and the future, to our surroundings, the world in which we live; with the result that our lives appear in our own conception as total entities ... These are the forms of order and interpretation which the modern writers here under discussion attempt to grasp in the random moment – not one order and one interpretation, but many, which may either be those of different persons or of the same person at different times; so that overlapping, complementing, and contradiction yield something that we might call a synthesised cosmic view or at least a challenge to the reader's will to interpretative synthesis (Auerbach, 1953, p485).

The notion of a 'cosmic view' is, of course, what Lyotard sees as irrevocably vanished in the postmodern condition. What is interesting is that he should accept such a construction of the modern in the first place. It is time to see what happens if the 'autonomy' construct is challenged by returning the passage to its historic aesthetic context illuminated by a retrospective view from the postmodern as a contemporary context of reception.

III

Life as Art

Postmodernism Reading To the Lighthouse

Perhaps we can begin to shift towards a 'postmodern' reading of *To The Lighthouse* by considering its treatment of representation as a philosophical and aesthetic problem. We may then return to the 'core of darkness' passage. Throughout, Mr. Ramsay struggles with the problem of subject and object and the nature of reality: contemplating the table; thinking about the possible existence of the table when no-one looks at it; invoking the ruminations of Locke, Berkeley and Hume on such problems of existence and perception. Indeed, the structure of the novel itself reflects such preoccupations. Proceeding from an initial section called 'The Window', it is concerned with the way in which human memory and desire determines the perception of or even constructs the objects of the quotidien world. Section one looks at the activities in the house through this window. In the middle section, however, the house stands empty of occupants: the equivalent of a table without a perceiver in a world of inevitable natural decay indifferent to human significance (Time Passes). In the final section, perception (light) and object (house) is transmuted into symbolic vision (the actual and symbolic lighthouse). Journey, mourning, painting and novel are completed with the redemptive phrase: 'It is finished'. Human significance is seen to be an aesthetic accomplishment premised on loss but offering the possibility of symbolic recovery and agency. This is not aesthetic withdrawal, but a plea for the recognition that all human activity is suffused with aesthetic impulses. How we gather and use them determines what we see in the world and what we do with our lives.

Earlier, Lily ruminates on the problem of perception and meaning as presented to her by Mr. Ramsay:

> 'Think of a table', he told her, 'when you're not there'. So she always saw, when she thought of Mr. Ramsay's work, a scrubbed kitchen table. It lodged now in the fork of a pear tree, for they had reached the orchard. And with a painful effort of concentration, she focussed her mind, not upon the silver-bossed bark of the tree, or upon its fish-shaped leaves, but upon a phantom kitchen table, one of those scrubbed board tables, grained and knotted, whose virtue seems to have been laid bare by years of muscular integrity, which stuck there, its four legs in the air. Naturally, if one's days were passed in this seeing of angular essences, this reducing of lovely evenings, with all their flamingo clouds and blue and silver to a white deal four-legged table (and it was a mark of the finest minds so to do), naturally one could not be judged like an ordinary person. (pp40–1).

The parenthesised irony is aimed of course at the 'girders' of the masculine intellect and is part of the continuous exploration in the novel of the relations between gender and forms of perception. When Lily tries to imagine an abstract essential 'philosopher's' table, her efforts comically fail. Having managed to banish the associative possibilities that connect the inert table to the beauty of the living tree with its silver-bossed bark, Lily still cannot prevent herself from anthropomorphising the table through physical description which locates it in a framework of moral value: 'muscular integrity'. It is still a 'masculine' table. Lily is pondering the relation of angular essences to lovely evenings. What has an abstraction which carves up the world, a concept, to do with perception as part of the flow of experience in all its mingling of imagination, desire and memory? Lily is struggling for a clarity of 'autonomous' perception which will allow her to put her own view of the world and of Mrs. Ramsay, in particular, on canvas. Even so, she still paints her as an abstraction: the purple triangle. For all perception is abstraction from the world. After Mrs. Ramsay's death, the problem becomes more acute: 'How could one express in words these emotions of the body? . . . It was one's body feeling, not one's mind' (p275). How to move beyond abstraction and arrive at the thing itself? Earlier, Lily thinks how she wants unity not knowledge, becoming the thing, not representing it, 'nothing that could be written in the language of men' (p82).

Woolf explores through Lily, problems about art which have profound implications for life. What 'autonomy' theory sets up as a self-reflexive concern with aesthetic status, is actually an exploration of the place of the aesthetic in all fundamental human experience: love, mourning, loss, death. Lily probes issues about art and representation as existential and not simply aesthetic problems. She explores the Symbolist aesthetic in order to move beyond it. In the conclusion to *The Renaissance* (1873), Walter Pater had expressed one means of responding to the collapse of the metaphysical framework of Romanticism and the loss of a self-evident correspondence between orders of mind and those of nature. Subjective experience becomes all; any order we perceive is 'but an image of ours'. We must live by seeking moments of heightened perception and represent that experience through a new expressive symbolism. The symbol can no longer express an *anologia entis* but only one of experience and expression through a heightening of Style. Both Pater and Wilde, however, retained the notion of an inner Soul to be expressed and can be seen to develop the Coleridgean sense of the imagination. But it is the internal coherence of style which must stand as the guarantor of any possibility of correspondence of mind with anything outside itself. W. B. Yeats was to express the feeling in these terms: 'solitary men in moments of contemplation . . . make and unmake mankind, and even the world itself, for does not "the eye altering alter all"' (Yeats, 1961, p159). An organicist concept of form shifts to the idea of form as conscious craftsmanship: the attempt through Style to articulate the intensity of the moment arrested from the flow of experience. It is not a very big step from here to the idea of art as an autonomous internally coherent world which is an 'iconic' or non-conceptual simulacrum of that ontologically distinct world outside from which it must withdraw to be itself.

But I do not believe Woolf took that step, though 'autonomy' readings have assumed that she did. Lily paints Mrs. Ramsay as a purple triangle; Mrs. Ramsay sinks into a wedge-shaped core of darkness. In both cases a shape in space comes to stand in some way for self experienced as an emotion of the body. What does the passage we are concerned with here seem to say about the self? To be oneself is to shrink, to lose personality, to be silent, alone, to be opaque, free to roam and have adventures, to visit all the places one has not seen. Freedom depends on opacity and invisibility for as soon as one rises to the surface, one is consummated as a personality in someone else's gaze: glittering maybe, doing and expansive, but caught in the fret and stir of others. What has the surface we are seen by to do with the invisible depths in which we roam unseen? Once the personality, the self of surface, has shed its attachments, then the dark core is free to choose its own connections. Instead of being lost through incorporation into other, it is thus freed to lose itself in identification with objects of its own choice: 'and this thing, the long steady stroke, was her stroke' (p100).

The influence of Bergson (1910) as well as Pater is evident. Self is subjective impressionism and profound élan vital. But, although the passage is preoccupied with self as surface and depth, it offers no obvious way in which to connect them: the dark core seems in no way to determine or even connect with the life of the glittering social self. The passage suggests that to look for the determinants of Mrs. Ramsay's social behaviour in some deep but causally related core essence of self is to discover that if such connections exist they are not amenable to the rationalisations of deductive logic. At the end of the passage Mrs. Ramsay attaches herself 'in this mood' to the last, long, steady stroke of the lighthouse. The last section of the book, long and steady and arriving at experiential and aesthetic completion, is an attempt to convey the realisation of Mrs. Ramsay for each of the characters. But only because Mrs. Ramsay is consummated through death. Artistic expression is premised upon loss but is also a liberation from the pain of loss: for Woolf (writing to lay the ghosts of her parents), as for Lily mourning Mrs. Ramsay. In the terms of a Nietzschean postmodern fictionality, however, the implications reverberate beyond the issue of painting and novel. Why not maximise the liberatory potential of art by aestheticising the totality of one's experience so that instead of preserving art by withdrawing into an autonomously self-referential aesthetic realm one bursts out of the enclosed circle and treats the world as a work of art giving birth to iself and the self as an infinitely plastic entity which is free to 'author' its own life. Does Woolf advocate a Nietzschean aestheticism familiar to us in its various postmodern guises?

Not quite. Mrs. Ramsay can be seen as caught in a Kierkegaardian 'either/or' of ethic and aesthetic, expressed through the two modes of self. The surface self is one of attachment, at the beck and call of children, guests and husband; defined through the relational identities of wife and mother which confer upon it the ethical imperatives of consistency, unity, reliable coherence, fixity, 'the things you know us by'. This self is situated in a traditional structure of external obligation where social functions place severe constraints upon any possibility of personal autonomy. But beneath it is all dark, not to be contained but all spreading, unfathomable, and capable, in its opacity, of a liberatory aesthetic negative capability which can transform itself in its plasticity into all things. Desire may travel to all places. But this Dionysian self achieves its dynamism only through its non-materialisation. And in this form it is also the inscription on a gravestone: 'this peace, this rest, this eternity'. The aestheticising impulse towards the liberatory creation of new selves, new worlds, is held in check by the everyday 'surface' preoccupations of the self concerned with the ethics of being in the world and having responsibilities towards other people. Such obligations require consistency, necessitate one's availability: Mr. Ramsay seeks sympathy, like a child, and 'drops off satisfied' (p64) when he has received it. He requires that his wife is there for him, sitting at the window, whilst he acts upon the world through his categories of abstract conceptualisation. If Mrs. Ramsay's aesthetic, as Woolf's, is one of autonomous withdrawal, it is because the instrumental world of doing refuses it admittance. Held utterly in check by externally imposed obligations, the iron girders of Victorian marriage for women, the energies of the dark core may never actualise themselves in the world. The imaginative, affirmative possibilities of life may be strangled at this very core.

Woolf is drawn to a Nietzschean conception of self and recognises some of its potential for an emancipatory politics. Elsewhere, she asked whether it is 'only when we give rein to its wishes and let it take its way unimpeded that we are, indeed, ourselves'. But, 'circumstances compel unity; . . . The good citizen when he opens his door in the evening must be banker, golfer, husband, father, not a nomad wandering the desert'. (Woolf, 1928a, p161). As Mrs. Ramsay sits alone knitting, in her imagination she stitches a personality, weaving dispersed elements into her own 'admirable fabric'. A woman, in particular, is a 'vessel in which all sorts of spirits and forces are coursing and flashing perpetually' (1928b, pp66–7). Women are represented as woven into, stitched out of, a social fabric produced through the machinery of patriarchy. However, they have the capacity to weave themselves. If they cannot travel, Flâneur-style, tasting the freedoms of the new urban metropolis, they can imaginatively inhabit exotic landscapes of the mind, adrift with an even greater anonymity and opacity than the self-created Dandy. They are nomads of endless mental landscapes. If the Angel is killed but there is no essence to take its place, then women must weave and fabricate new and colourful selves. Mrs. Ramsay, like Clarissa Dalloway and indeed Molly Bloom, responds imaginatively to the new possibilities of modernity, the gradual break from traditional social structures where self is fixed in an identity wholly through social obligation. Modernity offers the possibility of authoring one's own aesthetic scripts of identity. But such autonomy may exist for Mrs. Ramsay only in the mind. And for Woolf too, killing the Angel completely involves telling the truth of oneself as a *body*: it is as *bodies* that women enter the world disenfranchised of autonomously created identity. To live in the female *body* is still to exist as an object in the instrumental conceptualisation of the male *gaze*. When Mr. Ramsay walks past his wife sitting at the window, he observes her remote in her beauty. He sees the otherness of her body but cannot fathom the imaginary desire pressing against its maternal boundaries. How to find ways of rising to the surface with these newly, profoundly fabricated identities, of finding the means of giving them social expression and recognition in the world? How to roam in physical space?

Immediately after Mrs. Ramsay's experience of the core of darkness, she returns to her knitting and sternly composes the lines of her face. Mr. Ramsay passes, chuckling to himself 'at the thought that Hume, the philosopher, grown enormously fat, and had stuck in a bog'. Hume, that early philosopher of the self as fiction, a flux of ever-changing particulars endlessly and freely recombined and composed into new forms, is suddenly transformed into a very substantial body. It is a body comically fixed and absurbly non-fluid as it struggles with the recalcitrance of that most solid and yet shifting of earthly substances: mud. How to achieve the solidity of materialisation for aesthetically shaped identity? Woolf poses questions which the Nietzschean strand of Postmodernism has also foregrounded. How to discover and represent experience beyond the rigidifying and self-conscious modes of conceptual thought; how to create or discover the self as what Lyotard in his *Economie Libidinale* (1974) referred to as a 'libidinal band': self as an event or entity before the splitting into mind and body which arises with the emergence of self-consious subjectivity. In the philosophical discourses of Modernism: those of James, Bergson, Nietzsche, the image used to convey this desire is that of a fluid world of becoming fixed by the imposition on it of an abstract and static system of concepts. For Nietzsche and postmodernists who develop his thought, fluidity is simply chaos. All meaning is a projection onto it of rationalised desire, the body as a will to power masquerading as a will to knowledge. Only through fully acknowledging this, can we liberate ourselves from oppressive situatedness in world through self-conscious aesthetic shaping. The idea is perhaps more familiar to us now in Foucault's later work on 'technologies of the self' (1986, 1988a, 1988b).

In this philosophical mode, subject is always a fiction: a willed unity masking a chaos of conflicting and contradictory desires. Definitions of self and world are always struggles for conceptual mastery. The most persuasive have been those Platonic forms of thought which persuade us that mental and conceptual representations can reflect the structure of an ultimately fixed and unchanging reality of essences: 'think of a table when no one is there' or 'women can't write; women can't paint'. One can simply respond passively and, in herd-like fashion, allow others to impose their definitions upon one. Alternatively, in recognising that existence is entirely an aesthetic act, one can become the author of one's own life, become one's own supreme fiction. Nihilism as affirmation cannot be accomplished, however, through the imposition of the ready-made concept, fashioning oneself according to pre-given goals. As Nietzsche argued in *Ecce Homo*:

> That one becomes what one is presupposes that one does not have the remotest idea what one is. . . . The entire surface of consciousness – consciousness is a surface – has to be kept clear of any of the greatest imperatives. . . . For the task of a revaluation of values more capacities perhaps were required than have dwelt together in one individual, above all antithetical categories which are not allowed to disturb or destroy one another. Order of rank among capacities; distance; the art of dividing without making inimical; mixing up nothing; a tremendous multiplicity which is nonetheless the opposite of chaos – this has been the precondition, the protracted secret labour and artistic working of my instinct (Nietzsche, 1979, pp64–5).

Nietzsche talks of the self in terms which post-Kantian criticism has reserved for art. Authentic creation is a suspension of the consciously directed and formulated will in life as well as art. He extends the Romantic concept of the imagination to predict the Freudian sense of the unconscious as a primordially aestheticising mode arising out of body: out of instinct and desire. He looks forward also to Foucault's postmodern articulation of the body as both source of resistance to and locus of power. Here body must be harnessed to a 'technology of self' where self-construction displaces self-knowledge. For Foucault, as Nietzsche, human nature is not a hidden essence waiting to be discovered through self-analysis, but an artefact, a sedimented aggregate of those available forms we have chosen to shape into a coherent identity. Otherwise, if we have shunned the responsibility and anxiety of authentic aesthetic self-creation, we are entirely a fabrication of others. Self may be a genealogical chain, an entity which shapes itself consciously or unconsciously according to available theories. It is not, as in the Freudian account, fixed in some past determining moment which shall ever shape its future. Even the 'dark core' is a place of fictions. There is no originary moment establishing pure identity which can be rationally analysed, but only a flux of experiences ever being shaped into new wholes, reproduced through new vocabularies and new stories. Nietzsche famously argued in *Beyond Good and Evil*:

> The falseness of a judgement is not for us necessarily an objection to a judgement.... the question is to what extent it is life-promoting, life-preserving, species-preserving, perhaps even species-cultivating ... To recognise untruth as a condition of life – that certainly means resisting accustomed value feelings in a dangerous way: and a philosophy that risks this would by that token alone place itself beyond good and evil (1966, p4).

If human truths are fictions, they must still be experienced as discoveries, not creations, in order to be effective. We need to believe in them and to know that they are lies: at the same time. This is a description of all aesthetic experience: if I read a novel I enter into its fictional world and 'believe' in it, but if I fail to retain a sense of its fictionality I fall into a dangerous condition of myth. What Nietzsche never proclaims, despite popular notions of his thought, is that we can simply fashion at will a new self, be whatever we want to be. We are born into a web of relations: past creations become truths which place constraints upon our own aesthetic creations: Zarathustra says 'Some souls one will never discover, unless one invents them first' (Nietzsche, 1954, p18). We can redescribe the past but only create an authentic self by acknowledging past actions. We must struggle to recognise the defensive screening process which allows us to cohere as a fragile unity; try to break down such screens in order to admit as much of the multiplicity and fragmentariness of existence as possible. Woolf too saw that authenticity lies only in the impossible but necessary struggle to 'have no screens, for screens are made out of our own integument; and get at the thing itself, which has nothing whatever in common with a screen. The screen-making habit, though, is so universal that it probably preserves our sanity ... But the screens are in excess' (Woolf, 1978, p100).

What sort of nihilism if any is articulated in the Woolf passage? The passage hovers over a number of ways of seeing. The darkness is profoundly ambiguous. It may be an attempt to express an aestheticist negative capability in a Nietzschean sense of the liberatory potential of positive nihilism: if there is only chaos we are free to impose our own shapes upon it, to create the self. On the other hand, it seems to express a Bergsonian possibility of the self as an essential entity pre-existing divisions into body and mind, distorted through conceptualisation, available within the forms of the aesthetic. This would be a flux so profoundly ordered that conceptual thought, the language of habit, must always betray it. The aesthetic is then a means of discovery through creation. Art tears away the veil of habit from the world, breaks up routinised habits of perception: it is an idea expressed throughout Romantic and modernist aesthetics. T. S. Eliot stated the idea thus:

> Poetry may help to break up the conventional modes of perception and valuation which are perpetually forming and make people see the world afresh, or some new part of it. It may make us from time to time a little more aware of the deeper unnamed feelings which form the substratum of our being, to which we rarely penetrate; for our lives are mostly a constant evasion of ourselves, and an evasion of the visible and sensible world (*UPUC*, 1966, p155).

The Nietzschean mode of fictionality is an extension of a Coleridgean aesthetic shorn of its secure metaphysical underpinnings. Eliot articulates an alternative sense of situatedness: that we exist in a world which provides the structures through which we arrive at understanding and which must always restrain the fictionalising impulse, valuable as it may be. Woolf hesitates between the two. Her famous description of life as a luminous halo tends to be read as an expression of Paterian subjective impressionism. One could equally relate it to that passage in William James where he discusses the stream of consciousness:

> Consciousness, then, does not appear to itself chopped up in bits. Such words as 'chain' or 'train' do not describe it fitly as it presents itself in the first instance. It is nothing jointed; it flows. A 'river' or a 'stream' are the metaphors by which it is most naturally described. In talking of it hereafter, let us call it the stream of thought, of consciousness, or of subjective life (James, 1983, p233).

Like Bergson, James believed that such a flow could realise a deeper order beneath the world of discrete entities and definitions. The being and the doing which you see us by is Woolf's expression of the Bergsonian sense that 'our life unfolds in space rather than in time; we live for the external world rather than for ourselves; we speak rather than think; we "are acted" rather than act ourselves' (Bergson, 1960, pp231–32). Immediately before Mrs. Ramsay sits down at the window, we are told: 'No, she thought, putting together some of the pictures he had cut out – a refrigerator, a mowing machine, a gentleman in evening dress – children never forget. For this reason, it was so important what one said, and what one did, and it was a relief when they went to bed'. For Woolf, issues of fictionality and situatedness, creation or discovery, are traversed by those of gender. To be a woman in the modern world is to confront the contradiction that self is defined in terms of autonomy, whether Kantian or Nietzschean, but women remain positioned in traditional discourses of obligation which *deny* them identity in these terms of modernity. In 'A Sketch of the Past', she recognised:

> What immense forces society brings to play upon each of us, how that society changes from decade to decade; and also from class to class; well, if we cannot analyse these invisible presences, we know very little of the subject of the memoir; and again how futile life-writing becomes. I see myself as a fish in a stream; deflected; held in place; but cannot describe the stream (Woolf, 1976, p80).

Sinking into the wedge-shaped core of darkness may be a form of liberation from the violences of constructed and unified ego. However, in either Bergsonian terms of a descent into a deeper situatedness or in the Nietzschean terms of fictionality, there are dangers for women. The first may involve an implication in a traditional world where women are simply caught and immobilised by the invisible stream, rather than free to flash and swim in the opacity of subterranean darkness. The second may succumb to a negative nihilism, a suicidal impulse, negative capability as a desire for merger and peace, utter dissolution into the chaos of sensation. Mrs. Ramsay's experience of solitude is both exhilarating and terrifying. What is Mrs. Ramsay when husband and children disappear? What happens when the Angel in the House is an isolated body? There appears to be no identity, no autonomous self. The negative capability becomes an extension into non-being of a gendered relational identity: Mrs. Ramsay ceasing without pain on the stroke of the lighthouse beam. Woolf, like postmodernists after her, is caught between ethics and aesthetics. To embrace a Nietzschean mode of self-creation seems to offer the possibility of liberation from the narratives of others. But this may be at the expense of those external obligations which form the basis of our ethical relation to those others. Mrs. Ramsay is caught between her traditional situation as a maternal body with all its ethical imperatives inscribed upon it, and her imaginative reconstruction of identity as the aesthetic act of a modern mind. The poles of fictionality and situatedness form an intense dialectic with profoundly political and existential implications. The imaginary shape can only as yet realise itself as an abstract triangle: even then it is only represented when the living body is dead. Otherwise it is an invisible wedge-shaped core of darkness. Lily can only paint by denying relational ties, traditional situatedness as a woman: by moving the purple triangle off-centre, refusing the ethical imperative to comfort others, to give sympathy to the male, marry and have children; repressing the erotic nature of the impulses towards Mrs. Ramsay herself. How to reconcile the possibilities for aesthetic self-creation offered by modernity and there for women to seize, with ethical obligations which tie women to traditional fixed identities shaped by others and lived out every moment in the body itself? Woolf wrote the novel to lay the ghosts of obligation, recognising as she wrote it that if her father had been alive then Mr. Ramsay would never have been born.

Readings of Woolf through 'autonomy' constructions of Modernism tend to remind the reader of her association with Clive Bell. Here is Bell's concept of autonomy in art:

> If a representative form has value, it is as a form, not as a representation. The representative element in a work of art may or may not be harmful; always it is irrelevant. For, to appreciate a work of art we need to bring with us nothing from life, no knowledge of its ideas and affairs, no familiarity with its emotions. Art transports us from the world of man's activity to a world of aesthetic exaltation (Bell, 1987, p25).

I hope that I have already shown the inadequacy of readings which project such an aesthetic onto Woolf's writing. The next stage is to extend this discussion of autonomy theory and gender by examining these issues more generally in Modernism and Postmodernism.

8

MODERNISM, POSTMODERNISM, GENDER

The View from Feminism

I
Introduction

The discourses of feminism clearly arise out of and are made possible by those of Enlightened modernity and its models of reason, justice and autonomous subjectivity as universal categories. Feminist discourses, however, have been powerful forces in exposing some of the most entrenched and disguised contradictions and limitations of Enlightenment thought. Simply in articulating issues of sexual difference, the very existence of feminist discourses weakens the rootedness of Enlightenment thought in the principle of sameness; it exposes the ways in which this 'universal' principle is contradicted by Enlightenment's construction of a public/private split which consigns women to the 'private' realm of feeling, domesticity, the body, in order to clarify a public realm of Reason as masculine. In this sense at least, feminism can be seen to be an intrinsically 'postmodern' discourse. Until very recently, however, debates within feminism have tended to be ignored within discussions of Postmodernism and vice versa. Things have begun to change. Feminist theory has developed a self-conscious awareness of its own hermeneutic perspectivism based on the recognition of a central contradiction in its attempts to define an epistemology: that women seek equality and recognition of a gendered identity which has been constructed through the very culture and ideological formations which feminism seeks to challenge and dismantle. Awareness of such contradictions, in fact, start to emerge as early as 1971 with the publication by Kristeva of the essay 'Women's Time'. The concept of a 'woman's identity' functions in terms both of affirmation and negation, even within feminism itself. There can be no simple legitimation for feminists in throwing off 'false consciousness' and revealing a true but 'deeply' buried female self. Indeed, to embrace the essentialism of this notion of 'difference' is to come dangerously close to reproducing that very patriarchal construction of gender which feminists have set out to contest as *their* basic project of modernity.

Feminism of late, therefore, has developed a self-reflexive mode: questioning its own legitimating procedures in a manner which seems to bring it close to a Postmodernism which has absorbed the lessons of post-structuralism and consists at the most general level of a crisis of legitimation across culture, politics and aesthetic theory and practice. The slogan 'Let us wage war against totality', however, could be seen as Postmodernism's response to that earlier slogan of the feminist movement, 'the personal is political'. But if the latter can be seen as a rallying cry, the former implies a hostile attitude towards its implicit ideals of collectivism and community. The feminist cry situated its politics firmly within what Lyotard wishes to denounce and Habermas to affirm in modified form as the 'project of modernity'. In fact, at this point in my argument, I will have to declare my own situatedness and argue that if feminism can learn from Postmodernism it has finally to resist the logic of its arguments or at least to attempt to combine them with a modified adherence to an epistemological anchorage in the discourses of Enlightened modernity. Even if feminists have come to recognise in their own articulations some of the radical perspectivism and thoroughgoing epistemological doubt of the postmodern, feminism cannot sustain itself as an emancipatory movement unless it acknowledges its foundation in the discourses of modernity. It seems to me, however, it is possible to draw on the aesthetics of Postmodernism as strategies for narrative disruption of traditional stories and construction of new identity scripts, without embracing its more extreme nihilistic or pragmatist implications. Surely to assume otherwise is in itself to embrace a naively reflectionist aesthetic which sees representation as necessarily reflective of prior structures or ideologies. A number of questions arise out of this: can feminism remain opposed to Postmodernism's circular tendency to project itself onto the contemporary world and thus, not surprisingly, to find in that world an affirmation of its own theoretical presuppositions? Can it resist the implicitly religious vocabulary of apocalypse while acknowledging the force of its critique of Enlightenment epistemology as rooted in the instrumental domination of inert object (body, world, nature, woman), by a detached and transcendent subject (mind, self, science, man).

These issues can usefully be approached, it seems to me, through further consideration of that central Enlightenment concept, autonomy, and its role in the construction of various models of subjectivity. What the preceding discussion has suggested is that the epistemological and ethical contradictions now confronting postmodernists and feminists are fundamentally issues about identity and difference. Subjective transformation has been central to feminist agendas for political change. Similarly, over the last thirty years, the deconstruction of liberal individualism and the dissolution of traditional aesthetic conceptualisations of character have been central to postmodern art and theory. Like feminism, Postmodernism (in theoretical and artistic modes), has been engaged in a re-examination of the Enlightenment concepts of subjectivity as autonomous self-determination; the human individual as defined without reference to history, traditional values, God, nation. Both have assaulted aesthetic or philosophical notions of identity as pure autonomous essence. Ethical and epistemological contradictions have crowded onto the modern scene. Peter Berger, for example, defined the shift from traditional to modern identity as one from a world of honour to one of 'dignity': 'in a world of honour the individual discovers his true identity in his roles, and to turn away from the roles is to turn away from himself', but in a world of 'dignity' the individual can only discover his true identity by emancipating himself from his socially imposed roles' (Berger, Berger and Kellner, 1974, p91). We have already seen some of the contradictions involved in this, for it can only be fully accomplished through the refusal of history and institution. Even if such a self could internally formulate itself, without engagement with history or institution it could not act upon the world. Agency would exist only within a sealed aesthetic realm. This is the force of the Woolf passage examined earlier.

Everyone agrees that Postmodernism is much concerned with frag-mentation. Either it sees the world fragmenting or it sets out to discover modes which will fracture and dissolve old and supposedly exhausted unities. Numerous examples could be offered of this, from Lyotard's competing language games to the emphasis on the local, or from Barth-elme's declaration 'Fragments are the only forms I trust' to Nietzsche's proclamation of that condition of linguistic materiality which Jameson has seen, with that of nostalgia, as basic to the postmodern condition. One could view the impulse to fragment in psychoanalytic terms. The desire to destroy that which we cannot possess has long been recognised as a strategy of the child persisting into adult behaviour. The destruction of the other, however, cannot be accomplished without an accompanying effect of fragmentation of the self. This is the experience of the postmodern condition as expressed by Jameson:

> Schizophrenic experience is an experience of isolated, discontinuous material signifiers which fail to link up into a coherent sequence. The schizophrenic thus does not know personal identity in our sense, since our feeling of identity depends on our sense of the persistence of the 'I' and the 'me' over time (1985, p119).

Although Jameson draws his model of schizophrenia from Lacan, it was Melanie Klein who first showed the fragmentation of subjectivity to be a final defence against the fear of annihilation. It is preceded by a desire to destroy that which threatens to annihilate oneself: the object of desire which tantalises but can never be possessed. In my view, versions of Postmodernism which simply celebrate radical fragmentation can be seen to be a collective psychological response to the recognition that the ideal autonomy of Enlightenment cannot be possessed. Not only this, pursuit of it may have produced the worst sort of violence. Similarly, aesthetic autonomy theory may have done violence to the identities of those modernist artefacts reconstructed through it since the 1940s. As Adorno and others began to recognise earlier in the century, one of the effects of idealist philosophy has been to empty out the self into an abstract form. This may appear to confirm its transcendence. It has actually reflected its real condition of systematised negation through abstraction within the instrumental rationalism of the liberal political economy. My argument has been that the concept has functioned similarly within aesthetic discourses to suppress the historical identity of works of art, the political commitments of writers, their challenges to traditional ethics. In New Critical or later Structuralist or post-Structuralist formalisms, literature is understood as a system which allows us access to a purified autonomy for it condenses and foregrounds the existence of the linguistic sign as a reflexively self-constituting object 'purged' of reference. Thus purged: of history, ethical insights, the 'contaminations' of a debased mass cultural mode of communication, however, the literary text paradoxically becomes identified in the very terms of abstraction its existence is supposed to resist. In reaction to this, many postmodern texts flaunt their implication in and complicity with Late Capitalism by deliberately incorporating aspects of mass culture or by drawing on parodic forms which implicitly deny the possibility of pure autonomy or original self-determination (parody is always and openly parasitic upon an earlier text). Many of the discourses of Postmodernism, however, employ the more radical and desperate remedy of extreme fragmentation: a way of coping with an inability to give up a profound desire for autonomy in the pure terms of its promised Enlightenment forms. Here lies the crux of its problematic relationship with feminism.

Jameson connects this 'schizophrenic' tendency in Postmodernism with a pervasive nostalgia. In my view it is the nostalgia which produces the desire to fragment, the impossible yearning for the lost (imaginary) object of desire which issues in the frustrated and atavistic smashing of the ideal object. Although Nietzsche is often seen as the first postmodernist, he was also one of the first to connect the nostalgic impulse with nihilism. One sees in the writings of Deleuze, for example, or the fictions of Kathy Acker, the possibility of humanist affirmation destroyed by an insistent and excessive nostalgic sense of loss of pure Being (translated often from Spirit to Instinct) whose impossible realisation produces the urge to destroy altogether what can be: the representation of the human subject as an ethical, affective and effective historical agent. If things are fragmenting, let's fragment them utterly. This is the violent face of Postmodernism. Of course, it is often difficult to know if extreme fragmentation or dehumanisation is being used parodically as a mode of critique, or as an extension of a fragmented and dehumanised world. Here is a description of the character V, goal and negation of Stencil's quest in Thomas Pynchon's postmodern novel of that name:

> Skin radiant with the bloom of some new plastic; both eyes glass but now containing some photoelectric cells, connected by silver electrodes to optic nerves of purest copper wire leading to a brain exquisitely wrought as a diode matrix ever could be. Soleroid relays would be her ganglia, serio-actuators move her flawless nylon limbs, hydraulic fluid be sent by a platinum heart-pump through buthyrane veins and arteries (1979, p406).

For some critics, this dissolution of human subjectivity into textual play has been seen as a means of resisting the oppressive structures of global capitalism: fragmentation into atoms becomes the means of escaping patriarchal surveillance and control of the pleasure principle. Fragmentation and dehumanisation are part of a 'postmodern' assault on the bondage of thought to regulative ideals such as 'unity' and 'truth'. But for a feminist, the first difficulty with this argument must surely be that V is a woman and even if she is constructed to expose the dehumanising effects of idealististic patriarchy, she also perpetuates them in her very form. We should remember too that when Nietzsche recommended fragmentation, he represented the regulative ideals of Enlightenment thought as tied to what he saw, in fact, as phallic castration: an emasculation of the intellect which he associated particularly with emancipatory movements and especially with feminism. The idea of truth as untruth has a long history of articulation through the image of the seductive woman: a Salome who is only her veils, whose adornments cover over a gaping absence. She continues to appear with monotonous frequency in the metaphorical femininity of some postmodern writing. Her otherness is the possibility of a space of immediacy, outside language, an incitement to transgression: the postmodern version of that Romantic sublime which must forever remain outside the workings of power and history. This grotesque version of the metaphor, for example, appears in Nietzsche's *My Sister and I*: 'Truth is still elusive. However, she is no longer a young girl but an old bitch with all her front teeth missing' (1990, p114). Before examining in more depth what such rhetorical tropes might mean for actual women, and whether, indeed, they assault the oppressive structures of Late Capitalism for women, in particular, we need to return to some of the key ideas in postmodern theory which impinge on the issue of personal identity.

II
Founding Assumptions
Feminism and Postmodernism

Fredric Jameson is probably the best known commentator on Postmodernism to connect its insights with a radical critique of the Enlightenment ideal of personal autonomy. In his seminal 1984 essay, he argued that its most radical insight is the view that the bourgeois individual subject is not only a thing of the past but also a myth. We have never possessed this kind of autonomy: 'Rather this construct is merely a philosophical and cultural mystification which sought to persuade people that they 'had' individual subjects and possessed this unique personal identity' (1985, p115). Yet as we have seen, this insight is far from new. One philosopher has suggested that Descartes himself had to suppress his awareness of the contradictions of self-grounding as the basis of modernity:

Nothing, as Descartes himself seemed to realise, in the methodological identification of these internal features, in clarity and distinctness, of itself justified any metaphysical result. Being, or substance as Descartes ended up understanding it, was only the result of the application of the method, and there was no convincing reason to think that what satisfies our self-certifying criteria for what there is, what is least susceptible to certain kinds of doubt, still gets us where we wanted to go, 'back' to the world we suspended in the moment of doubt . . . Given the self-understanding of an extreme break in the tradition, of a need for a new beginning not indebted to old assumptions, and so wholly self-grounding, the modern philosophic enterprise appears locked in a kind of self-created vacuum, determining by argument or reason a method for making claims about the world, but unable to argue convincingly that what results is anything other than what the method tells us about the world, be the 'real' world as it may (Pippin, 1991, p25).

Postmodernism has provided a radical critique of method both in its development of Nietzschean radical fictionality and of the idea of non-conceptualisable Being or pre-understanding from Heidegger. In the former version, the interest is in the way in which experience is aesthetically constructed and the self an ever-revisable script. In the second, the emphasis is on the possibility of recovering some immediate, primordial, authentic mode of being which is non-rationalisable and pre-conceptual and variously seen as the 'politics of desire' or 'against interpretation'. Both invoke the aesthetic as the mode of its realisation. Yet as I have tried to show, these two tendencies are derived from two modes of Romanticism which, in themselves, were powerful critiques of Enlightenment. Postmodernism, however, claims to have entirely left behind the metaphysical ground of Romanticism. But has it? The fictionality mode still reproduces a form of late Coleridgean aesthetics: self recreating itself through the (textual) imagination and still raising difficult ethical issues even as it claims to go beyond good and evil. The alternative mode, an extension of the Wordsworthian, often displaces the notion of nature with a notion of the body in a new instinctual foundationalism; or it displaces it with a notion of situatedness or tradition often still effectively grounded in a sacred mysterious Being.

One hears much in Postmodernism about the subject as myth and the notion that the master narratives of history are redundant illusions. Yet, I often have the feeling, as I read postmodernist writing, that its apocalyptic nihilism about the possibility of ethical and imaginative subjective existence is still grounded in a nostalgia for the ideal autonomous self as presented in Enlightenment thought. Nostalgia rewrites history in the terms of desire. In the case of apocalyptic postmodernism, it may be that its schizophrenic fragmentation is a response to a continuing obsession with an impossible ideal. Postmodernism, in this mode, may itself have rigidified autonomy into an absolute identity. Autonomy has been a powerful concept in philosophical and aesthetic writing, but even as they ascribe to the theory most people know it cannot be lived absolutely in this ideal form. Certainly, few women have attempted to live it, because women have been more or less excluded from its applications. They have developed alternative models of self-identity. A problem for feminists in relating to Postmodernism, is that they are highly unlikely to bear this sort of relationship to history or to the ideal autonomous self central to the discourses of modernity. Those who have been systematically excluded from the constitution of that so-called universal subject – whether for reasons of gender, class, race, sexuality – are unlikely either to long nostalgically for what they have never experienced or possessed (even as an illusion) or to revel angrily or in celebratory fashion in the 'jouissance' of its disintegration. To recognise the limitations of an ideal which was never one's own is to bear a very different relationship to its perceived loss.

The decentred and fragmented subject of the 'postmodern condition' is one which has been created, at least in part, by Postmodernism itself. It is in part the consequence of an inability to rethink a self not premised in some way on the pure idealism of the autonomous subject of Enlightenment thought, German Idealist philosophy and Kantian aesthetics. It is present in much postmodern writing at least as a structure of feeling. Recent feminist scholarship has shown why women are unlikely to have experienced history in this form. For feminists, therefore, the goals of agency, personal autonomy, self-expression and self-determination, can neither be taken for granted nor written off as exhausted. They are ideals which feminism has helped to reformulate, modify and challenge. Feminism needs coherent subjects and has found a variety of ways of articulating them which avoid the fetishisation of Pure Reason as the locus of subjecthood and the irrationalism born out of the perceived failure of this ideal.

III
Alternative Histories

Both feminism and Postmodernism have extended our awareness that one of the effects of modernity is that knowledge reflexively enters and shapes experience and is then shaped by it in an unprecedentedly self-conscious fashion. The ways in which we formulate notions of selfhood out of the models of subjectivity available to us shape our behaviour in the world and shape response to any new models consciously or unconsciously encountered. In such a climate, to talk of 'origins' is highly problematic. However, we have already examined a number of formulations of the postmodern, and seen that most of them begin to appear in the late 1950s. By the late seventies, in fact, both feminism and Postmodernism can be seen to have radically altered the way in which modern culture is understood and experienced. What I find astonishing is the fact that these discourses have had so little to say to each other. Even now, as postmodern theory increasingly draws on a highly idealised and generalised notion of femininity as 'other' in its search for a space outside the disintegrating logic of modernity, it rarely talks about (or to, one suspects) actual women or even about feminism as a political practice. I have been amazed at the number of general accounts of Postmodernism which do not even mention gender, when clearly one of the most obvious and radical shifts in late modernity has been in the relations between women and men. This shift has had all sorts of ramifications for modern concepts like nation, the aesthetic, epistemology, ethical systems, autonomy. And, indeed, there are obvious points of historical contact between Postmodernism and feminism. Both have undermined the Romantic-Modernist cultivation of the aesthetic as an autonomous realm and helped to expose it as a critical construction. Each assaults Enlightenment discourses which universalise white, Western, middle-class male experience. Both recognise the need for a new ethics responsive to technological changes and shifts in knowledge and power. Each has offered critiques of foundationalist thinking: gender is not a consequence of anatomy nor do social institutions so much reflect universal truths as construct historical and provisional ones. Postmodernism too, is 'grounded' in the epistemological problem of grounding itself, of the idea of identity as essential or truth as absolute.

Feminism has provided its own critique of essentialist and foundationalist assumptions. Arguably, however, even if it draws upon postmodern aesthetic forms of disruption, it cannot repudiate entirely the framework of Enlightened modernity without perhaps fatally undermining itself as an emancipatory politics. In proceeding through the demands of political practice, feminism must posit some belief in the notion of effective human agency, the necessity for historical continuity in formulating identity and a belief in historical progress. Even if people are shaped by historical forces, they are not simply reflexive epiphenomena of impersonal deep structures or of a global agonistics of circulating and competing language games. Feminism must believe in the possibility of a community of address situated in an oppositional space which can allow for the connection of the 'small personal voice' (Doris Lessing's term) of one feminist to another and to other liberationist movements. One writer producing personal confessional novels about 'women's identity' can then be seen to connect with the activity of another woman rewriting the history of slavery or one camped on the mud of Greenham Common, even as they recognise and accept each other's differences. All are ultimately engaged in practices which involve an adherence to a shared ideal of truth and justice grounded in fundamental human needs, but as the embeddedness of each of us in the world is different, so we shape different styles of living, of aesthetic expression and political action for ourselves. It seems to me that all along feminism has been engaged in a struggle to reconcile context-specific difference or situatedness with universal political aims: to modify the Enlightenment in the context of late modernity but not to capitulate to the postmodern condition.

Glancing through the various postmodernisms, in fact, one can see how the full range of conceptualisations of difference has entered feminist theory and aesthetic practice. An invigorating imaginative playfulness has entered feminist writing: a sense of the importance of the aesthetic in the imaginative and embodied projection of alternative futures. Too often though, political claims are made for avant-garde formal disruption which are difficult to justify. One sort of disruption is assumed to be the mirror of another. Once epistemology becomes so problematic, however, such category mistakes are bound to occur. Real and fictional may be entirely conflated. Concepts are transferred unproblematically from the context of aesthetic to political practice. But surely feminists should keep in mind the centrality to his work of Lyotard's assertion that emancipatory discourses are no longer possible because there can no longer be a belief in privileged metadiscourses which transcend local and contingent conditions in order to ground the 'truths' of all first order discourses (Lyotard, 1984). According to this view, gender cannot be used cross-culturally to explain the practices of human societies. In one sense this is the state of affairs feminism is aiming for in the ideal society it imagines to be possible. It should not, however, mean that feminists abandon their struggle against sexual oppression because 'gender' as a metanarrative is necessarily a repressive enactment of metaphysical authority. Lyotard unnecessarily conflates the concept of totality with that of totalitarianism. Feminists should remember that 'totalities' such as the concept of political unity, need not mean uniformity, that they can be enabling and liberating. Globalisation may be a critical mode of knowledge as well as a functional mode of capitalism or of reigns of terror.

The postmodern concept of language games, dissensus and dispersal developed in Lyotard's reading of Wittgenstein, is one postmodern discourse often naively appropriated by an avant-garde desire to conflate artistic textual disruption with political subversion. Analogy may be confused with causality in order to claim a massive political significance for formally innovative writing. The position is as strongly identified with postmodernists like Lyotard as with feminists such as Kristeva. Its immediate impulses can be traced back to Tel Quel influences, to Barthesian jouissance and to the avant-garde manifestos of the twenties and thirties. Critics such as Peter Bürger have argued that Postmodernism has failed to challenge the institutionalisation of modern art as autonomous practice because of the post-structuralist persistence in viewing the sign as self-reflexive (Bürger, 1984). Although I have suggested alternative ways of reading Postmodernism and of viewing the issue of aesthetic autonomy, there are implications here for feminism. I must confess to some suspicion about the way in which some postmodernist discourses have developed the concept of femininity. The dangerous use of the metaphor of 'femininity' to designate a linguistically non-reproducible 'otherness' effectively redescribes a space of the sacred. Its roots are in Romanticism. Such a 'feminine' space has always been used to deny the *material* existence of actual women. From Nietzsche through Hassan and Lacan, femininity has been used to signify an 'otherness' which has effectively been essentialised as the disruption of the legitimate or the Law of the father. This 'otherness' has been variously expressed as the repressed other; the hysterical body; the semiotic; the pre-oedipal; the ecstatic, fluid, maternal body. It is associated with the transgression of Christian mysticism. In 'Women's Time', for example, Kristeva writes:

> It seems to me that the role of what is usually called 'aesthetic practices' must increase not only to counterbalance the storage and uniformity of information by present-day mass media, data-bank systems and, in particular, modern communications technology, but also to demystify the identity of the symbolic bond itself, to demystify therefore, the community of language as a universal tool, one which totalises and equalises ... what I have called 'aesthetic practices' are undoubtedly nothing other than the modern reply to the eternal question of morality (Kristeva, 1982, p53).

We have seen this argument reproduced throughout an aesthetic tradition of Enlightenment critique from Romanticism to Postmodernism. The danger is to assume that because it is often articulated through metaphors of femininity, women, in particular, will be liberated through it. It may indeed function as an agent of women's oppression. In Kristeva's own account, women have no special access to this pre-conceptual space of the 'maternal body', and even as avant-garde artists they receive little attention. It seems to be male experimental writers who can speak it. In fact, as often as not, this celebration of 'difference' goes hand in hand with an amazing *indifference* to the material and psychological circumstances of actual women. The postmodern espousal of psychotextual decentring as liberatory says little about women as beings in the world who continue to find themselves displaced and invisible even within a critique of epistemology which has supposedly, in deconstructing the centre, therefore done away with the margins to produce the possibility of a new emancipatory liminality. As in most religious discourses, Postmodernism in this 'desire' mode promises a beyond to the sense of an ending: a conversion of chronos to kairos, beyond language, concept, time. Within postmodern psychoanalytic discourse, for example, it has been described as 'the body without organs' (the small boy's view of the mother?), 'becoming woman' (the male fantasy of plenitude?) and the 'hysterical body') (the female object through which psychoanalysis first arrived at its definition of the implicitly masculine subject). It seems that as postmodernists obsessively register their sense of the collapsing legitimacy of the frameworks of Western knowledge, they are also registering, unconsciously and metaphorically, a fear specifically of the loss of the legitimacy of western *patriarchal* grand narratives. This may even reproduce aspects of the new forms of fear of women evident in other ways in contemporary culture: addictions to body building, violence to women, a resurgence of religious fundamentalism, new forms of pornography which present women literally in bondage to men, the popularity of films like 'Fatal Attraction' and the current cult of serial killer movies. Is it a coincidence that at the very historical moment when (male) postmodernists intensify their interest in (and master through their own discourses) a (religious) space described as the 'feminine' and nothing to do with actual women, feminists are establishing an (Enlightened modern) sense of their coherent identity as women through the very categories and discourses which postmodernists claim to have dismantled and done away with in the name of this 'femininity'. Surely this has an ominously familiar ring to it? Could one see the oppressed (women) returning in the form of the repressed (femininity) in postmodern discourse only to be worked through and mastered yet again in the language of theory?

If femininity has become, once more, a metaphor for a state beyond metaphysics, feminists should be certain that its tenor is not simply the contemporary theoretical counterpart to the Victorian parlour. If they have any suspicions then they should continue to hammer through its boundaries, those between public and private, in an assertion of their continued belief in their own capacity for agency and historical reconstruction. If Barthes writes a pseudo-autobiography to articulate the idea that 'to write an essay on oneself may seem a pretentious idea, but it is a simple idea, simply as the idea of suicide' (1977, p56), feminists should remind themselves that the shelves of books by Barthes in libraries all over the world proclaims a confidence in his authorship even as he disclaims it. They should not be surprised then that so many women writers in the seventies articulated a desire to become 'authors of their own lives' at precisely the moment that Barthes was announcing the death of that concept. Whose death?

Jean Baudrillard's work, it seems to me, is even more problematic for feminism. For him postmodernity signifies the state of contemporary culture which exists as a simulacrum of signs where the information age has utterly dissolved identity through reflections to maskings to complete absence. In this perspective all that literature can do is to play off 'alternative worlds' in a state of pluralistic anarchy where the subject is simply a simulating machine of commercial images, the mass a silent majority and the very idea of resistance, an absurdity. Simulation replaces imagination and human beings are left with no capacity to reshape their world even in their own heads. They act like the characters in Robert Coover's novel *Gerald's Party* (1986), as dense points of transmission for all the cop and thriller and porn movies which construct their desires and which churn out incessantly throughout this text in an orgy of hedonistic sensationalism. It may be that Coover is using the parodic mode of the postmodern to offer a critique of postmodernity from within its own codes, but again one is left with the claustrophobic sense that there can be no real opposition to it because no place outside. In most versions of the postmodern, in fact, any claim to a substantive reality outside representation is discredited and there can be no escape from the prison house of language.

One difficulty in discussing Postmodernism is that the apocalypticism of the theory may have unduly affected our response to the fictional artefacts (if I may be so old-fashioned as to hang onto such a distinction). It seems to me this *is* an important distinction to hang onto, because it is evident that many women writers are using postmodern aesthetic strategies of disruption to re-imagine the world in which we live, while resisting the nihilistic implications of the theory. Certainly one can see the writing of Angela Carter, Jeanette Winterson, Margaret Atwood, Maggie Gee, Fay Weldon, to name but a few, in this way. This is perhaps not so very surprising since women have, in practice, always experienced themselves in a 'postmodern' fashion – decentred, lacking agency, defined through others. Which is why, it seems to me, they had to attempt to occupy the centre in the early seventies. It is why women began to seek a subjective sense of agency and collective identity within the terms of the discourses of modernity at precisely the moment when postmodernists were engaged in the repudiation of such discourses, proclaiming the 'death of the author' and the end of humanism. Much feminist fiction of this period, therefore, was either confessional or concerned with the idea of discovering an authentic identity. If its philosophical roots are clearly anywhere it is in existentialism rather than post-structuralism. It may now appear to be philosophically naive and formally unadventurous, espousing an uncontested aesthetics of expressive realism or a simple reversal of the romance quest plot which did little to problematise ideologies of romantic love or essential identity. I have argued that perhaps feminist writers needed to formulate a sense of identity, history and agency within these terms before they could begin to deconstruct them. However, feminist writers did not subsequently rush off to embrace the postmodern – indeed they have largely maintained a cautious distance, certainly from much of the theory. This is where I shall declare my own distance as a feminist in offering some 'grand and totalising' narratives which allow us to think of subjectivity in ways which neither simply repeat the Enlightenment concept of modernity nor repudiate it in an embrace of anarchic dispersal.

IV
Rethinking Subjectivity and Aesthetics
Alternative Feminist Positions

I want to suggest, somewhat tentatively, that despite differences in the theoretical construction of modernity and postmodernity, common to them both is the inheritance of a particular ideal of subjectivity defined in terms of transcendence and pure rationality. Postmodernism can be seen as a response to the perceived failure of this ideal. This notion of subjectivity, whether expressed through Descartes' rational 'I' and refined into Kant's categorical imperatives, or through Nietzsche's 'übermensch' or Lacan's phallogocentric symbolic order, has not only excluded women but has made their exclusion on the grounds of emotionality, failure of abstract intellect or whatever, the basis of its own identity. This position has been reproduced across philosophy, psychoanalysis and literature. In viewing this situation as fundamentally unchanged, I am, in effect, repudiating the postmodern notion that there are no longer any generally legitimated metanarratives. What I am saying is that patriarchal metanarratives function just as effectively within our so-called 'postmodern age' as in any other age and in its metaphorical play on notions of the feminine they continue insidiously to function powerfully within postmodern theory itself.

Jameson has diagnosed postmodernism as the schizophrenic condition of late capitalism, but I would argue that the autonomous transcendent self of German idealism, Enlightenment humanism, European Romanticism and realist aesthetics and the impersonally fragmented self of Postmodernism are products of the same cultural tradition. Schizophrenia is clinically defined as a splitting of thought and feeling: the 'schizophrenia' of Postmodernism can be seen as a fin-de-siècle parody or caricature of a dualism inherent in the Western tradition of thought where the self is defined as a transcendent rationality which necessitates splitting off what is considered to be the irrational, emotion, and projecting it as the 'feminine' onto actual women. It is to see T. S. Eliot's 'dissociation of sensibility' from a feminist rather than a High Tory position. Freud, of course, has taught us that reason and feeling are inextricably bound up with each other, but even he believed that ego could and should master id, that impersonal reason is the basis of personal autonomy. Increasingly in this century, such a contracted 'rational' self cannot make sense of the world: whether in the fictions of Kafka or Bellow, for example, or in the aetiolated dramas of Samuel Beckett. When transcendence fails, however, the threat of disorder is seen to come from the split off (and therefore uncontrollable) aspects of the psyche, the non-rational projected onto and thus defining women, racial minorities, so-called 'sexual deviants' or even 'the masses'.

Postmodernism may seek to locate the possibility of disruption or 'jouissance' in this space, but in continuing to regard it as 'feminine', whether it speaks of actual women or not, then it simply continues the process of projection and does little to overcome the dualism and psychological defensiveness inherent in it. Often in postmodernist fiction, for example, traditional images of the castrating female, the unknown and therefore uncontrollable woman, are overlaid in a technological age with their representation as machines which have outstripped the controlled and rational dominance of the male (one thinks of V again). The 'emotionality' thus projected onto the feminine or onto woman in order to retain rationality and autonomy as the core of masculine identity produces both images of woman as the 'other' of romantic desire and woman who, thus beyond control, threatens annihilation or incorporation. If feminists wish to argue a politics of feminity as avant-garde disruptive desire they should first think about some of the meanings of, for example, V or Nurse Ratched.

In fact, in both modernist and postmodernist writing, when order conceived of as a circumscribed rationality seems no longer to cohere in either the self or in history, then it is projected onto the impersonal structures of language or of history conceived of as myth, a static and synchronic space. Despite the new 'perspectivism' which enters literary history in the early part of the century, the potential for the re-evaluation of the relations between subjectivity and objectivity, so many of the aesthetic manifestos of the time and later critical accounts of the period emphasise 'impersonality', 'autonomy', 'objectivity', universal 'significant form', 'spatial form', 'objective correlative' – even when most of the artefacts, such as *Ulysses*, clearly problematise such notions. The New Critical theorisation of literature, in particular the modernist text, as an autonomous linguistic structure, reinforced these ideas. Since then the increasing professionalism of literature has extended the vocabulary of form and structure: defamiliarisation, systems of signs, the death of the author, the free play of the signifier, simulations . . .

One can see in much modernist literature both the attempted assertion and the failure of Enlightened modernity's ideal of autonomy. The belief in absolute self-determination, whether that of Stephen Dedalus or Mr. Ramsay, is always discovered to be dependent on the desires of others. Whereas a transcendent Being could anchor desire as absolute, to express it in relation to others is always seen to produce delusion, deception, jealousy, a whole variety of epistemological crises which modernist texts offer. The possibility of Art itself as an absolute autonomous realm, however, often comes to take the place of the sacred here. Art, as religion, seems to offer precisely that illusion of utter self-determination and transcendence which relations with other mortals must always shatter. It is interesting how many of the male heroes of modernist literature achieve an apparent self-determination in aesthetic terms through a refusal of social relationship. Hence the figure of the alienated artist who affirms his own autonomy, his independence from the mediation of others at the price of the cessation of human relationship and desire: Marcel writing in his room, Ralph Touchett vicariously living through Isabel, Malone talking to himself, Mann's Leverkühn, Hesse's Steppenwolf. Art as the impersonal focus for desire displaces the possibility of human relationship because it involves no mediation through the desire of the other. Hovering behind these texts is Nietzsche's self-creating and self-affirming artist for whom to recognise the other would be to fall into a slave mentality.

In my view it is the identification of self with an impossible ideal of autonomy which can be seen to produce the failure of love and relationship in so many texts by male modernist and postmodernist writers. Can one rethink the self outside of this concept without abandoning subjectivity to dispersal and language games? Not only do I believe that one can, I also believe that many feminist writers have done so. This is the really 'grand and totalising' part of my argument. It seems to me that autonomy defined as transcendence, impersonality and absolute independence, whether an idealised goal or a nostalgic nihilism, whether informing the aesthetics of Modernism or those of Postmodernism, is not a mode with which most feminists, nor indeed, most women, can very easily identify. Feminist theory, though drawing on anti-humanist discourses to sharpen its understanding of social processes, has emphasised that 'impersonal' historical determinants are lived out through experience. This distance from anti-humanist discourse has allowed feminist academics to connect with grass roots activists outside the academy. Their own historical experience has tended to develop in women strongly 'humanist' qualities in the broader sense of the term and feminism has always been rooted in women's subjective experience of the conflicting demands of home and work, family and domestic ties and the wider society.

V

Psychoanalysis, Gender and Aesthetics

Jürgen Habermas has recently suggested that modernity is not exhausted, simply unfinished. His view of this is not incompatible with some of the ideas I am trying to develop here. What he has argued is that instead of abandoning its ideals we need to modify them by redefining the model of Reason which underlies them. His work is part of a tradition of critical thinking which sees Enlightenment reason failing because defined too narrowly in the terms of an instrumental, purposive or utilitarian epistemology. He proposes instead a model of what he calls 'communicative reason', based on speech act theory and emphasising not individual autonomy but intersubjectivity (1987). Like so many theorists within the postmodern debate, however, he seems singularly unaware of many of the developments in feminist thinking over the last twenty years. It seems to me that many feminists have been working for some time with models which are not fundamentally incompatible with Habermas's whether or not they have used them in specifically theoretical ways. I will now examine some of these ideas and suggest that through them it is possible to arrive not only at an alternative definition of the aesthetic but also of subjectivity itself.

According to most psychoanalytic theories and their popularly disseminated forms, subjecthood is understood as the achievement of separation. Maturity is seen to be reached when the dependent infant comes to regard its primary caretaker (nearly always a woman) as simply an object through which it defines its own identity and position in the world. This is then maintained through the defensive patrolling of boundaries. Implicit then in most theories of identity is the assumption that the 'otherness' analysed by feminists from de Beauvoir on, is the necessary condition of women – certainly as long as women mother. Separation and objectivity rather than relationship and connection become the markers of identity. Freudian theory has been used to support this view. Both the liberal self and the postmodern 'decentred subject' can be articulated through Freud's notion of the unconscious, dominated by instinctual and universal drives seeking impossible gratification. In the liberal version, ego as rationality can master the drives either intrapsychically or with the help of the silent, impersonal and objective analyst who will be uncontaminated by countertransference. In the postmodern version, rationality breaks down and the anarchy of desire as impersonal and unconscious energy is unleashed either in the freeplay of the signifier of the avant-garde text or that of the marketplace of Late Capitalism. Freud's infant hovers behind both: an autoerotic isolate, inherently aggressive and competitive, its sexuality and identity oedipally resolved only by fear, seeking to discharge libidinal energy which is necessarily in conflict with 'rational' and 'enlightened' concern for others and for society as a whole.

Can we imagine alternative models of subjectivity? If knowledge is inextricably bound up with experience then it seems that we certainly can, for this is not a description of universal experience. In fact Freud himself hints at other possibilities in less familiar parts of his writings. In the paper 'On Narcissism', for example, he says: 'A strong egotism is a protection against falling ill, but in the last resort we must begin to love in order not to fall ill and we are bound to fall ill if in consequence of frustration, we are unable to love' (1914, p85). In fact, in the development of selfhood, the ability to conceive of oneself as separate from and mutually independent with the parent develops with the ability to accept one's dependency and to feel secure enough to relax the boundaries between self and other without feeling one's identity to be threatened. Why, then, is autonomy always emphasised as the goal of maturity? Why not emphasise equally the importance of maintaining connection and intersubjectivity? As Joan

Rivière has argued 'There is no such thing as a single human being pure and simple, unmixed with other human beings . . . we are members one of another' (1986). Parts of other people, the parts we have had relationships with, are parts of us, so the self is both constant and fluid, ever in exchange, ever redescribing itself through its encounters with others. It seems to be this recognition of mediation as that which renders total self-determination impossible which so many male modernist and post-modernist writers find unacceptable. Yet much women's, particularly feminist, writing has been different in that it has neither attempted to transcend relationship through the impersonal embrace of Art as formal autonomy or sacred space nor through rewriting its own Apocalyptic sense of an ending.

Returning to psychoanalysis, however, one can see some of the reasons why the definition of subjectivity as transcendence and autonomy has been so powerful and why it has come to be seen not as a description of the experience of most white, Western males, but of universal structures of subjectivity. In psychoanalytic terms, if subjectivity is defined as separate-ness, its acquisition will involve radical disidentification with women in a society where women are normally the exclusive caretakers of children. This will be true even for girls who, at the level of gender, will also seek to identify with the mother. Fathers are not perceived as threatening non-identity for in classical analysis they are seen as outside the pre-oedipal world of primary socialisation with its intense ambivalences and powerful Imagos. They are from the start associated with the clear, rational world of work and secondary socialisation. Object relations theorists like Nancy Chodorow (1978), however, have pointed out that the desire for radical disidentification with the mother will be more acute for boys for the perception of women as mothers will be bound up with pre-oedipal issues of mergence and potential loss of identity requiring a culturally reinforced masculine investment in denial and separation. The world of secondary socialisation associated with the father comes to be seen as superior and as inherently male. Subjectivity thus comes to be seen as autonomy or as role-definition through work. Truth is defined as objectivity and transcend-ence. Science in the form of an instrumental technology will be overvalued and defined in terms of objectivity; philosophy comes to deal only with universal and metaphysical truths (whatever the theoretical challenges to these notions). Women (or the 'feminine') come to be identified in Cartesian or post-structuralist philosophy with all that cannot be rationally controlled and thus threatening dissolution or non-identity: mortality, the body, desire, emotionality, nature. Post-structuralist 'femininity' is simply another way of making actual femininity safe, of controlling through a process of naming which in post-structuralist fashion prises the term utterly away from the anatomical body of woman.

If the female sex thus represents, in Sartre's words 'the obscenity . . . of everything which gapes open' (1985), then men seem to be justified in their instrumental attitude to women and to everything, including nature, which has been 'feminised' and which must therefore be distanced, controlled, aestheticised, subdued (one might call this the Gilbert Osmond syndrome). Women appear threatening in this way because they carry the

culture's more widespread fear of loss of boundaries, of the uncontrollable, more threatening because unconsciously split off in order to retain
the purity of a subjectivity, a human-ness defined as autonomy, pure
reason and transcendence. Cartesian dualism thus persists along with
strict empiricism in science and impersonality and formalism in literary
theory and criticism.

What I have tried to argue here, therefore, is that an examination of
alternative feminist models of identity can add a further and important
dimension to the debates considered earlier about the construction of
Modernism in terms of formal autonomy. The exclusion of gender from
postmodern discussions has left its theorists largely blind to the possibilities of challenging autonomy through a relational concept of identity. If
women's identity has tended, broadly, and allowing for differences across
this, to be experienced in terms which do not necessarily see separation
gained only at the expense of connection, one would expect some sense of
this to be expressed in discourses other than the theoretical and psychoanalytic. Women's sense of identity is more likely, for psychological and
cultural reasons, to consist of a more diffuse sense of the boundaries of self
and their notion of identity understood in relational and intersubjective
terms. I am certainly not claiming that this is exclusive to women, for
clearly gender is a continuum, and there are several theoretical models
often invoked in the postmodern debate which articulate a similar sense of
identity. It provides a further perspective on the Woolf passage. Certainly,
I believe that Woolf's work has been so important for feminists because
both formally and thematically it articulates a critique of patriarchal
institutions through its exploration of the relatedness of subjects and
objects. Beyond this, however, she offers a critique of the exclusive
identification with relational modes of identity as they have functioned
within patriarchy. She shows their negative as well as positive potential in
characters such as Mrs. Ramsay and Clarissa Dalloway. In a society where
women are perceived as culturally inferior, relationality as the basis of
identity has often reinforced their desire to please, to serve others and seek
definition through them, internalising any anger about this as a failure of
(essential) femininity. Mrs. Ramsay's desire for autonomy, her travels in
the imagination, remain a dark core. If it could rise to the surface, tempered
by a relational sense of connection to others, then it might no longer hover
as a suicidal impulse. It could fully realise the sense that human beings are
fundamentally bound to and produced through each other as well as
fundamentally separate. Indeed, the recognition of the co-existence of
these states might be essential for the survival of the human race. If ego is
the product of culture, as Freud argued, and if ego may only be defined in
terms of separateness, impersonality, containment and pure reason, then
culture has produced only divided and deformed human beings. Feminist
discourses suggest that the dissolution of containment into irrational desire
or the dispersal of jouissance are not the only alternatives to a discredited
Enlightenment. My hope is that these perspectives may be fairly represented in future accounts of the postmodern debate and the condition of
late modernity.

9

FROM IMPERSONALITY TO SITUATEDNESS

Reading T. S. Eliot on Tradition

No discussion of Modernism would be complete without some attention to the criticism of T. S. Eliot, for it was this body of writing more than any other which institutionalised Modernism and provided an alternative theoretical base to the earlier provocative *Blast*-style proclamations. Eliot's concern with 'impersonality' fed into the 'autonomy' construction of Modernism. Drawing on Postmodernism, I will explore ways in which this reading of Eliot may be challenged.

Woolf's question of how to write the body emerged from the pressure of a desire to begin to dismantle the fetters of gender: a possibility both facilitated and retarded by that shift in 'all human relations' which was her experience of modernity. In an essay on 'American Literature and American Language' written a quarter of a century later, T. S. Eliot also addressed the notion of a shift in literature:

> From time to time there occurs some revolution, or sudden mutation of form and content in literature. Then, some way of writing which has been practised for a generation or more, is found by a few people to be out of date, and no longer to respond to contemporary modes of thought, feeling and speech. A new kind of writing appears, to be greeted at first with disdain and derision; we hear that the tradition has been flouted, and that chaos has come. After a time it appears that the new way of writing is not destructive but re-creative. It is not that we have repudiated the past, as the obstinate enemies – and also the stupidest supporters – of any new movement like to believe; but that we have enlarged our conception of the past; and that in the light of what is new we see the past in a new pattern (1965, p57).

Although Eliot emphasises mutation of form, it is as a response to 'thought, feeling and speech' and to a self-conscious awareness of a shift in the relations of past and present. However, as with Woolf, the 'autonomy' reading of Modernism has ignored important aspects of the historical context of ideas which shaped his thought. Throughout his writing, Eliot is concerned with that same dialectic of self and history which we saw in Woolf, the same sense that knowledge cannot be pure and that the supposedly disinterested intellect is always driven by pressures of the body, of non-rational needs and desires. Hardly the stuff of New Critical objectivity. However, for Woolf, the body must function as the source of a fictionalising pressure which could bring about fundamental change in human relations. For Eliot, the body must remain situated in the unconscious rituals of a traditional culture. If it is to act effectively in the world, it must neither be paralysed by self-consciousness nor overwhelmed by irrational desire. If, for Woolf, the self-consciousness produced by modernity is potentially liberating, for Eliot, it may produce that paralysis which is a symptom of the proliferation of values: the necessity for choice and the inability to choose. It is the mode of 'Shall I' and 'Do I dare' and 'Should I' and 'How should I' and 'Would it have been worth it after all' which afflicts not only Prufrock but most of Eliot's poetic protagonists.

Both Eliot and Woolf, however, share a sense of the intellect as a conceptualising instrument, a secondary force overlaying a pre-existent flux which may or may not contain its own inherent order. Far from reflecting Platonic essences or pure structures of reason, the intellect may simply be that means of formulating experience in order to establish provisional, working order in the world. Mind and body, reason and desire, cannot be divorced. The insight, however, gives rise to very different aesthetic and political philosophies. Probably its most famous literary critical expression was in Eliot's 1921 essay on the metaphysical poets where Donne, for example, is admired not simply for his revolt against the ratiocinative, or for feeling his thought as immediately as the odour of a rose, but is praised for looking both into the heart and into 'the cerebral cortex, the nervous system, and the digestive tracts' (1953, p120).

For Woolf, the issue of the body was bound up with that of feminist politics. For Eliot, it was bound up with the concept of tradition, formulated in the famous essay of 1919, but reiterated in a variety of contexts each essentially articulating what is directly stated in *Notes towards the Definition of Culture* (1948): 'Culture cannot altogether be brought to consciousness; and the culture of which we are wholly conscious is never the whole of culture; the effective culture is that which is directing the activities of those who are manipulating that which they *call* culture' (1962, p107). It is a version of that well known modernist tenet: go in fear of abstractions. But it is also an expression of an orientation towards the notion of situatedness which I have suggested can be located in a Wordsworthian Romantic aesthetic but which surfaces powerfully as one of the basic branches of postmodern thought and aesthetics and is articulated in the hermeneutics of Gadamer as in the work of philosophers such as Richard Rorty. Eliot's notion of culture as an embodied experiential mode of the present arising out of and continuously reformulating the past is close to a current postmodern sense that what we experience in the present as valuable has arisen through the values of the past. This allows us not only to understand the past but to experience continuity of value even if we cannot step out of our own temporal situation to find 'disinterested' conceptual terms, abstractions, which may describe this experience. We are situated in a history which cannot be grasped conceptually but which shapes what we are, including how we attempt to conceptualise it.

Woolf's Bergsonian sense of the possibility of depth as an essential flux irreducible to rational formulation, shares the concern of Eliot with relations between form and contingency as problems of experience and history as well as art. Both see 'personality' as a convenient and pragmatic fiction. For each, 'impersonality' represents the possibility of expressing a deeper, latent, non-conceptualisable reality. For neither, is it simply an 'escape from personality'. Impersonality can function, however, in positive and negative modes. Woolf, for example, expresses the view that 'one is living all the time in relation to certain background rods or conceptions' (1976, p73) and in this very book talks of one of them as that 'looking glass shame' which women experience about their bodies as a consequence of the work of culture. Impersonality here articulates that divorce from one's own deeper sensations when one is forced habitually to experience oneself as an object in another's gaze. Eliot famously defended the notion of impersonality in poetry as a suspension of the rational intellect, allowing feelings to enter into new combinations. But there are times in his writing when impersonality constitutes that force of social convention which imposes identities upon us in an oppressive and destructive fashion. In the essay on Blake in *The Sacred Wood* (1920), he argues that 'the ordinary processes of society which constitute education for the ordinary man ... consist largely in the acquisition of impersonal ideas which obscure what we really are and feel, what we really want, and what really excites our interest'. He goes on to describe Tennyson as a poet, 'almost wholly encrusted with parasitic opinion, almost wholly merged into his environment' (1960, p154). In contrast, Blake is a 'naked poet': able to see with the intensity of a vision uncontaminated by formal education. But Blake's genius is defective and eccentric because it was never 'controlled by a respect for impersonal reason, for common sense ... what it sadly lacked was a framework of accepted and traditional ideas' (pp157–8). Eliot sets *authentic* impersonality (poetic talent growing out of situation in a nourishing cultural tradition) against *inauthentic* impersonality (talent assimilated to the rationalising abstractions of the modern world).

By 1933 he was arguing explicitly that 'culture is the one thing we cannot deliberately aim at', just as he believes that poetry restores us to the 'deeper unnamed feelings which form the substratum of our being' (1964, 155). Woolf, however, knows that without conscious deliberation (without Lily's conscious aesthetic decision to place the purple triangle off-centre), for women, at least, the authentically impersonal sphere (the wedge-shaped core) will simply not achieve expression at all. For Eliot, authentic cultural expression and subjectivity is dependent upon a full acknowledgement of 'situatedness': of the way in which one's fundamental emotional and personal life arises out of and is expressed through a being in the world which cannot be rationally formulated and understood but exists as an embodied condition. Only a gifted and enlightened few are capable of bringing any of it to consciousness. For Woolf, however, such embodiment is alienation: tradition is patriarchal oppression. The potential of the conscious mind to seize and shape the all-spreading dark is a necessary aspect of the attempt to articulate a new identity for women. Consciousness-raising as oppositional political practice has always been as important to feminists as it has tended to be threatening to conservative High Anglicans like Eliot. He prefers 'situatedness' in the mode of Heideggerian pre-understanding, just as Woolf prefers the possibilities opened up by radical fictionalisation. Her desire is not to change art in order to preserve culture but in order to effect an emancipatory break with tradition. In each, however, there is a central dialectic of consciousness as rationality and unconsciousness as body where the latter is seen to be more authentic. For Woolf, collective emancipation is desired and explored through the possibility of conscious articulation and shaping of unconscious desire. This is implicit in the fiction, explicitly argued in texts like *Three Guineas* (a conscious articulation of many of the concerns of her preceding novel *The Years* (1937)). For Eliot, however, consciousness as will is that shaping of experience which produces social engineering: rational planning, destruction of tradition, paralysis of authentic poetic expression. The view is harnessed to a neo-Tractarian Christian Toryism where a defence of art as situated and embodied experience is linked to a conservative organicist philosophy designed to preserve the sort of social structure Eliot saw capable of nourishing genuine aesthetic experience.

In Eliot and Woolf the aesthetic is actively constructive of the lifeworld. Despite their very different modes of engagement with that world, their art is as much part of an 'aestheticising' impulse as any Postmodernism. Its construction through the concept of 'autonomy' is a retrospective critically imposed narrative identity which takes up some explicit and intentional proclamations of modernist writers themselves and suppresses others. The (conscious) intentionalism of the manifestos (which deny the authenticity of consciousness) is grafted onto the imaginative texts themselves. Impersonality seems to support an autonomy reading and it is not difficult to find any number of modernist declarations of 'impersonality': Stephen's famous identifcation with an Aquinean aesthetic of static contemplation in *A Portrait of the Artist as a Young Man* (1916); the construction of the artist as a departed Deity paring his fingernails in the background; Eliot's numerous allusions to the idea of the poem as an escape from not an expression of personality, or of its 'reality which is not simply the reality of what the writer is trying to "express", or of his experience of writing it, or of the experience of the reader or of the writer as reader' (1964, p30); Pound's description of the ideogrammatic method as analogous to a biologist assembling slides. These statements of impersonality are used to give an intentionalist foundation to the construction of Modernism through theories of autonomy. Yet to re-examine the full context of any one of these statements is to recover a much more complex articulation. In his 1919 essay on Ben Jonson, for example, Eliot described Jonson's characters conforming to the logic of their world and argued that such worlds are like systems of non-Euclidean geometry. When Eliot wrote these words, non-Euclidean geometry had already ceased to be the provenance of mathematicians describing ideal structures with no application to the world outside. Einstein was already developing its implications to produce profoundly new articulations of the human experience and understanding of time and space. Recognition of this context is important for without it one can easily see how the assertions about Jonson's 'worlds' can be used to support an 'autonomy' reading of Eliot. In fact, a non-Euclidean world does not simply provide a perspective outside from which to see the actual world of human experience, but offers a way of understanding situated experience *in the world* as itself a perspectival and shifting construction. Even in this apparently 'autotelic' early claim for art, one sees a greater complexity in Eliot's thought than formalist 'objectivity' theories have recognised.

The New Critical reading of Eliot has already been subject to revision by a number of critics such as C. K. Stead, Frank Kermode, Robert Langbaum and, more recently, Edward Lobb and Harold Bloom, who have shown his connection to a continuing tradition of Romantic aesthetics.[17] Lobb, for example, has pointed out how Eliot's notion of 'dissociation of sensibility' is a Fall myth for the modern age, 'the story of Eden applied to the secular history of literature' (p5) which originates in a Romantic conception of history. The preference for image over idea, embodied over conceptual, has its roots in Coleridge and Keats. The notion of perception through the whole mind and not just the intellectual faculty, can be traced back to Wordsworth and Schiller. Lobb points out other features in common such as the use of myth and the search for mythical constructions to ground individual voice. Both Keats and Eliot make explicit their suspicion of poetry which has a palpable design on us; Coleridge and Eliot offer accounts of the mind which reject empiricism and psychologism as extremes; Wordsworth and Eliot emphasise the importance of unwilled memory. However, the recognition of this connection with Romanticism has not entirely succeeded in prising the construction of Modernism away from its New Critical formulation because more attention needs to be paid to the precise history of the concept of autonomy. This is where Postmodernism is valuable in focusing attention on its historical contradictions. Probably the most famous New Critical formulation of autonomy was in Brooks and Warren's *Understanding Poetry* (1938), where they argued that the poem is an organic system of relationships, an autonomous entity or heterocosm irreducible to content or 'message' or historical contexts and essentially what Jakobson had defined as a message focused on itself for its own sake. This definition itself owes much to Coleridge and the organicist concept of the image. However, as I argued earlier, the Coleridgean concept of the work of art as the expression of imagination is tied to an essentially Kantian sense of autonomy as self-determination though grounded in a metaphysical concept of Divine Mind. Once the metaphysical ground disintegrates, whether conceived of as Imagination or Reason, the concept of autonomy as self-identity and self-expression comes under strain. I have argued that the New Critical formulation of it is an attempt to

---

[17]   See C. K. Stead *The New Poetic: Yeats to Eliot* (1964); Frank Kermode *Romantic Image* (1957); Robert Langbaum *The Poetry of Experience* (1957); Harold Bloom *Poetry and Repression; Revisionism from Blake to Stevens*; Edward Lobb *T. S. Eliot and the Romantic Critical Tradition* (1981).

transfer the notion of self-grounding from the existential subject to the work of art conceived of as a heterocosm: a self-contained world produced through particular linguistic relations and essentially related to the historical world through analogy rather than existentially extended experience.

Eliot himself, of course, challenged the formulation of his work through the terms of the New Criticism. Discussing pervasive references to him as a New Critic or the founder of New Criticism in an essay entitled 'The Frontiers of Criticism', he said of this: 'I fail to see any critical movement which can be said to derive from myself' (1957, p107). He goes on to argue that just as poetry is the expression of the poet's experience and thinking and thus of the whole person, so too is the practice of criticism. The discussion which ensues of the limitations of consciously articulated interpretation and understanding, in fact, would not look out of place in any of the so-called postmodern, post-Heideggerian versions of 'practical wisdom' (what I have called 'situatedness'). For Gadamer, for example, to offer a critique of Cartesian method, of the idea that rationality can only be founded on scientific foundationalist principles of verification, is not to collapse into a total relativism and chaos of value and meaning but to develop instead a version of practical wisdom which accepts situatedness in a lifeworld out of which deliberate intelligence arises and can have meaning and value. For Heidegger this is what allows us to understand: we approach literary works with some pre-understanding arising from our common situatedness in a culture and each work will contribute its own modifying effect on that understanding in a continuously revolving process. Eliot expressed precisely this view in his 1929 essay on Dante:

> The enjoyment of the Divine Comedy is a continuous process. If you get nothing out of it at first, you probably never will; but if from your first deciphering of it there comes now and then some direct shock of poetic intensity, nothing but laziness can deaden the desire for fuller and fuller knowledge . . . it is a test . . . that genuine poetry can communicate before it is understood. The impression can be verified on fuller knowledge. I have found that about such impressions there was nothing fanciful. They were not due, that is, to misunderstanding the passage, or to reading into it something not there (1975, p206).

It is more famously expressed perhaps in the well-known line from the *Four Quartets* reminding us that there is only 'limited value in the knowledge derived from experience': the pattern imposed by the knowledge will always be provisional for it 'is new in every moment'. Eliot expresses the hermeneutic recognition that as we enter the experience of a literary work, we already have some preconceptual sense of its meaning for us. If the work is successful, we will come away from it with those meanings and the sense of who we are ever so slightly modified. To enter the work is in some way to renounce the self and never quite to capture that self again, just as culture itself will have been forever modified by the entry into it of the work. There may be a foundation but it cannot be formulated, fixed or ultimately known. So, as Eliot argued in *The Aims of Education*, 'the past has to be reinterpreted for each generation, for each generation brings its own prejudices and fresh misunderstandings' (1965, p119). Similarly, he argued in several essays against the concept of interpretation as knowledge or possession, for there is nothing to possess: 'Qua work of art, the work of art cannot be interpreted; for there is nothing to interpret . . . and for 'interpretation' the chief task is the presentation of relevant historical facts which the reader is not assumed to know' (1953, pp46–7). Again what Eliot presents is the view that we can only make sense of ourselves, of works of art, of others, because we exist in a tradition, but tradition itself only exists through a community's practice and understanding of it. This understanding is always being modified: past is continually shaped by present and present by past. This notion of situatedness, that human meaning exists only in embodied, contextualised terms, is central to what I have identified as one of the two basic strands of postmodern thought. Implicitly, it refutes the Kantian transcendental ego: the view from nowhere. Again, we see Postmodernism *in* Modernism as much as *after* it.

   Eliot's first most explicit statement of distance from linguistic theories of autonomy came in 1933 in *The Use of Poetry and the Use of Criticism* when he argued that the experience of literature is shifting, transient, existential. He warns that poetry must not be cut off from ideas or beliefs and criticises writers like I. A. Richards for suggesting that 'poetry can save us' because it does not involve beliefs about life (1964, pp130–1). The poet creates a world, but one arising out of and co-extensive with that historical one which is the world of the reader. This sense of existential extension is central to all Eliot's criticism (and poetry, though there is not space to go into this here: what is Prufrock, man and poem, if not a self-consciously constructed longing to attain the existential condition of embodied unself-consciousness; let us go then you and I). In modified versions of formalist autonomy theory, 'poetry is a complex kind of verbal construction in which the dimension of coherence is by various techniques of implication greatly enhanced and this generates an extra dimension of correspondence to reality, the symbolic and analogical' (Wimsatt, 1964, p241). Wimsatt tries to argue for a form of iconic relation between word and object, so that the more complex self-enclosed coherence of poetic language produces new *analogical* relationship: in its structural autonomy the poem constitutes a different ontological order (and required therefore a new 'ontological critic'). For Eliot, however, the world produced in the poem is an amalgam of disparate experiences formed into new wholes, a coming into Being (in the Heideggerian sense) which is not a transcendence of the world of experience but part of it: 'unconcealing' by concealment (showing forth not naming) our grasp of understanding of our own existence in the world. 'I could not speak' and 'my eyes failed' and 'I knew nothing' (*The Wasteland*) is a necessary acknowledgement of humility before the world. One knows only by returning to where one started from and recognising that self is not separate from it. Throughout Eliot's poetry the method of working by amalgamating disparate experiences functions to dissolve the boundaries of different orders of experience. He achieves this less through the violent and abrupt juxtapositions of Pound's ideograms, but more through a process whereby it becomes difficult to separate one order of experience from another, past from present, subject from object. Often this seems to express a desire to 'lose personality' by merging into a more fundamental collectivity (a poem like *The Wasteland* draws on Jungian, Darwinian, Christian and Fraserian senses of primordial cultural mind). However, the process always involves an impetus to *withdrawal* from such ego-threatening modes: in *Hysteria* (1917), it is clear that although the hysterical subject appears to be the laughing woman with her cavernous mouth, it is actually her gentleman companion who experiences himself engulfed by a primordial feminity which is a projection of his own fear. In such circumstances, 'I decided that if the shaking of her breasts could be stopped, some of the fragments of the afternoon might be collected, and I concentrated my attention with careful subtlety to this end' (Eliot, 1969, p32).

For Eliot only a theory of cultural tradition could provide that recognition of the condition of situated embodiment from which all human activity arises and also offer a structured 'impersonality' through which the desires of the body could enter into controlled form. That this essentially *hermeneutic* understanding of art and culture should have been read in terms of New Critical autonomy only goes to illustrate Eliot's own articulation of the way in which the past is continuously reformulated through the present. It is surprisingly close to the different versions of 'embodiment' in postmodern theory. Let us return to the famous 'Tradition and the Individual Talent' (1919) essay in the light of these observations. Tradition, of course, is itself always an abstraction, as numerous critiques of Eliot from Raymond Williams (1958) onwards have in effect pointed out. In the concept of tradition, however, Eliot finds the equivalent of Woolf's wedge-shaped core of darkness, for if tradition is an abstraction, it may also be experienced as a lived condition. It is a timeless monument and an existential state: consciously crafted High Art and embodied and situated unconscious practice out of which such art arises in its purification of the dialect of the tribe. Rather than an autonomy theory of art, this is an aestheticisation of the historical world as a culturally shaped body providing the groundless ground for that conscious High aesthetic expression. The essay was the first of many statements which articulate an aestheticist understanding of culture where art shapes life and is always implicated in it. However, its affinities with Postmodernism do not extend to an optimism about the democratising potential of art viewed in this fashion. For Eliot, resistance to democratisation is the only means of preserving High Culture as the conscious articulation of a deeper (unconscious), embodied condition, lived out (silently) by the majority of those who share the culture in the broader, anthropological sense of the word. The 'living' must be rejuvenated by a knowing but the general public, almost by definition, cannot 'know' (and ought not to). Tradition, in one sense, is precisely not to know, for as soon as one has consciously articulated a 'tradition' one is no longer in it in the same way. Modernity, as a condition opposed to tradition, entails the assumption that one can formulate, self-consciously, an identity for oneself. For Eliot, there must be an unconscious (traditional) 'tradition' for the majority and a (self-contradictorily) consciously articulated tradition for the educated and conscious few. In Woolf, the aesthetic, in its fictionalising mode, represents that impulse of modernity towards new identity, control and emancipation. In Eliot, the aesthetic, in its mode of 'situatedness', acts as a brake on these impulses. The impossibility of an epistemological position from outside becomes the justification for resistance to any attempt at social change through rational planning or ideological critique. The position, as we shall see, is a common one in some versions of the postmodern. It is Postmodernism in its neo-conservative mode. It is hardly a radical break.

In *Truth and Method* (1975), Gadamer offered a defence of interpretation intended to affirm why truth cannot be limited to what is confirmable by method. It is essentially a statement of the unavoidable existence of a 'hermeneutic circle' and the notion that, as for Heidegger, prejudice is a condition of consciousness: no method can be foundational because we always understand the world (or a text in it) before we begin to reflect upon it. We always find ourselves situated in an ongoing process where knowledge can never be absolute return or arrival because the object is always expanded by the attempt to know it. Objectivity is always something which cannot be grasped because it arrives too late: in Eliot's words, 'History has many cunning passages, contrived corridors/and issues, deceives with whispering ambitions,/Guides us by vanities . . . We have not reached conclusion . . . (*Gerontion*, 1969, p38). Gadamer's version is this: 'understanding is always a movement in such a circle, for with reason the repeated return from the whole to the parts and vice versa is essential. In addition, this circle continually expands itself in that the concept of the whole is relative and the inclusion in ever larger contexts alters the understanding of single parts' (1975, p167). As in the *Four Quartets*, exile is homecoming for the process involves loss of self and return to an expanded self. Gadamer refers to this possibility of maintaining an openness to what is other than oneself (what Eliot means by impersonality) as a process of 'tact'. It is an *aestheticising* mode, an empathetic awareness based on imaginative projection. It has associations with Kant's notion of 'taste' in that it connects us to each other as human beings. However, for Gadamer, as Eliot, the aesthetic impulse arises much more extensively and inextricably out of (and pervades) the communal life of human beings: an expression of a sensus communis which grounds experience but in an historically changing and non-conceptualisable way. Actual works of art exist always in a context of interpretation which is historical. Authentic encounters with them open out the self to redefinition through an historical otherness which allows one to repossess that self expanded through the incorporation of other ways of seeing and experiencing it. Prejudice becomes a *precondition* of enlightenment, rather than its negation, for only if we are *interested* can our prejudices be challenged. As we are expanded out of them, we come to see in part what they are. Im-mediacy can be achieved only through mediation, one's own self or world only made apparent through experience of another's. Enlightenment as faith in method is seen as the crippling of tradition: not the determination of self by self but the loss of self:

> To come into our very own requires an excursion into the alien that is also a
> return to ourselves because our identity is not a given but a task, not the unity
> of a self-presence but a reunion with the past. When we interpret the artwork,

we interpret ourselves and as the work comes to be interpreted so we come to be also. (Weinsheimer, 1985, p115).

As for Heidegger, knowledge of the world cannot be divorced from being in the world. Neither self nor world can ever be foundationally conceptualised: knowledge and experience, body and mind, are essentially inextricable. We have already seen how such a view has been developed in the postmodern critique of Enlightenment and was implicit in the contradictions of Conrad's *Heart of Darkness*. It is entirely explicit in T. S. Eliot's critical writing though obscured by its historical framing through later theories of autonomy. The 'Tradition' essay appears, for example, in David Lodge's 1972 anthology *Twentieth Century Literary Criticism*, introduced as an early precursor of that 'objective' anti-affective and anti-intentionalist New Critical mode to be developed by Wimsatt and Beardsley and others. Lodge includes it with the essay 'The Function of Criticism' as representative of Eliot as ahistorical, anti-Romantic, supporting an 'autonomy' reading of literature. There are, in fact, strong strains of Romanticism throughout the essay. The incongruous use of scientific images to describe the artistic process, is an attempt to reconcile an imagist sense of closeness to the object with a symbolist sense of art as the expression of an unconscious not so far removed from the Romantic concept of the Imagination. The poet escapes not from personality but deeper into it. The poet's mind is a receptacle for storing up numberless feelings, phrases, images which unite under the unconscious pressure of the artistic process rather than through any willed search for emotions to express. Consciousness is secondary, willed originality simply eccentricity. But, if this presses towards a Romantic orientation, there is also a Classical countermovement. If Pound ordered modernists to make it new, Eliot is suspicious of the new. Just as he criticised Blake for eccentricity, he would later argue: 'I believe it to be a condition of success, that the view of life which (poets) attempt to express in poetry, should be one which is already accepted. I do not think you can make poetry out of ideas when they are too original, or too new . . . For the business of the poet is to express the culture in which he lives, and to which he belongs, not to express aspirations towards one which is not yet incarnate' (Eliot, 1945, p145). Poetry arises out of what is incarnated, individual body and social body. It is nourished by the culture and nourishes it; ideas as disembodied concepts are dangerous because they attempt to step outside. The Tradition essay reveals the roots of Eliot's later cultural conservativism though his concern in it may seem to be more with opposing Romantic egotism and searching for something outside the self which could provide allegiance and anchorage. The unspoken fear is of the political potential of the radical fictionalising mode of the Romantic imagination.

Poetry arises as a fundamentally unconscious incarnation of culture (here tradition). The role in it of conscious shaping or craft is secondary. Poetry is a dialectic of embodied cultural experience and conscious formulation. This is not to say that poetry does not express ideas. But ideas which are not embodied in this way, but are consciously articulated, may produce that argumentative dissent which can challenge cultural authority and tradition. Eliot does not develop these implications in this essay but he lays the seeds for later works such as *Notes towards the Definition of Culture* (1948) which extend the description of ideal poetic practice into a blueprint for an entirely aestheticised culture. A broadly similar dialectic of consciousness and unconsciousness expresses an essentially unchanged political philosophy in these later works. *Notes* is probably best read as a response to the post-war reconstruction programme of the Labour government: to Butler's education reforms and to those in health, welfare, nationalisation of industry. It expresses a fear of centralised state planning as the political arm of a new managerialism harnessing the powerful but fragmenting forces of mass society through a burgeoning instrumental technologism. As in the early essay, the theme of resistance to the will of consciousness is foregrounded: just as a poem cannot be consciously willed into existence so too a culture cannot be planned and rationally engineered. A culture, like a poem, is the incarnation and organic outgrowth of existing traditions, unself-consciously persisting as well as consciously articulated. Just as feeling and emotion never coincide in the creation of a poem, so too, belief and behaviour never entirely merge in a culture. An elite conscious minority must articulate belief, while a passive, unconsciously driven majority enacts cultural tradition through everyday behaviour. Eliot fears uniformity as the spectre haunting mass society. In the early essay, tradition is both a timeless monument and a temporal order which can be revised: it is to offer the security and restraint of a stable order which can contain unbounded individualism but not stifle those necessary (individual) impulses of the imagination without which new cultural artefacts, including poems, cannot be produced. In tradition, intellect and feeling, mind and body, can be reconciled in a resistance to the arid intellectualising modes of rationalist social planning. What functions in the earlier essay as a critique of Romantic expression is transformed in *Notes* into an assault on both socialism and liberalism as philosophies arising out of an Enlightenment belief in rational self-determination. For Eliot, as for writers on the left in the thirties and forties, the progressivist ideals of Enlightenment seemed to have facilitated capitalist instrumental rationality: a mechanisation of the lifeworld which had created a moral and spiritual vacuum which liberalism could not fill. This world was now threatened by those irrationalist forces evident in Fascism. A new paganism might unite belief and behaviour through the technological manipulation of the mob (a fear expressed in *The Idea of a Christian Society*). Eliot offers a return to 'tradition' as the only viable alternative to what he sees as the connected poles of rational social engineering and irrational Fascism. Specifically, of course, it must be a return to Christian tradition.

Even in the 'Tradition' essay, Eliot is struggling to find some foundation for knowledge outside the self which would still allow that self as poet freedom of expression. The essay shifts confusingly from a positivist language of science (which gives it an apparently New Critical orientation) to a hermeneutic vocabulary of consensus which has become familiar to us in the work of Gadamer. It emerges also in the more developed postmodern position of writers like Richard Rorty with the pragmatist concept of truth as whatever a community agrees it should be. At times, particularly in the concept of mind as inert shred of platinum, receptacle for impressions, Eliot seems to be striving towards an idea of impersonality as annihilation of personality. It is the opposite of the Romantic concept of mind as a lamp. Here, poetry is the registration of immediate sensation. It is a version of the Imagist sense of ideas only in things, objects in the world: an attempt to circumvent the theoretical and conceptual abstractions of thought in a 'situatedness' in the object which is later developed as one mode of the postmodern. It is a precarious objectivity, however, for how could such impressions be communicated or object distinguished from subject? It threatens, paradoxically, to collapse into solipsism.

The more developed sense of impersonality, one which enters much of Eliot's critical thinking after this essay, is that which is bound up with the notion of tradition. It is this concept which can be illuminated by the work of Gadamer and his notion of the sensus communis. For Eliot in 1919, however, the notion of tradition as a timeless monument must have seemed rather more secure in its foundationalism than the temporality of a hermeneutic view of tradition. Accordingly, the essay tends to slide from one definition to another (much as the later essay on culture will conflate the concept of Culture as High art with its anthropological sense as the way of life of a community of people). Once Eliot has entirely abandoned a mirror concept of truth, what is central to his work is the notion of tradition conceived of as an ongoing fusion of the horizons of past and present in a continuous 'living' reconstruction of the past, expanding our identity in the present, but in a way which cannot be known in the terms of a definitive rationalism. Meaning in the world is always a function of situatedness in a common tradition, though what is common is constantly being modified through our present immersion in that tradition. Gadamer's concern with 'situatedness' is virtually indistinguishable from Eliot's concept of 'tradition' and this consideration of Eliot through hermeneutic theory reveals again a continuous development from Modernism to Postmodernism (and, indeed, as I have already argued, of Romanticism too). Granted that each represents different moments in an ongoing aesthetic critique of Enlightenment, can one argue that the postmodern position is distinctively different? If the 'post' phenomenon is basically a manifestation of a general refusal to accept the possibility of any theory claiming a vantage point of truth or knowledge outside of culture (and hence a shift to the idea of local knowledges, language games, specific intellectuals, interpretative communities), then the roots of that 'post' would seem to be in Modernism itself and not in something which comes after it. Yet Lyotard for one has defined Modernism as the articulation of a belief in grand narratives arising out of the conviction that rational procedures can establish foundational truth. Rorty has seen Postmodernism as fully acknowledging a pragmatist recognition that truth is consensually constructed and cannot 'reflect' a deep structure of world for which Modernism still nostalgically longs. We need finally to look more closely at these arguments and in particular the way in which they raise issues about the relation of ethics and aesthetics. Again I will offer a reading of a key modernist work – Joyce's *Ulysses* – as a way of addressing this: a final demonstration of how one might 'work with' Postmodernism.

ETHICS
AND THE POSTMODERNITY
OF PARODY

Reading James Joyce's Ulysses

Joyce built his city of words, *Ulysses* (1922), to be a world of the imagination so exact in its extratextual reference that he claimed it could serve as a map of the real city of Dublin. Edmund Wilson (1931) found the experience of reading it akin to that of entering a city existing in real space and time: the fictional 'as if' taking on what Henry James had referred to as the 'solidity of specification' in monumental fashion. The idea of a city of words, or of the world as a book written by a Divine Author, has a long history with which Joyce was entirely familiar. More recently, Wittgenstein has likened the entire language system itself to a city. If Wilson's comment confers upon the verbal sign qualities associated with the quiddity of the phenomenal, Wittgenstein extends this:

> Our language can be seen as an ancient city: a maze of little streets and squares, of old and new houses, and of houses with additions from various periods; and this surrounded by a multitude of new boroughs with straight regular streets and uniform houses (Wittgenstein, 1978, p8).

Wittgenstein's description is taken up as a central image in Lyotard's *The Postmodern Condition* as the impetus for the idea that modernity can no longer be understood through master narratives but must be seen as a proliferation of local and agonistic language games which conform to no single overarching set of rules. Lyotard suggests that as Enlightenment metanarratives become obsolete, those institutions founded upon them, such as the university or metaphysical philosophy, similarly find themselves in a crisis of legitimation. In such a world, language becomes unstable, people find themselves at the intersection of many agonistic discourses whose truth effects are specific to their own different sets of rules and which collide in ever shifting and heterogeneous combinations. As the distinction between critical and functional knowledge breaks down, the criteria for value shift from indicators of truth to those of performance.

Ulysses certainly appears 'postmodern' in these terms for it presents itself as a vast concert hall staging, from its profane theatrical opening to Molly's last histrionic imaginative simulation of High Romance, an opera comique of contestatory generic and rhetorical performances. If Joyce is the impresario, Dublin, in its linguistic guises, provides the material for the score: political, journalistic, medical, ecclesiastical, literary, scientific, philosophical, proverbial to pubtalk itself. Molly is a singer, Bloom an 'ad. man' and Stephen a would-be writer and literary critic. In such a world, as Lyotard later recognises, to exist is to perform in a network of colliding and intersecting 'little narratives': dramatic games with language. If for Lyotard, however, the self is little more than a point of intersection of numerous language games, for Joyce, this sense of modernity can be reconciled, as we shall see, with a more substantive and less unstable sense of personal identity.

Wittgenstein's image actually invokes the idea of a *palimpsest* as much as a network, suggesting diachronic depth and historical anchorage as much as synchronic surface and kaleidoscopic theatrical performances. The regular streets of rationalised modern urban planning are superimposed upon an ancient labyrinthine structure, glimpsed through the new uniform houses. It is a recurrent image in modernist writing. It appears literally in E. M. Forster's *A Passage to India* where the sensibly planned civil station rests on the low indestructible moving mud which is the ancient Ganges and below the overarching sky which 'settles everything' (1947, p11). Joyce's Dublin also invokes an ancient, mythic, as well as modern labyrinth, but always a self-consciously verbal one. The only exit points will be through a craft of fabulous artifice involving words. Inhabiting it are characters like Gerty McDowell who will never find their way out. Gerty exists entirely and unself-consciously within a language game over which she has little control. She is unaware of her reproduction through Joyce's parody of the popular women's literature of her day, comically and pathetically perceiving the masturbating Bloom in the terms of sentimentally domesticated Romance as 'a steadfast, a sterling man, a man of inflexible honour to his fingertips' (1986, p299). Indeed, she is unable to experience even the most basic desires of the body except in the euphemistic maudlin sentimentality of the Lady's Pictorial. But, even for Gerty, implication in one language game releases her from another. If the Lady's Pictorial conceals the truth of the body, at least it gives Gerty some access to aspects of bodily experience which the discourses of popular Catholicism may have denied her altogether.

Other inhabitants of this verbal labyrinth include Stephen and Bloom, who are given a much greater capacity for self-conscious manipulation of language games. Indeed, both characters create new linguistic combinations in order to reconstruct fundamental emotional responses. The chapter mentioned above ends with the evocation of bird sound 'Cuckoo/cuckoo/cuckoo': a displacement of language which allows Bloom also to conceal from and reveal to himself his 'construction' (as cuckold) within the language game of middle class respectable Dublin. Later, he finds greater peace in an emotional accommodation to his circumstances through an ability to switch linguistic register and control the language game for his own effective ends. Returning to the marital bed after Boylan's visit, he reconstitutes himself as an insignificant speck through the impersonal vastness of the Ithacan scientific speculation on the cycles of the universe: 'To reflect that each one who enters imagines himself to be the first to enter whereas he is always the last term of a preceding series even if the first term of a succeeding one, each imagining himself to be the first, last, only and alone whereas he is neither first nor last nor only nor alone in a series originating in and repeated to infinity' (p601). Who has not discursively impersonalised an unbearable personal situation through similar linguistic displacement? Bloom shows how some measure of autonomy may be achieved even in a world which is, literally and metaphorically, a tissue of allusions, parodies, popular songs, legal, medical, scientific, journalistic, literary, philosophical and proverbial discourses. By examining Joyce's presentation of his characters' linguistic manipulations, we may discover our own possibility of freedom in a world where, we are told, Enlightenment emancipatory discourses have further broken down and context-specific rhetorical performance has displaced altogether universal ethical foundation.

A metropolis which is a network of proliferating and intersecting language games would seem, necessarily, to produce or rest upon multiple value systems. The problem of moral evaluation becomes acute. How can one talk of justice if one cannot talk of truth? If truth is an effect of successful rhetorical performance, history a respository of available styles, is 'universal' ethics simply a rationalisation of desire, of a will to power? Lyotard's recent work has been much concerned with these issues. Since *Au Juste* (1985), he has consistently argued that we must give up the search for universal foundations of justice in a world of incommensurable language games. Ethical decisions will always be context-specific; what is 'just' within the terms of one language game may be the worst sort of injustice within the terms of another:

> Yes, there is first a multiplicity of justices, each one of them defined in relation to the rules specific to each game. These rules prescribe what must be done. . . . Justice here does not consist merely in the observance of the rules; as in all the games, it consists in working at the limits of what the rules permit, in order to invent new moves, perhaps new rules and therefore new games (1985, p100).

Joyce's city is full of characters unilaterally attempting to fix the rules for all through the attempted universalisation of specific language games. Such attempts are consistently viewed in a negative light, from Mr. Deasey's construction of political history to the sentimental and violent jingoism parodied in the Cyclops chapter. Even when a more positive code of value strives for universal legitimacy, it tends to be recontextualised in more equivocal terms. So Bloom resists political violence, for though he recognises his own racial victimisation, he rejects 'force, hatred, history and all that', declaring it is the opposite of life: 'Love . . . I mean the opposite of hatred' (p273). Later, however, he copes with the pain of Boylan by deciding that 'love' like 'hate' is just a word. Even if Joyce's perspectivism entails a context-specific ethics (and I will argue that it does not entirely), however, one sees the inadequacy of the metaphor of 'rhetorical performance' to describe it. Even the most artificial 'rhetorical performance' in *Ulysses* is not delivered in cold blood. If existence *is* theatre, in Lyotard's sense, then behind the 'wind and piss' of the worst bigot lie powerful human emotions which, culturally constructed or otherwise, are still experienced as 'truths' of a kind. Simply to rewrite the rules of a language game will not displace the emotions invested in existing ones. It seems to me that Joyce's text, more than Lyotard's account, probes the complex psychological investments which people have in 'grand narratives' of whatever kind. Bloom may theoretically relativise 'love' as a language game, but if he still invests in it psychologically, then to all intents and purposes, it continues to exist. If people continue to invest in any 'grand narrative', fictional or otherwise, such a narrative can be said to exist. In all human cultures, feeling is bound up with personal, artistic and political history which, if ever hermeneutically shifting and overlaid with new language games, provides depth of a sort. Joyce is perhaps closer than Lyotard to the full implications of Wittgenstein's image. Even in mechanistic, mercantile or colonised cultures, human beings are not so easily converted into automatons occupying an arterial surface of impersonal communication systems.

Not only does Joyce's universe show that rhetoric is not necessarily inconsistent with depth, even more than this, he reveals how grand narratives are modified rather than entirely displaced by the proliferation of little ones. There is no key to all mythologies in *Ulysses*, but there is a recognition of the way in which myths survive and inform our behaviour even as we believe we have divested ourselves of them. In recognising this, we may begin to unlock areas of human experience which seem resistant to reformulation through a new 'language game'. Throughout the novel, though, we should remember that there is no stable 'master' key. Like those of Stephen and Bloom, keys are always subject to loss, dispossession, lack of fit, commercial appropriation, displacement: their usefulness may be no more than provisional. There is an overarching code in the novel: the invocation of heroic values in the use of Homeric myth. It does inform human behaviour, as we shall see. But it has little stabilising effect on the protean flux of the novel in its phenomenologically realised temporarily. It does, however, provide us with another way of approaching the problem of establishing ethical value in a linguistically perspectival world. With this in mind, first let us look at the shifts.

Everything in the novel appears protean. The reader is continuously and immanently situated in an ever moving vantage point in relation to events which acquire new shapes through the language which constructs them. He or she is deprived of those basic rules of perspective laid down in the fifteenth century by Alberti and Brunelleschi, rules which established the premises of Cartesian dualism and the consensus aesthetics of the omnisciently narrated realist novel. The effect gathers force as we move further into the novel. Until the Hades chapter there is a reasonably stable narrative alternation of interior monologue interspersed with covert narration which often takes on the vocabulary and syntax of the idiolect of each character. After Hades, however, there is no clearly discernible external stable narrative perspective. If Postmodernism is, indeed, the rejection of the possibility of a view from outside then, in this sense alone, the novel would appear to be postmodern. However, if Joyce creates a perspectival Einsteinian world, I believe that he also shows how one might preserve some ethical generality and consistency in the midst of epistemological relativism. He suggests ways in which one might respond to Lyotard. Instead of abandoning grand narratives, we need to recognise our embeddedness in a culture which they have helped to shape. Instead of imagining that we can simply manipulate our own language games, or believe that we have entirely fragmented into the rules of the various contexts in which we find ourselves, we can learn to recognise ways in which we have continuous identity within a culture which, though it shapes us, does not leave us simply at the mercy of its diverse codes. In my view, ever postmodern before his time, Joyce achieves this through recognition of the ethical potential in an aesthetic mode: parody. Before we examine how he achieves this effect, we must look at the most obvious 'Master Narrative' in the novel: the heroic Homeric frame.

This is not to deny that Joyce also enjoys 'just gaming' himself. The Homeric myth, on one level, is simply an ironic literary equivalent of the dream of a scientific unified field theory: a fantasy of total correspondence in a world where, if the technician and the scientist play God, then the artist too must be allowed divinity. If the tiny, moving points of Stephen, Bloom and Molly appear to correspond in any way to the vast and unchanging figures of Telemachus, Odysseus and Penelope, then we are never allowed to forget that this correspondence is simply a metaphor, an arbitrary projection of mind upon random experience. Such self-conscious theatricality, however, preserves the opacity of character. In flaunting his artifice, Joyce refuses to ingest others entirely into his own order and similarly ensures that he is not ingested himself. The myth is not imposed as a straitjacket. Its ironic and parodic use recognises the possibility of creative deformation as an acknowledgement of pre-given orders existing in historical traditions which have shaped the present, but an acknowledgement which also facilitates their repossession for oneself in one's own terms. The new freedom is not purchased at the expense of another's annihilation or the denial of one's own cultural situatedness. The parody of grand narratives becomes a way of acknowledging cultural implication without being ingested by culture. In *Ulysses*, it becomes a means of emotional accommodation, allowing characters to wrest some sort of freedom without denying or consuming the other. For Stephen, for example, it facilitates a mode of heresy which allows him to recognise and acknowledge the way in which his identity has been constructed through an orthodoxy which he cannot simply transcend, because to do so would be to deny his own flesh in all senses of the word. His aesthetic mode of displacement is not the cold-blooded mockery of a Buck Mulligan but a mode which offers a dialectic of involvement and distance which has positive moral implications.

The mythic frame can be read as ironic, parodic or mock-heroic: a substitute for that metaphysical ground which once supported the notion of a teleologically plotted world presided over by a Providential form. Joyce uses it both to demonstrate the importance of fictional projection in a world which has lost such ground, but also to show that it has not been entirely lost. If we no longer inhabit an heroic world as a coherent social formation, we still make investments in structures which have arisen out of that world and thus profoundly inform our own. Joyce chose *this* myth rather than any other for particular reasons. The choice was not arbitrary because Joyce is doing more than flexing his artistic impressario's muscle. The Odyssey is the least violent of Greek heroic myths: the most concerned with intimate filial relationships and friendship, a narrative which explores homecoming as continuity but also as new ways of seeing and connecting. The only overtly violent deed committed by its hero – the slaying of the suitors – significantly disappears in Joyce's text. Bloom modernises the text by acknowledging the emotional force of love and hate, but also coming to recognise that they are provisional language games. He manages to believe and not to believe. For this, he suffers the ignominy of the biscuit tin and Molly's tendency to see him as weak and masochistic. But, in the civic as the domestic space, his capacity to believe in a state which he also represents in inverted commas actually facilitates the positive opening up of definitions of institutions in the world: marriage and citizenship. Each are seen as conditions which should involve attitudes of tolerance and acceptance of the other rather than his or her annihilation through projected fear or exclusive possession. Joyce wrote that he intended Bloom to be seen as a good man not a weak or masochistic one. In connecting him to Odysseus, Joyce shows that the pain of jealousy may persist in unaltered form through ancient to modern worlds. The proliferation of language games does not alter the pain. However, whereas Odysseus could only respond to it within his culture's code of honour with bloody revenge, Bloom can sift through the language games available to him and produce new combinations, exercise his powers of linguistic displacement. His heroism lies in the self-control and imagination required in such aesthetic reshaping of attitudes. The aesthetic has ethical implications. Fictions produce change in the world: in institutions, relationships, feelings. In this sense, as Joyce saw, it becomes truth. If this is 'postmodern', then Joyce is.

Ulysses leads us to question whether an heroic concept of 'virtue' cannot be reformulated to provide an ethical basis for the good life in that it may facilitate recognition of elements of human emotional need ignored in Enlightenment definitions of justice. Kantian universalism cannot accommodate variations in context, the specificity of culture, pressures of race, class, gender, or emotional investments which cannot simply be rationalised away. As much as that earlier epic, *Paradise Lost*, *Ulysses* uses its heroic framework self-consciously to explore the issue of ethical value for its own (and our) time. Its modernity lies in its recognition that although moral significance can no longer be revealed, it may, indeed, be positively renegotiated. Bloom refuses to slay the suitors or respond with one eye for one eye to the citizen. Stephen refuses to pray at his mother's bedside but learns through his own bodily response that he must temper his egotistic desire for freedom by extending his artistic negative capability. Molly begins to renegotiate the traditional script of virtuous wife through a reformulated demotic version of the language of courtly love. Each character explores new possibilities of friendship and filial relationship. If there is no longer a self-evident metanarrative to ground ethical value, we must refashion the materials given to us in the world: as Joyce must parodically reshape its aesthetic languages. Nourishment through food, care, shelter, friendship and imaginative play are shown to be perennial human needs, but in seeking to satisfy them we may encounter jealousy, remorse, fear, racism and violence: particularly in a world politically structured through the stimulation of consumerist desire and the cannibalism of Imperialist force. The way in which we seek to fulfil those needs will be shaped by our cultural circumstances, but this does not mean we are at their mercy: even in the postmodern condition. Values mean nothing until they are situated in specific contexts. Bloom's own heroic disinterestedness can be read within the terms of a different language game as an extension of a pathological desire for emotional gratification without the immersion and messy negotiation of intimate human relationship. His voyeuristic activities maintain a sexual distance which is present to some extent in his relations with Molly and with all women. His introduction of Stephen into 7 Eccles Street, may be a way of completing a tragically and prematurely severed Oedipal triangle (after the death of Rudy), but may also be another means of continuing to avoid sexual intimacy with a wife who is terrifyingly Calypso, Gaea, Tellus and Penelope in one. After all, it is not an uncommon male fantasy.

Human desire, like human language, is never whole and never pure. As with sex, so with food. Bloom's kidney is hardly the sole disconnected organ in the novel. Lips, fingers, stomachs, sexual organs, noses, press, seemingly autonomously, for satisfaction. The body does not submit as unified entity to systems of moral codification. Lestrygonians, a chapter specifically about hunger and the consumption of food, introduces the concept of parallax (the apparent change in the position of an object resulting from a change in the position from which it is viewed). It is the basic formal principle of the novel. As ever, there are ethical implications. Food is represented here as both a source of life and pleasure, a vital requirement of the body associated with the conviviality of the city and the care of the family, but also and equally as a source of greed; painful nostalgia for Bloom (where the experience of taste reminds him of past sensuous enjoyments with Molly); disgust (phlegm-like oysters feeding on filth, dogs lapping up their vomit); power: the desire to consume another. Joyce, the fabulous artificer, weaves his patterns of correspondence (consumption, commerce, ingestion, greed, nutrition, desire, biology) in an arbitrary demonstration of his talents as impressario. But the Homeric parallel also allows him to transport the heroic values to the rhetorically excessive world of petit-bourgeois Dublin. It allows him to explore ways in which an ethical framework might be formulated for a self-reflexive modern world of disembedded and proliferating styles of existence. If the ultimate 'good' of this world remains unclear, it is manifestly peopled by characters seeking the embeddedness of shared community and human relationship as well as imaginative freedom and personal autonomy. The achievement will require varieties of conversation and negotiation. *Serious* games with language.

How does Joyce present the possibility of avoiding moral solipsism or unthinking emotivism in a world in which epistemological certainty seems impossible? Throughout the novel, Stephen reflects upon the instability of this world. Allusions which produce a sense of its material fixity: 'knocking his sconce against' it (p31), are set against those which suggest a radical Nietzschean perspectivism. Indeed, in reading Joyce through Postmodernism, the Nietzschean may seem to be the only viable ethical, as well as epistemological, mode. Here is Nietzsche's famous declaration of his notion of truth:

> A mobile army of metaphors, metonymies, anthropomorphisms: in short a sum of human relations which have been poetically and rhetorically intensified, transposed, adorned, and after long usage seem to a nation fixed, canonical, and binding; truths are illusions of which one has forgotten that this is what they are; metaphors which have become worn out and have lost their sensual power (1979, p184).

Nietzsche praised art not because of its capacity to give us insight into reality, but because it flaunts itself explicitly as a realm of illusion. It reveals that 'truth' has nothing to do with the chaos which is world but everything to do with the aestheticising impulses of the human mind. This may seem entirely compatible with the aesthetic self-consciousness of *Ulysses*. Its implication though, is that morality is only ever the imposition on us of another's contingent and aesthetically produced order. If, for Kant, morality was categorical, for Nietzsche it is *always* hypothetical: the good is simply another private possession. 'Good is no longer good when your neighbour takes it into his mouth. And how could there exist a "common good"! The expression is a self-contradiction: what can be common has ever but little value' (1973, p53).

Unlike Bloom, Nietzsche would clearly not have shared Molly with Boylan. But Joyce does not reject all possibility of 'common good'. He sees that a notion of becoming oneself which makes no provision for one's relations with and obligations to others can only be a recipe for self-destruction. The world is not simply one's interpretation of it. One lives its materiality all the time in the very real limits of the physical and social body through which every individual has to negotiate his or her identity. The only Overmen in this world are fascistic fantasists like the Citizen who are blinded by their own myths.

Stephen is ever conscious that the 'cords of all link back, strandentwining cable of all flesh', just as *Ulysses* itself is the great twentieth-century epic of the body: of its sensuous pleasures, its frustrations, its ingesting, excreting, coupling, sweating, tensing, resting and dying. The city is itself a body, of that earth which Joyce recognised as pre-human. Mind recycles human civilisation as it floats over the world's body but mind is also a product of body and cannot systematise its own source through any one explanatory system. Myth has become ironic. For Nietzsche, heroic Greek culture was ideal precisely because it was unified by an overarching narrative which gave purpose and public cohesion. The embodied mode of myth allowed an immediacy of experience and connection of subject and object which he saw fragmented in the modern world. Without such foundation in myth, he believed that modern man grubs about for roots, desperately turning to the abstractions of scientific knowledge for a nourishment it cannot find, for 'what does our great historical hunger signify, our clutching about us of countless other cultures, our consuming desire for knowledge, if not the loss of myth, of a mythic home, the mythic womb? Let us ask ourselves whether the feverish and frightening agitation is anything but the greedy seizing and snatching at food of a hungry man' (Nietzsche, 1956, p137). Bloom fries his kidney and draws into his body the various noonreeks of Dublin, hot mockturtle vapour and jam rolypoly. Stephen ingests words, but his emotions too insistently force into his mind images of the all-wombing tomb. Each seeks a lost immediacy of experience tied to the expression of social purpose. They seek each other and find each other because human necessity requires it and mythic form facilitates it. Even irony cannot entirely displace need.

Nietzsche came to argue that if modern culture lacked a mythic ground then a myth must be created. Joyce saw the extreme political dangers lurking in such a view. Few of us would want to inhabit a materialised world of the citizen's imagination. But Joyce also recognised that even in the impersonal world of the modern city our language games are, as often as not, fragments of earlier myths. We do not simply leave them behind and if we attempt an intellectual break, our physical bodies, shaped by such fragments, may begin to protest. Grand narratives are ways of formulating fundamental human needs and their 'grandness' is a measure of the urgency and intensity of the need. They are unlikely simply to die, though they may be profoundly transformed. If this seems to limit our power to fabricate entirely new identities for ourselves, it provides an anchorage in community which the concept of 'language games' severely challenges. Because we are modern, we do not unself-consciously inhabit one myth, but we may self-consciously manipulate the fragments of a diverse range of them: heroic Greece, Medieval scholasticism, Enlightenment reason, Celtic Twilight. Even in a colonised culture where myth has been imposed with violence and has produced an equally distorting nationalistic countermythology perpetuating rigid notions of insider and outsider, to be modern is to recognise the possibility of choosing other myths or of creatively reformulating those myths which anchor one to the world in ways which produce frustration or oppression. To be free of the narratives of the past is to acknowledge their persistence in the present and to begin to reformulate their terms. Stephen is able to meet Bloom because Joyce's ironic use of myth allows for the coincidences which lead them to each other. Eliot, of course, partially recognised what Joyce was doing in his 1923 review, noting that the narrative method may have suited an 'age which had not sufficiently lost all form to feel the need for something stricter'. He argued that only the mythic method could control and 'give shape and a significance to the universal panorama of futility and anarchy which is contemporary history' (1975, p177). *Ulysses* is also, however, a self-conscious examination of the ethical implications of the loss of the grand narratives of history. Myth is not presented simply as an arbitrary and ironic imposition of an author playing God, but as a viable and inescapable narrative mode existing in the world.

In his discussion of the postmodern condition, Lyotard assumes the demise of customary knowledge and the narrative forms which accompany it. Joyce shows the continuing deep embeddedness in culture and in our very bodies of such forms. Lyotard himself admits that 'no self is an island', but he expresses self as 'a post through which various kinds of message pass' and over which we exercise only rhetorical power. Lyotard uses the language of speech act theory and produces an image of life as rhetorical performance. He does this to make the point that we can no longer look to the grand narratives of the past whose form provided the foundation both for customary and Enlightenment knowledge. We should accept the redundancy of these narratives and look to the new possibilities of a technological age for narrative disruption. In the skirmishes of many competing language games lie any opportunities remaining to us to construct identities for ourselves. We cannot make the fragments cohere in terms of correspondence to an underlying narrative, but if we accept this, we may achieve a shifting and provisional autonomy in each of the various incommensurable contexts which make up our lives. We must accept that justice is now dependent on dissensus alone. Let us now see how Joyce combines a similar epistemological scepticism with a much less relativistic notion of ethics.

In invoking the concept of justice, Lyotard uses a term much favoured by the Enlightenment he sees as exhausted. A more ancient way of formulating the problem might be to ask about the possibilities of the *good life* in such a world. Lyotard might talk of the forms of justice, but in remaining silent about its substantive ends, its content, he reproduces a familiar absence within the discourses of modernity. The response of some philosophers involved in discussions of postmodernity has been to argue that in a world of moral incommensurables, the only way to retain a coherent ethical system (without resorting to the anarchy of emotivism or outworn rhetorical postures of universalism) is to return with a more open mind to a pre-modern, specifically Aristotelian, notion of virtue. If modernity offers us a new freedom to manipulate the world and to create new identity scripts, this freedom may be exercised through a subjective colonisation of the world which involves an egotistical manipulation of it. A reinvigorated sense of a situation in a tradition of ongoing practices may temper the heady Nietzscheanism implicit in this possibility. It offers the creative tension of shaping the new through a reformulation of the old. (The project is most closely associated with the work of Alisdair MacIntyre.) In such a world, we will not find absolute anchorage, but neither will we float dangerously adrift. For Aristotle, a virtue was a disposition to act in a particular way which contributes to some ideal of the good life both for the individual concerned and his or her society. What this consists in need not be absolutely specifiable as a conceptual goal and indeed cannot be discovered through the application of rigid pre-existing formulae. Such a concept of the ethical life is broadly compatible with the two modes of Postmodernism I have outlined in this book: the aestheticising mode of radical fictionality or the search for a new immanence or 'embeddedness' in some version of 'situatedness'. For Aristotle, the ethic of virtue was addressed to the citizen and identity assumed to arise out of the political and cultural activities involved in membership of the community of a city state. There was no space in it for choice, for identity was conceived as the fulfilment of one's place in a social order (and not to have a place was to be less than human). Modern identity concepts involve notions of self-fulfilment as matters of free choice but, as we have seen with Woolf and Eliot, that freedom is always constrained by obligations to others which may well involve a sense of 'virtue' in this more traditional sense. Such commitments are bound very often to complex emotional attachments which cannot simply be thrown off (Mrs. Ramsay's emotional investment in being a 'good' wife and mother). This recognition hovers somewhere behind all Postmodern accounts of failure of Enlightenment.

It seems to me that a consideration of *Ulysses* may throw light on some of these dilemmas. Joyce's commitment to art is also a commitment to an image of the good life as one lived through a self-consciously held belief that to be fully human is to exist in the world through a strenuous effort to imagine the situation of others. This involves the recognition that personal freedom from cultural constraint is always a reformulation of particular narratives of that culture in a way which does not annihilate the narratives of others who share it or are excluded from it, nor does it necessitate the total withdrawal of complete social alienation. If MacIntyre rescues us from fragmentation, he threatens to plunge us back into oppressive restraint. Joyce recognises the potential of the aesthetic to negotiate a position between these two poles. He is not usually read in these terms, however, for he tends to be identified with Stephen Dedalus's comments at the end of *A Portrait*: 'I will tell you what I will do and what I will not do. I will not serve that in which I no longer believe whether it call itself my home, my fatherland or my church; and I will try to express myself in some mode of life or art as freely as I can, using for my defence the only arms I allow myself to use – silence, exile, cunning' (1960, p247). Joyce's own mode was one of exile, cunning and silence. Despite his support for Irish independence, he would not use his art to propagandise for any political cause. He chose to leave Ireland and renounce Catholicism and to write in a mode of ironic indirection (but thereby find directions out). In a lecture delivered in Trieste in 1907 he summed up his culture as one where 'individual initiative is paralysed by the influence and admonitions of the church, while its body is menaced by the police, the tax office and the garrison (Ellmann, 1983, p258).

Dublin is seen to be paralysed by church, colonialism and petit-bourgeois greed. In early essays like 'The Day of the Rabblement' too, Joyce argued for the need of the artist to withdraw into imaginative autonomy (Ellmann, pp88–90). The destiny of Stephen, we are told in *A Portrait*, is to 'be elusive of social or religious orders – he was destined to learn his own wisdom apart from others, or learn the wisdom of others himself wandering among the snares of the world' (p162). Joyce too fashioned a new identity free of Ireland, even signing his letters 'Stephen Dedalus'. But he recognised that one cannot simply fly the nets of one's culture. *Ulysses* is a linguistic world in which he explores the sense that a dialectic of radical fictionality *and* situatedness is a necessary prerequisite for self-fulfilment within a 'virtuous' notion of the 'good life'. *Ulysses* is a city of words, but it is not an 'autonomous' artefact. Its very aesthetic processes are bound into an exploration of ethical values. Stephen wishes to fly tradition in the form in which he has received it. I believe Joyce developed a more complex relationship to tradition. For in the modern impersonal world of commodified commercial relations and scientific values, cultural tradition may, in modified form, provide some sense of that embeddedness whose more complete disappearance produces the Angst and anomie of developed capitalist societies. Joyce's Dublin is not an advanced capitalist society, but there is more than a hint that the commercially stunting effect of colonisation may have emotional benefits as well as producing emotional casualties.

It is possible that we can derive insights into the problems of our own later modern condition from Joyce's representation of an earlier one. This Dublin is closer than most later modern cities to Aristotle's polis. It has not witnessed the same intense separation of the public and the private which characterises advanced liberal democracies. This separation can often disguise the perpetuation of a double standard of ethics where, for example, women may be publically included in the rhetoric of Enlightenment morality but find themselves in 'private' domestic roles which tie them invisibly to fixed pre-modern concepts of virtue. This is not to say, however, that Molly or any of the other women characters in the novel have the freedom of the city. Unlike the men, none of them enter its political and literary debates or wander its streets and visit its public houses, libraries, hospitals, newspaper offices and other civic spaces. If cultural embeddedness is in some way desirable to those inhabiting the impersonal structures of the modern capitalist state, as Joyce well knew, embeddedness without choice is likely to produce quite other desires. Molly may not freely wander the streets like Bloom, but, from her domestic bed, she wanders through the exotic locations of numerous (imaginary?) amours and breaks out of her embeddedness as wife in at least one physical realisation in the world which perhaps even more than her career as a singer involves a considerable renegotiation of the traditional script of virtuous wife. Molly flouts her embedded condition by flaunting her bed. In a limited fashion, though, even she realises a new identity script through a reformulation of the limits of her condition. She does not fully disembed herself (and the obvious failure of the naive sexual liberationism of the sixties suggests very good reasons why a less radical gesture might be more preferable). She cannot fully disembed herself because she is bound in by real emotional ties arising out of that very condition (affection for Poldy). Like Nietzsche's yes-sayer, and without the destruction, however, she does affirm life and modify a customary identity script (marriage) to confirm the human need for both intimate connection and personal autonomy, the freedom of fictionality and the attachment of situatedness.

Molly goes some way towards making public her private space (and gossip supplies whatever her narrative fails to account for). But in the life of the Dublin streets, as well as in its private spaces, there exist modes of relationship where identity is negotiated through face to face conversation. Negotiation suggests modernity, but the conflation of public and private suggests that Dublin is not fully modern. It is true that conversation often amounts to no more than exclusionary gossip: speculation on Bloom's ethnic origins or Molly's (easy) 'virtues'; the violent non-negotiable rhetoric of the citizen. Much, however, is about cementing relations which arise out of a more positive sense of cultural community. As we have seen, values always point both ways: the violence of the citizen (an utter debasement of the traditional virtues of the hero) is based on a nationalism where the emotions connected with the desire to belong, to feel cared for, nurtured, which arise for all of us in the context of affective familial ties, are reduced to 'one-eyed' and monologic racism where power, fear and exclusion have entirely displaced altruistic sentiments.

Joyce produces the effect of world as a texture of lived possibilities in which we are involved in ongoing action and world as our imaginative capacity to reshape that condition of situatedness in the spheres of personal relationships, politics, ethics, as well as High Art. Existence is a continuous process of renegotiation involving creative freedom but also recognition of limitation. First are the physical boundaries of the body itself: Joyce described the novel as 'the cycle of the human body' (1966, pp146–7). These limitations introduce Bloom relishing the anticipated breakfast kidney. In a different way, they introduce Stephen, subject to the mocking Mulligan's liturgical parody on the first page of the novel and immersed in the problems of Aristotelian materialism at the beginning of the third chapter. Though less direct, these too are indications of a physical situatedness which provides the boundaries of the embodied self. Mulligan's incantatory 'Introibo ad altare Dei' serves only as a reminder that even if Stephen has refused to pray for his mother, he still has the 'cursed Jesuit strain' in him 'only it's injected the wrong way' (p7). Even the image of the shaving bowl is bound emotionally with the guilty sense of her last moments. He may use artistic licence to transpose the image into the Swinburnean terms of sea as 'great sweet mother' or muse poetically upon the whitening mirror of water, but he knows that he is 'a horrible example of free thought' and one who serves two masters: the Imperial British state and the 'holy Roman catholic and apostolic church' (p17). A self cannot be a free thinking intellect shaping itself at will, because self is also a driven body, instinctually shaped by the parameters of the soil in which it has grown. If Stephen feels he has acted ethically in accordance with a rationalist Enlightenment sense of moral self-determination, his bodily emotional protest registers the extent to which Enlightenment which ignores the demands of custom as it enters into the very formulation of that self and its emotional bonds with others will fail to nourish. Stephen is haunted throughout by the image of the 'allwombing tomb'. He muses on the possibility of procreation without sexual contact and involving an absence of maternity. He develops a reading of Shakespeare's genius as a product of his betrayal by Ann Hathaway. Hydrophobic and refusing to wash himself in either the bowl of water or the great sweet mother of the sea, he is hardly a good Kantian subject. Wherever he turns it is to face an anxiety of influence which is more than simply literary.

Even in the earlier novel (which might appear to be a less equivocal exposition of the possibility and desirability of flying, skylark fashion the nets of culture), Cranly tells Stephen that his mind is 'supersaturated' with the religion in which he says he disbelieves (p240). Allusion and intermittent pastiche reveal the extent to which Stephen's mind is structured through the languages of a cultural tradition: the aesthetics of Newman and Pater, English Romanticism, Shakespeare, Dante. Yet he continues to search for the immediate presence of 'voice' as the articulation of his unique being. The paradox he discovers is that his chosen aesthetic of impersonality, a reconciliation of classicism and Romanticism engineered to give him psychological distance from a world he finds oppressive and ugly, alienates him even more. In its terms, he can only voice who he is through a language already voiced by others, already, therefore, contaminated by world. Discovering his vocation, 'his throat ached with a desire to cry aloud, the cry of a hawk or eagle on high . . . not the dull gross voice of the world of duties and despair. . . . An instant of wild delight had delivered him and the cry of triumph which his lips withheld cleft his brain' (pp169–70). But the newly born can only be delivered into a linguistic world through which it must learn its voice. The very first sentence of the novel is that 'Once upon a time' which introduces all of us to the stories, the narratives, grand and little, which will continue to shape our identities in the world.

Stephen's refusal to accept cultural embeddedness is presented ironically by Joyce, but in a manner which allows him to discover an aesthetic resolution of the problem. The mode discovered becomes the aesthetic foundation for the Ulyssean ethics of imaginative tolerance. As we have seen, *Ulysses* opens with an act which simultaneously conveys a cluster of 'structures of feeling' which determine the form and themes of the novel. These are: exile, heresy, parody, parallax, inversion. What is common to these concepts and forms is that each recognises the existence of a current implication in a given system which cannot be denied utterly but which can be reformulated, creatively deformed, dissolved into elements which can be recombined into a new vocabulary. This cluster of activities allows Joyce to represent modernity as a proliferation of mutually contradictory language games but, as in Wittgenstein's city, ancient grand narratives still provide some anchorage in a world of modern technological rhetorics. Joyce produces a dialectic of fictionality and situatedness which offers a genuinely ethically motivated aestheticism.

Yet Joyce has also been assimilated to theories of aesthetic autonomy which close off consideration of the ethical implications of his technical virtuosity. It is not difficult to see why this should be the case: *Ulysses* is a highly self-reflexive text, conscious of itself as a city of words. Stephen Dedalus himself tends to perceive the world as a network of texts. He wanders along the beach at Sandymount Strand thinking 'See now. There all the time without you, and ever shall be, world without end' (p31). No amen though and no you without tome as well as time. Almost everything that enters Stephen's consciousness is mediated through a pre-existent literary or scholastic discourse. What Stephen sees on the beach is a semiotic problem: 'These heavy sands are language tide and wind have silted here' (p37). He knows that the ground of his identity is not simply the earth upon which he walks, but also the language of those writers and thinkers who have already deposited the sedimented bed from which consciousness arises. In such a condition of embeddedness in pre-established linguistic orders, how can one see anew, how to find in oneself an originary moment of being from which to bring forth a loveliness which has not yet entered the world? Stephen is caught in a Heideggerian recognition of situatedness within the structures of a world he finds either banal or oppressive. He seems unable to escape anxiety of influence and liberate himself into what that philosopher expressed as an 'even more original and more universal horizon from which we may draw the answer to the question, "What is Being"' (1962, p26). Most immediately of course, Stephen is a 'character' in the Greek and modern sense of the word in Joyce's linguistic world. If he never explicitly addresses his maker (unlike Molly who begs him 'oh Jamesy, let me up out of this pooh', p633), Stephen is allowed to see that his city of dreams is Joyce's city of words: modern metropolis of unholy loves. St. Augustine and Baudelaire amongst others have already been there. More than Bloom, however, he does know, most of the time, whose thoughts he's chewing: 'ineluctable modality of the visible: at least that if not more; thought through my eyes' (p31). How not to be imprisoned in a point of view: how to see the thing in itself as it really is?

If *Ulysses* flaunts its textuality, however, we should not see it simply as a world of words, modernist heterocosm or 'book which is a model of itself' (Eco, 1989, p1). Its concern is to explore through a secular and often profane lens the world as book of modern loves. The postmodern recognition of the implication of the aesthetic in the moral facilitates a reading of the novel which refuses to reduce it to self-reflexive aesthetic autonomy. In *A Portrait* Stephen arrives aesthetically at a Symbolist appropriation of a Thomist position which would see art as an autonomous laboratory of language offering at most analogous truth, but more likely substituting itself entirely for life. The position is close to some New Critical formulations, such as Wimsatt's, examined earlier. For Aquinas, the work of art was an object with its own internal structures which were nothing to do with the expression of individual mind. Stephen attempts to reconcile Thomism with a fully non-utilitarian Symbolist aesthetic. In Thomist terms, the work of art exists in its integritas, proportio and claritas as a self-contained object 'luminously apprehended' in a context of space and time which is radically other than its own. Stephen imports a Romantic theory of creative expression into this stark neo-classical view of art. Yet, as with Eliot's 'impersonality', this buried Romantic modification tends to be ignored in the construction of Joyce as purveyor of modernist 'autonomy' and Joyce's intentions are read off from Stephen's declared preference for the 'dramatic' as the highest form of art:

> The personality of the artist, at first a cry or cadence or a mood and then a fluid and lambent narrative, finally refines itself out of existence, impersonalises itself so to speak ... The mystery of esthetic like that of material creation is accomplished. The artist, like the God of the creation, remains within or behind or beyond or above his handiwork, invisible, refined out of existence, indifferent, paring his fingernails (p215).

So Joyce beomes the God-like impersonal 'arranger' of the self-contained and ontologically distinct possible world of *Ulysses*. Some versions of post-Structuralism have reinforced this reading: those derived from a post-Saussurean theory of textuality which view language entirely constituting the world as text. For some, this would be the obvious way to draw out Joyce's affinities with Postmodernism or to postmodernise him for our own age. But as I have tried to show, Postmodernism, and Joyce, have more to offer than this. Indeed, *Ulysses* plays with such textualist ideas, holding them up to critical gaze. It is full of hidden, misplaced, misspelt letters (always a favourite with post-Structuralists). Letters walk through the city. H.E.L.Y.S. wander its streets, latter day Scarlet Letters of commercial modernity, displaying the commodification of language and the human body. Letters determine plot (such as it is): Boylan's confirmation of the sexual assignation with Molly. Bloom conducts an epistolary affair. He spends almost the entire novel ruminating and avoiding rumination on letters. The indeterminacies of linguistic existence are addressed directly in the letter from Martha Clifford. She has written: 'I called you naughty boy because I do not like that other world. Please tell what is the real meaning of that word' (p131). Martha Clifford is not the only female character in the novel to use a different language game to create a world which will displace the moral injunctions of the language games through which her identity has been shaped. Just as Gerty can perceive but not see Bloom as a masturbating voyeur (or herself as exhibitionist) because the language of popular romance does not admit such possibilities, Martha's schoolmistressy euphemisms allow her to avoid acknowledgement of implication in what is, in the terms of another language game, adulterous sexual deception (to sin in word being as heinous as to sin in deed). Each reshapes ethical engagement through a shift of vocabulary. *Ulysses* is as much about the difficult ethics of modernity as about its need for a new aesthetic. Its aesthetic suggests ways in which Kantian universalism may be modified without collapsing entirely into ethical relativism or inert consensus. Postmodernists may learn from Joyce. The end of Cyclops is not an outright victory for Proteus.

I
CONCLUSION
The Logic of Both/And

This book has foregrounded Postmodernism in its *aesthetic* aspects, in part, because my own understanding of it began here. If it is a 'perspective' on the postmodern, however, the logic of my argument suggests that it is 'truth' of a kind. It is not the kind of truth which can be verified, but the sort which can carry the investments of human belief as truth-*effect*. I believe that we can live without truth, but not without truth-effect. As I have suggested in relation to Joyce, 'grand narratives' may be seen (on a purely theoretical level) to have collapsed. However, if people still continue to invest in them, then they can be said still to exist. If they are ways of formulating fundamental human needs, their 'grandness' is a measure of the urgency and persistence of the need invested in them. They are unlikely to die, though they may be profoundly transformed. If radical theologians discuss 'God' as a projection of a human impulse towards transcendence, then the narratives of emancipation and knowledge may be viewed in the same light. It may not matter whether they are 'true' as long as they function in terms of 'truth-effect'. I suspect that Postmodernism will increasingly come to be seen as a strategy for exposing oppressive contradictions in the enlightened discourses of modernity, but I would wish to resist the idea that we should all embrace the postmodern condition in whatever form it is articulated and repress or give up our impulses towards the 'transcendence' offered through enlightened discourses. In some contexts, it may be appropriate to shape our behaviour according to universal emancipatory or epistemological ideals, in other contexts, to recognise the lurking cultural imperialism always potential in such practices and thus to draw on the postmodern as a strategy of disruption. If Freud was right (and how can we know) that maturity is the ability to live with ambiguity, hesitation, contradiction and paradox and still be capable of belief, then to grow up may be to live suspended between the modern and the postmodern, resisting the temptation to come to the security of ground on either side. The controversies over interpretation within literary criticism have taught us that art is an ever open dialogue of self and other. Perhaps the most positive lesson of Postmodernism is that to see existence in terms of such an aesthetic model may be to recognise that 'autonomy' can still be achieved but in ways which do not necessarily assert self by annihilating other.

SELECT BIBLIOGRAPHY

ADAMS, R. 1977: *After Joyce: Studies in Fiction After Ulysses*. New York: Oxford University Press.

ADORNO, THEODOR 1986: *Negative Dialectics* E.B. Aston (tr.). London: Routledge Kegan & Paul.

ALLEN, D.M. and TALLMANN, W. 1985: *The Poetics of the New American Poetry*. New York: Grove Press.

ALTER, ROBERT 1978: 'Mimesis and the motive for fiction', *Triquarterly*, Spring, pp228–50.

ALLEN, J. and YOUNG, I.M. 1989: *The Thinking Muse: Feminism and Modern French Philosophy*. Bloomington and Indianapolis: Indiana University Press.

ALTIERI, C. 1973: 'From Symbolist thought to the ground of Postmodern American Poetics', *Boundary 2*, 2,1, pp605–41.

ANDERSON, PERRY 1984: *In the Tracks of Historical Materialism*. London: Verso.

ANTIN, DAVID 1972: 'Modernism and Postmodernism: Approaching the Present in American Poetry', *Boundary 2*, 2,1, pp98–133.

ARAC, J. 1987: *Critical Genealogies: Historical Situations for Postmodern Literary Studies*. New York: Columbia University Press.

AUERBACH, ERIC 1953: *Mimesis*. New York.

BAKHTIN, M. 1981: 'Forms of time and the chronotope in the novel', *The Dialogic Imagination: Four Essays*, M. Holquist (ed.), C. Emerson and M. Holquist (tr.). Austin: Texas University Press.

BALDICK, C. 1983: *The Social Mission of English Criticism 1848–1932*. Oxford: Oxford University Press.

BARTH, JOHN 1969: *Lost in the Funhouse*. New York and London: Secker and Warburg.

—— 1967: 'The Literature of Exhaustion', *The Atlantic* 220, 2, pp29–34.

—— 1980: 'The Literature of Replenishment: Postmodernist Fiction', *The Atlantic* 245, 1, pp65–71.

BARTHELME, DONALD 1967: *Snow White*. London: Cape.

—— 1971: *City Life*. London: Cape.

BARTHES, ROLAND 1977: 'From Work to Text'. In *Image-Music-Text*, S. Heath (ed.). London: Fontana Cape.

BATAILLE, GEORGES 1985:   *Visions of Excess*. Minneapolis: Minnesota University Press.

BAUDELAIRE, CHARLES 1972:   'The Painter of Modern Life'. In *Selected Writings on Art and Artists*. Harmondsworth: Penguin, pp390–435.

BAUDRILLARD, JEAN 1975:   *The Mirror of Production*. St. Louis: Telos Press.

—— 1983a: *Simulations*. New York: Semiotext(e).

—— 1983b: *In the Shadow of the Silent Majorities*. New York: Semiotext(e).

—— 1987:   *Forget Foucault*. New York: Semiotext(e).

—— 1988:   *The Ecstasy of Communication*. New York: Semiotext(e).

BELL, CLIVE 1987:   *Art*. Oxford: Oxford University Press (1913).

BELL, DANIEL 1973:   *The Coming of Post-Industrial Society*. New York: Basic Books.

—— 1976:   *The Cultural Contradictions of Capitalism*. New York: Basic Books.

BELL, MICHAEL 1980:   *The Context of English Literature 1900–1930*. London: Methuen.

BENHABIB, S. and CORNELL, D. 1987:   *Feminism as Critique*. London: Polity.

BENJAMIN, A. (ed.) 1989:   *The Problems of Modernity*. London and New York: Routledge.

BENNETT, DAVID 1985:   'Parody, Postmodernism and the politics of reading', *Critical Quarterly 27*, **4**.

BENNINGTON, G. 1988:   *Lyotard: Writing the Event*. Manchester: Manchester University Press.

BERGER, P., BERGER, B. and KELLNER, H. 1974:   *The Homeless Mind*. New York: Vintage.

BERGSON, HENRI 1947:   *Time and Free Will: an essay on the Immediate Data of Consciousness*, F.L. Pogson (tr.). New York: Macmillan.

—— 1913:   *An Introduction to Metaphysics*, T.E. Hulme (tr.). London: Macmillan.

BERMAN, MARSHALL 1982:   *All that is Solid Melts into Air*. New York: Simon and Shuster.

BORGES, JORGE LUIS 1970:   *Labyrinths*. Harmondsworth: Penguin.

BRADBURY, MALCOLM 1973:   *Possibilities*. Oxford: Oxford University Press.

BRENNAN, T. (ed.) 1989:   *Between Feminism and Psychoanalysis*. London and New York: Routledge.

BRONNER, S. and KELLNER, D. 1989:   *Critical Theory and Society: A Reader*. London and New York: Routledge.

BROOKE-ROSE, CHRISTINE 1981:   *A Rhetoric of the Unreal: Studies in Narrative and Structure especially of the Fantastic*. Cambridge: Cambridge University Press.

BÜRGER, PETER 1984:   *Theory of the Avant-Garde*, M. Shaw (tr.). Minneapolis: Minnesota University Press.

BURGIN, VICTOR 1986:   *The End of Art Theory: Criticism and Postmodernity*. London: Macmillan.

BUTLER, C. 1980:   *After the Wake*. Oxford: Clarendon.

CALINESCU, MATEI 1987:   *Five Faces of Modernity*. Durham: Duke University Press.

CALLINICOS, ALEX 1990:   *Against Postmodernism: A Marxist Critique*. Cambridge: Polity.

CARAMELLO, CHARLES 1983:   *Silverless Mirrors: Book, Self and Postmodern American Fiction*. Florida State University Press.

CASSIRER, ERNST 1951:   *The Philosophy of the Enlightenment*, F. Koellen and J. Pettegrove (tr.). New Jersey: Princeton University Press.

CHODOROW, NANCY 1978:   *The Reproduction of Mothering: Psychoanalysis and the Sociology of Gender*. University of California Press: Berkeley, Los Angeles, California.

COLERIDGE, SAMUEL TAYLOR 1956:   *Bigraphia Literaria*, George Watson (ed.). London: Dent.

—— 1957:   *Notebooks*, K. Coburn (ed.). London: Routledge & Kegan Paul.

COLLINS, J. 1989:   *Uncommon Cultures: Popular Culture and Postmodernism*. New York and London: Routledge.

CONNOR, STEPHEN 1989: *Postmodern Culture*. Oxford and New York: Blackwell.

CONRAD, JOSEPH 1969: *Letters to R.B. Cunninghame Graham*, C.T. Watts (ed.). Cambridge: Cambridge University Press.

—— 1973: *Heart of Darkness*. Harmondsworth: Penguin.

COUTURIER, M. 1982: *Representation and Performance in Postmodern Fiction*. Proceedings of the Nice Postmodernism Conference.

DEBORD, GUY 1976: *The Society of the Spectacle*. Detroit: Black and Red.

DELEUZE, GILLES 1983: *Nietzsche and Philosophy*. New York: Columbia University Press.

—— and GUATTARI, FELIX 1983: *Anti-Oedipus*. Minneapolis: Minnesota University Press.

DE MAN, PAUL 1971: *Blindness and Insight*. London and New York: Oxford University Press.

DERRIDA, JACQUES 1989: 'Structure, Sign and Play in the Human Sciences'. In *Modern Literary Theory: A Reader*, Philip Rice and Patricia Waugh. London: Edward Arnold.

—— 1976: *Of Grammatology*. Baltimore: Johns Hopkins.

—— 1981: *Margins of Philosophy*. Chicago: Chicago University Press.

—— 1984: 'Of an Apocalyptic Tone in Recent Philosophy', *Oxford Literary Review*, 6, **2**.

DESCARTES, R. 1970: *The Philosophical Work of Descartes*, E.S. Haldane and G.R.T. Ross (ed.). London: Cambridge University Press.

DIAMOND, L. and QUINBY, L. 1988: *Feminism and Foucault*. Boston: Northeastern University Press.

DURING, SIMON 1987: 'Postmodernism or Post-colonialism Today, *Textual Practice*, 1, **1** pp32–47.

EAGLETON, T. 1986: *Against the Grain*. London: Verso.

—— 1987: 'The Politics of Subjectivity'. In ICA Document Identity: L. Apignanesi (ed.). London: ICA.

—— 1990: *The Ideology of the Aesthetic*. Oxford: Blackwell.

ECO, UMBERTO 1989: *The Aesthetics of Chaosmos*, Ellen Esrock (tr.). Oklahoma: Tulsa.

ELIOT, GEORGE 1972: *Middlemarch*, W.J. Harvey (ed.). Harmondsworth: Penguin.

ELIOT, T.S. 1960: *The Sacred Wood*. London: Methuen.

—— 1975: 'Ulysses, Order and Myth'. In *Selected Prose of T.S. Eliot*, Frank Kermode (ed.). London: Faber.

—— 1964: *The Use of Poetry and the Use of Criticism*. London: Faber.

—— 1945: 'The Social Function of Poetry', *Adelphi*, xxi.

—— 1948: *Notes Towards the Definition of Culture*. London: Faber.

—— 1953: *Selected Prose*. Harmondsworth: Penguin.

—— 1957: *On Poetry and Poets*. London: Faber.

—— 1965: *To Criticise the Critic*. London: Faber.

—— 1969: *The Complete Poems and Plays*. London: Faber.

ELLMANN, M. 1987: *The Poetics of Impersonality*. Brighton: Harvester.

ELLMANN, R. 1983: *James Joyce*. Oxford: Oxford University Press.

FEDERMAN, RAYMOND 1975: *Surfiction: Fiction Now and . . . Tomorrow*. Chicago: Swallow Press.

FEKETE, J. 1988: *Life After Postmodernism*. London: Macmillan.

FELSKI, R. 1989: *Beyond Feminist Aesthetics*. London: Hutchinson.

FLAX, J. 1990: *Thinking Fragments: Psychoanalysis, Feminism and Postmodernism in the Contemporary West*. Berkeley: California University Press.

FOKKEMMA, D. 1984: *Literary History: Modernism and Postmodernism*. Amsterdam: John Benjamins.

—— and BERTENS, H. 1986: *Approaching Postmodernism*. Amsterdam: John Benjamins.

FOSTER, HAL 1985:   *Postmodern Culture*. London and Sydney: Pluto.
—— 1985b: *Recordings: Art, Spectacle, Cultural Politics*. Washington.
FORSTER, E.M. 1947:   *A Passage to India*. London: Edward Arnold.
FOUCAULT, M. 1974:   *The Order of Things*, London: Tavistock.
—— 1977:   *Language, Counter-Memory, Practice*. D. Bouchard (ed.). Oxford: Blackwell.
—— 1980:   *The History of Sexuality*. New York: Vintage.
—— 1986:   *The Uses of Pleasure*. New York: Vintage.
—— 1986:   *The Foucault Reader*, P. Rabinow (ed.). Harmondsworth: Penguin.
—— 1988a: *The Care of the Self*. New York: Vintage.
—— 1988b: *Technologies of the Self*, L.H. Martin, H. Gutman, P.H. Hutton (eds). London: Tavistock Press.
FRANK, J. 1958:   'Spatial form in Modern Literature'. In *Criticism: The Foundations of Modern Literary Judgement*, M. Scorer, J. Miles and G. Mckenzie (eds). Berkeley, Los Angeles and London: California University Press.
FRASCINA, F. 1985:   *Pollock and After: The critical debate*. London: Harper and Row.
FREUD, S. and BREUER, J. 1955:   *Studies in Hysteria*, S.E. 2: London.
FREUD, S. 1957:   'On Narcissism: an introduction', S.E. 14: London.
—— 1950:   *Beyond the Pleasure Principle*, S.E. 18.
FRY, ROGER 1981:   *Vision and Design*, J.B. Bullen (ed.). Oxford: Oxford University Press.
GADAMER, HANS-GEORG 1975:   *Truth and Method*, G. Barden and J. Cumming (eds). New York.
GASS, WILLIAM 1970:   *Fiction and the Figures of Life*. New York: Alfred Knopf.
GIDDENS, ANTHONY 1981:   'Modernism and Postmodernism', *New German Critique*, 22, pp15–18.
GELPI, ALBERT 1987:   *A Coherent Splendour: The American Poetic Renaissance 1910–1950*. New York: Cambridge University Press.
GRAFF, GERALD 1979:   *Literature Against Itself*. Chicago and London: Chicago University Press.
—— 1980:   *Poetic Statement and Critical Dogma*. Chicago and London: Chicago University Press.
GRASS, GÜNTHER 1985:   *On Writing and Politics 1967–1983*. London: Secker and Warburg.
GREENBERG, CLEMENT 1973:   'Modernist Painting'. In *The New Art*, pp66–77, G. Battock. New York: Dutton.
GROSZ, E. 1989:   *Sexual Subversions*. Sydney: Allen and Unwin.
HABERMAS, JÜRGEN 1981:   'Modernity versus Postmodernity'. In Foster (ed.) (1985).
—— 1984, 1987:   *Theory of Communicative Action*, vols. 1, 2. Boston: Beacon Press.
—— 1987:   *The Philosophical Discourses of Modernity*, F.G. Lawrence (tr.). Oxford: Polity.
HARVEY, DAVID 1989:   *The Condition of Postmodernity*. London: Blackwell.
HASSAN, IHAB 1971:   *The Dismemberment of Orpheus: Towards a Postmodern Literature*. New York: Oxford University Press.
—— 1975a: 'Joyce, Beckett and the postmodern imagination', *Triquarterly*, **34**.
—— 1975b: *Paracriticisms: Seven Speculations of the Times*. Urbana, Chicago and London: Illinois University Press.
—— 1980:   *The Right Promethean Fire*. Urbana, Chicago, London: Illinois University Press.
—— 1987:   *The Postmodern Turn: Essays in Postmodern Theory and Culture*. New York: Columbia University Press.
HEIDEGGER, MARTIN 1962:   *Being and Time*. New York: Harper and Row.
—— 1972:   *On Time and Being*, J. Stambaugh (tr.). New York: Harper and Row.

—— 1975: *Poetry, Language, Thought*, A. Hofstadter (tr.). New York and London: Harper and Row.

—— 1977: *The Question Concerning Technology*, William Lott (tr.). New York.

HORKHEIMER, M. and ADORNO, T. 1972: *Dialectic of Enlightenment*. New York: Seabury.

HOFFMANN, G., HORNING, A. and RUDINGER, K. 1977: '"Modern", "Postmodern" and "Contemporary" as Criteria for the Analysis of Twentieth Century Literature', *Amerika Studien*, **22**, pp19–46.

HOWE, I. 1959: 'Mass Society and Postmodern Fiction', *Partisan Review*, **26**, pp420–436.

—— 1971: *Decline of the New*. London: Gollancz.

HUTCHEON, LINDA 1989: *The Politics of Postmodernism*. London and New York: Routledge.

—— 1990: *A Poetics of Postmodernism: History, Theory, Fiction*. New York and London: Routledge.

HUYSSEN, ANDREAS 1988: *After the Great Divide: Modernism, Mass Culture and Postmodernism*. London: Macmillan.

JAGGAR, A. 1983: *Feminist Politics and Human Nature*. Brighton: Harvester.

JAMES, WILLIAM 1975: *The Meaning of Truth*. Cambridge, Mass.: Harvard University Press.

—— 1983: *The Principles of Psychology*. Harvard University Press.

—— 1985: *The Varieties of Religious Experience: A Study in Human Nature*. Harmondsworth: Penguin.

JAMESON, FREDRIC 1971: *Marxism and Form*. Princeton: Princeton University Press.

—— 1972: *The Prison House of Language*. Princeton University Press.

—— 1981: *The Political Unconscious*. New York: Cornell University Press.

—— 1984: 'Postmodernism, or the Cultural Logic of Late Capitalism', *New Left Review*, 146, pp53–93.

—— 1985: 'Postmodernism and Consumer Society'. In Foster (ed.), pp111–126.

—— 1989: *The Ideologies of Theory: Essays 1971–86*. New York.

—— 1989: 'Periodising the Sixties'. In *The Ideologies of Theory*.

JARDINE, ALICE 1985: *Gynesis: Configurations of Woman and Modernity*. Ithaca and London: Cornell University Press.

JENCKS, CHARLES 1987: *The Language of Post-Modern Architecture*. London: Academy.

JOSIPOVICI, GABRIEL 1971: *The World and the Book*. London: Macmillan.

—— 1977: *The Lessons of Modernism*. London: Macmillan.

JOYCE, JAMES 1960: *A Portrait of the Artist as a Young Man*. Harmondsworth: Penguin.

—— 1986: *Ulysses*. Walter Gabler (ed.). Harmondsworth: Penguin.

—— 1957: *Letters, 1*, Stuart Gilbert (ed.). New York and London: Viking and Faber.

KANT, EMANUEL 1952: *Critique of Judgement*. J.C. Meredith (tr.). Oxford: Oxford University Press.

—— 1984: 'What is Enlightenment?'. In *German Aesthetic and Literary Criticism: Kant, Fichte, Schelling, Schopenhauer, Hegel*, David Simpson (ed.). Cambridge: Cambridge University Press.

KAPLAN, A.E. 1988: *Postmodernism and its Discontents*. London: Verso.

KAUFFMANN, WALTER 1974: *Nietzsche: Philosopher, Psychologist, Antichrist*. New Jersey: Princeton University Press.

KEARNEY, RICHARD 1988: *The Wake of Imagination*. Minneapolis: Minnesota University Press.

—— 1991: *Poetics of Imagining*. London: Harper Collins.

KELLNER, DOUGLAS 1989a: *Jean Baudrillard: From Marxism to Postmodernism and Beyond*. Cambridge: Polity.

—— 1989b: *Postmodernism/Jameson/Critique*. Washington D.C.: Maisonneuve.

KERMODE, FRANK 1966:   *The Sense of an Ending*. Oxford: Oxford University Press.

—— 1968:   *Continuities*. London: Routledge, Kegan and Paul.

—— 1988:   *History and Value*. Oxford: Oxford University Press.

KOLB, DAVID 1986:   *The Critique of Pure Modernity*. London: Chicago University Press.

KRAMER HILTON 1985:   *The Revenge of the Philistines: Art and Culture 1972–1984*. New York: Free Press.

KROKER, ARTHUR 1986:   *The Postmodern Scene*. New York: St. Martin's Press.

—— and KROKER, MARILOUISE 1988:   *Body Invaders: Sexuality and the Postmodern Condition*. London: Macmillan.

KRISTEVA, JULIA 1982:   'Women's Time'. In *Feminist Theory: A Critique of Ideology*, N. Keohane, M. Rosaldo and B.C. Gelpi, 1982. Brighton: Harvester.

LACLAU, E. and MOUFFE, C. 1987:   'Post-Marxism Without Apologies', *New Left Review*, 166, pp79–106.

LASH, SCOTT 1985:   'Postmodernity and Desire', *Theory and Society*, **14**, 1, pp1–33.

LESSING, DORIS 1973:   *The Golden Notebook*. St Albans: Panther.

—— 1976:   *The Memoirs of a Survivor*. London: Pan/Picador.

LEVENSON, M. 1984:   *A Genealogy of Modernism*. Cambridge: Cambridge University Press.

LEVIN, HARRY 1966:   'What was Modernism?'. In *Refractions*. New York: Oxford University Press.

LEVIN, D.M. 1988:   *The Opening of Vision: Nihilism and the Postmodern Situation*. London: Routledge.

LOBB, EDWARD 1981:   *T.S. Eliot and the Romantic Critical Tradition*. London: Routledge.

LOVIBOND, S. 1989:   'Feminism and Postmodernism', *New Left Review*, **178**, pp5–28.

LODGE, DAVID 1977:   *The Modes of Modern Writing*. London: Edward Arnold.

LUNN, E. 1982:   *Marxism and Modernism*. London: Verso.

LYOTARD, JEAN-FRANCOIS 1974:   *Economie Libidinale*. Paris: Minuit.

—— 1985:   *The Postmodern Condition*. Manchester: Manchester University Press.

—— 1988:   *The Differend*. Manchester: Manchester University Press.

—— 1989:   *The Lyotard Reader*, Andrew Benjamin (ed.). London and Cambridge, Mass.: Blackwell.

—— and THEBAUD, J.L. 1985:   *Just Gaming*. Minneapolis: Minnesota University Press.

MANDEL, ERNST 1975:   *Late Capitalism*. London: New Left Books.

MARCUSE, HERBERT 1964:   *One-Dimensional Man*. Boston: Beacon Press.

MACINTYRE, ALISDAIR 1985:   *After Virtue: A Study in Moral Theory*. London: Duckworth.

—— 1990:   *Three Rival Versions of Moral Enquiry*. London: Duckworth.

—— 1991:   *A Short History of Ethics*. London and New York: Routledge.

MANGANIELLO, D. 1980: *Joyce's Politics*. London: Routledge & Kegan Paul.

MARX, KARL and ENGELS, FRIEDRICH 1975:   *Collected Works*. New York: International Publishers.

MATEJKA, L. and POMORSKA, K. (eds) 1971:   *Readings in Russian Poetics*. London and Cambridge, Mass.: MIT Press.

MAZARRO, JEROME 1980:   *Postmodern American Poetry*. Urbana: Illinois University Press.

MCHALE, BRIAN 1987:   *Postmodernist Fiction*. London and New York: Methuen.

MEESE, E. and PARKER, A. (eds) 1989:   *The Difference Within: Feminism and Critical*

Theory. Amsterdam/Philadelphia: John Benjamins.

MEGILL, A. 1985: *Prophets of Extremity: Nietzsche, Heidegger, Foucault, Derrida*. Berkeley and London: California University Press.

MEISEL, P. 1989: *The Myth of the Modern: A Study in British Literature and Criticism After 1850*. New Haven and London: Yale University Press.

MENAND, LOUIS 1987: *Discovering Modernism: T.S. Eliot and his Context*. Oxford: Oxford University Press.

MELVILLE, S.W. 1986: *Philosophy Beside Itself: on Deconstruction and Modernism*. Minneapolis: Minnesota University Press.

MERQUIOR, J.G. 1986: 'Spider and Bee'. In *Postmodernism*. London: ICA Documents 4, 5, pp16–18.

NEHEMAS, A. 1985: *Nietzsche: Life as Literature*. Cambridge, Mass. and London: Harvard University Press.

NEWMAN, CHARLES 1985: *The Postmodern Aura*. Evanston: Northwestern University Press.

NICHOLSON, L. 1990: *Feminism/Postmodernism*. New York and London: Routledge.

NIETZSCHE, FRIEDRICH 1966: *The Birth of Tragedy*. New York: Vintage.

—— 1956: *The Birth of Tragedy and the Genealogy of Morals*. New York: Archer.

—— 1954: *Thus Spake Zarathustra*. In *The Portable Nietzsche*. New York: Viking.

—— 1973: *Beyond Good and Evil*. Harmondsworth: Penguin.

—— 1979: *Philosophy and Truth: Selections from Nietzsche's Notebooks of the Early 1870s*, D. Breazeale (tr.). New Jersey: Humanities Press.

—— 1979: *Ecce Homo: How One Becomes What One Is*. Harmondsworth: Penguin.

—— 1967: *The Will to Power*. New York: Random House.

—— 1990: *My Sister and I*. Los Angeles: Amok Books.

NORRIS, CHRISTOPHER 1985: *The Contest of Faculties: Philosophy and Theory after Deconstruction*. London and New York: Methuen.

—— 1990: *What's Wrong With Postmodernism*. Brighton: Harvester.

OLSON, CHARLES 1984: 'Human Universe' and 'Projective Verse'. In Allen and Tallman (eds), pp161–74, 147–58.

PATER, WILLIAM 1910: *Plato and Platonism*. London: Macmillan.

—— 1986: *The Renaissance*. Oxford: Oxford University Press.

PHILLIPSON, M. 1985: *Painting, Language and Modernity*. London: Routledge, Kegan and Paul.

PIPPIN, R. 1991: *Modernism as a Philosophical Problem: On the Dissatisfactions of European High Culture*. Cambridge, Mass. and Oxford: Blackwell.

POSTER, MARK 1990: *The Mode of Information: Post-structuralism and Social Context*. Cambridge: Polity Press.

POULET, GEORGES 1956: *Studies in Human Time*. Baltimore: Johns Hopkins.

RASKIN, JOHAN 1970: 'Doris Lessing at Stony Brook: an interview', *New American Review*, **8**.

RIVIERE, JOAN 1977: 'The Unconscious Fantasy of an Inner World Reflected in Examples from Literature'. In *New Directions in Psychoanalysis*, Melanie Klein (ed.). London.

ROBERTS, J. 1990: *Postmodernism, Politics and Art*. Manchester and New York: Manchester University Press.

RORTY, RICHARD 1980: *Philosophy and the Mirror of Nature*. Oxford: Blackwell.

—— 1989: *Contingency, Irony and Solidarity*. Cambridge: Cambridge University Press.

RUSHDIE, SALMAN 1983: *Shame*. London: Picador.

RUSSELL, BERTRAND 1961: *History of Western Philosophy*. London: Allen and Unwin.

RUSSELL, CHARLES 1985: *Poets, Prophets and Revolutionaries: The Literary Avant-Garde from Rimbaud through Postmodernism*. Oxford: Oxford University Press.

SARTRE, J.-P. 1956: *Being and Nothingness*. New York: Philosophical Library.
SARUP, M. 1988: *An Introductory Guide to Post-Structuralism and Postmodernism*. Brighton: Harvester.
SCHILLER, J.C.F. 1967: *On the Aesthetic Education of Man, in a Series of Letters*. Oxford: Oxford University Press.
—— 1988: 'On Naive and Sentimental Poetry'. In *The Origins of Modern Critical Thought*, David Simpson (ed.), Cambridge: Cambridge University Press, pp148–177.
SCHUSTERMAN, R. 1988: *T.S. Eliot and the Philosophy of Criticism*. London: Duckworth.
SCHWARZ, D.R. 1989: *The Transformation of the English Novel: 1890–1930*. London: Macmillan.
SCHWARZ, SANFORD 1985: *The Matrix of Modernism*. New Jersey: Princeton University Press.
SEARS, S. and LORD, G.W. 1972: *The Discontinuous Universe: Selected Writings on Contemporary Consciousness*. New York and London: Basic Books.
SIMPSON, DAVID 1984: *German Aesthetic and Literary Criticism*. Cambridge: Cambridge University Press.
—— 1988: *The Origins of Modern Literary Thought*. Cambridge: Cambridge University Press.
SILVERMAN, H.J. 1990: *Postmodernism: Philosophy and the Arts*. New York and London: Routledge.
SMYTHE, E.J. 1991: *Postmodernism and Contemporary Fiction*. London: Batsford.
SONTAG, SUSAN 1966: *Against Interpretation*. New York: Farrar, Strauss and Giroux.
SPANOS, WILLIAM 1972: 'The Detective at the Boundary: Some Notes on the Postmodern Literary Imagination', *Boundary 2*, 2, 1, pp147–68.
—— 1979: *Martin Heidegger and the Question of Literature*. Bloomington and London: Indiana University Press.
STEVENS, WALLACE 1951: *The Necessary Angel: Essays on Reality and Imagination*. London: Faber.
—— 1966: *Letters of Wallace Stevens*. New York: Knopf.
STRATTON, JON 1990: *Writing Sites*. Ann Arbor: Michigan University Press.
SVANY, ERIK 1988: *The Men of 1914: T.S. Eliot and Early Modernism*. Milton Keynes and Philadelphia: Open University Press.
VAIHINGER, H. 1924: *The Philosophy As If*, C.K. Ogden (ed.). London.
VONNEGUT, KURT 1973: *Breakfast of Champions*. St. Albans: Panther.
WAUGH, PATRICIA 1984: *Metafiction: The Theory and Practice of Self Conscious Fiction*. London and New York: Methuen.
—— 1989: *Feminine Fictions: Revisiting the Postmodern*. London and New York: Routledge.
WEIMANN, R. 1976: *Structure and Society in Literary History*. London: Lawrence and Wishart.
WELLEK, R. 1963: *Concepts of Criticism*. New Haven and London: Yale University Press.
WEINSHEIMER, J.C. 1985: *Gadamer's Hermeneutics: A Reading of Truth and Method*. New Haven and London: Yale University Press.
WILDE, ALAN 1987: *Modernism, Postmodernism and the Ironic Imagination*. Philadelphia: Pennsylvania University Press.
WILLIAMS, R. 1989: *The Politics of Modernism*. London: Verso.
WIMSATT, W.K. 1964: *The Verbal Icon*. New York: Farrar, Strauss and Giroux.
WITTGENSTEIN, LUDWIG 1978: *Philosophical Investigations*. Oxford: Blackwell.
WOLIN, R. 1984–5: 'Modernism and Postmodernism', *Telos*. **62**, pp9–29.
WOOLFF, J. 1990: *Feminine Sentences: Essays on Women and Culture*. Cambridge: Polity Press.

WOOLF, VIRGINIA 1979: 'Women Novelists' and 'Professions for Women'. In *Women and Writing*, M. Barrett (ed.). London: Women's Press.
—— 1967: 'Street Haunting'. In *Collected Essays*, **4**. London: Hogarth Press.
—— 1969: *To the Lighthouse*. London: Hogarth Press.
—— 1975: *Three Guineas*. Harmondsworth: Penguin.
—— 1976: *Moments of Being*, J. Schulkind (ed.). Brighton: Harvester.
WORDSWORTH, WILLIAM 1971: *The Prelude*, J.C. Maxwell (ed.). Harmondsworth: Penguin.
YEATS, W.B. 1961: *Essays and Introductions*. London: Macmillan.

INDEX